THE
2002 ANNUAL:
Volume 2
Consulting

(The Thirty-Ninth Annual)

Edited by Elaine Biech

JOSSEY-BASS/PFEIFFER
A Wiley Company
www.pfeiffer.com

Published by
JOSSEY-BASS/PFEIFFER
A Wiley Company
989 Market Street
San Francisco, CA 94103-1741
415.433.1740; Fax 415. 433.0499
800.274.4434; Fax 800.569.0443

www.pfeiffer.com

Jossey-Bass/Pfeiffer is a registered trademark of John Wiley & Sons, Inc.

Looseleaf ISBN: 0-7879-5966-9
Paperback ISBN: 0-7879-5962-6
ISSN: 1046-333X

Printed in the United States of America

We at Jossey-Bass strive to use the most environmentally sensitive paper stocks available to us. Our publications are printed on acid-free recycled stock whenever possible, and our paper always meets or exceeds minimum GPO and EPA requirements.

Acquiring Editor: Josh Blatter
Director of Development: Kathleen Dolan Davies
Developmental Editors: Susan Rachmeler and Rebecca Taff
Senior Production Editor: Dawn Kilgore
Manufacturing Manager: Becky Carreño

Printing 10   9   8   7   6   5   4   3   2   1

PREFACE

Welcome to the *2002 Annual: Volume 2, Consulting*. This year represents the thirty-first year the *Annuals* have been published. Through the years, trainers, consultants, and performance-improvement technologists have turned to the *Annuals* as a resource for experiential learning activities and instruments, a reference for cutting-edge articles, and a source of inspiration as they design their own materials. This year's *Annuals* will continue to provide that same support.

The *Annuals* have been published as a set of two since 1995: Volume 1, Training, and Volume 2, Consulting. The materials in the training volume focus on skill building and knowledge enhancement. The training volume also features articles that enhance the skills and professional development of trainers. The consulting volume materials focus on intervention techniques and organizational systems. The consulting volume also features articles that enhance the skills and professional development of consultants. As you might imagine, it can be difficult in some cases to place materials strictly in one volume or the other. As a fellow practitioner, I encourage you to examine both volumes to find the materials that will meet your needs.

As we look toward 2002, we see that many organizations are re-establishing the training departments that they outsourced in the 1990s or increasing the size of training departments that they previously downsized.

The consultants we speak with are busier than ever, as organizations continue to implement new initiatives with a short supply of employees. These situations require more and more productivity from you as a trainer or consultant, so make the *Annuals* your companions as you meet the needs of your employer or client.

To ensure that you receive the most of all the *Annuals*, be sure that you have a *Reference Guide to Handbooks and Annuals* to help you identify all the resources available to you. The *Reference Guide* is a giant index that helps you locate just what you need based on topics and key words.

The *Annual* series has been valuable to the training and consulting professions for the past thirty-one years for several reasons. First, and most important, the *Annuals* provide you with a variety of materials that cover many topics—from the basics to cutting-edge issues. The topics focus on what you as a trainer or consultant require in order to improve your own competencies in areas such as facilitating skills, team building, consulting techniques, and opening and closing techniques. The *Annuals* also provide content for you to use to design materials or to develop strategy for your internal or external clients.

Second, the *Annuals* are valuable because the materials are applicable to varying circumstances. You will find instruments for individuals, teams, and organizations; experiential learning activities to round out workshops, team building, or consulting assignments; and articles to assign as pre-reading, to read to increase your knowledge base, or to use as reference materials in your writing tasks.

Third, the *Annuals* are ready when you are. All of the materials contained in them may be duplicated for educational and training purposes. If you need to adapt or modify the materials to tailor them for your audience's needs, go right ahead. We only request that the credit statement found on the copyright page be included on all copies. In addition, if you intend to reproduce the materials in publications for sale or if you wish to use the materials on a large-scale basis (more than one hundred copies in one year), please contact us for prior written permission. Our liberal copyright policy makes it easy and fast for you to use the materials to do your job. Please call us if you have any questions.

While the *2002 Annuals* are the newest in the series, you will benefit from having the entire series for your use. They are available in paperback, as a three-ring notebook—and the Pfeiffer Library is available on CD-ROM.

The *Annuals* have always been a valuable resource to the profession. The key is that the materials come from professionals like you who work in the field as trainers, consultants, facilitators, educators, and performance-improvement technologists. This ensures that the materials have been tried and perfected in real-life settings with actual participants and clients, to meet real-world needs. To this end, we encourage you to submit materials to be considered for publication in the *Annual*. At your request, we will provide a copy of the guidelines for preparing your materials. We are interested in receiving experiential learning activities (group learning activities based on the five stages of the experiential learning cycle: experiencing, publishing, processing, generalizing, and applying); inventories, questionnaires, and surveys (both paper-and-pencil as well as electronic rating scales); and presentation and discussion resources (articles that may include theory related to practical application). Contact the Jossey-Bass/Pfeiffer Editorial Department at the address listed on the copyright page for copies of our guidelines for contributors or contact me directly at Box 657, Portage, WI 53901; on email at Elaine@ebbweb.com; or call our office at 608/742-5005. We welcome your comments, ideas, and contributions.

Thank you to the dedicated people at Jossey-Bass/Pfeiffer who produced the *2002 Annuals:* Josh Blatter, Kathleen Dolan Davies, Dawn Kilgore, Susan Rachmeler, Samya Sattar, and Rebecca Taff. Thank you to Beth Drake of ebb associates inc, who organized this huge task and ensured that all the deadlines were met.

Most important, thank you to our authors, who have once again shared their ideas, techniques, and materials so that the rest of us may benefit. Thank you on behalf of all training and consulting professionals everywhere.

Elaine Biech
Editor
June 2001

About Jossey-Bass/Pfeiffer

Jossey-Bass/Pfeiffer is actively engaged in publishing insightful human resource development (HRD) materials. The organization has earned an international reputation as the leading source of practical resources that are immediately useful to today's consultants, trainers, facilitators, and managers in a variety of industries. All materials are designed by practicing professionals who are continually experimenting with new techniques. Thus, readers and users benefit from the fresh and thoughtful approach that underlies Jossey-Bass/Pfeiffer's experientially based materials, books, workbooks, instruments, and other learning resources and programs. This broad range of products is designed to help human resource practitioners increase individual, group, and organizational effectiveness and provide a variety of training and intervention technologies, as well as background in the field.

CONTENTS

Preface   v

General Introduction to *The 2002 Annual: Volume 2, Consulting*   1

EXPERIENTIAL LEARNING ACTIVITIES

Introduction to the Experiential Learning Activities Section   3

Experiential Learning Activities Categories   6

*710. Internet Impressions: Responding to Different Levels
   of Self-Disclosure
   Lori Silverman and Karen Ostrov   11

711. Ask Everyone: Generating Solutions
   Yvette Delemos Robinson   21

712. Successful Leadership Traits: Reaching Consensus
   Robert Alan Black   25

713. Construction Project: Task vs. People Orientation in Teams
   Edward L. Harrison and Paul H. Pietri   31

714. Team Traps: Learning to Take Risks
   Lynn A. Baker, Sr.   37

715. Island Survival: Choosing Roles in a Group
   Nancy Jackson   41

716. Scrambled Words: A Problem-Solving Task
   Phyliss Cooke and Ralph R. Bates   45

717. Me in a Bag: Breaking the Ice in an Intact Work Team
   Steve Sphar   51

718. What's Next? Building an Agenda
   Kristin J. Arnold   55

719. Billboard Sentiments: Saying Goodbye
   Niki Nichols and Ed Werland   59

720. Supervisory Success: Balancing Followership with
   What Seems Right
   Bob Shaver   63

721. Futures: Planning Creatively
   Kevin J. Pokorny   71

---

*See Experiential Learning Activities Categories, p. 6, for an explanation of the numbering system.

722. Pink Slip: Dealing with Organizational Change
M.K. Key   79

INVENTORIES, QUESTIONNAIRES, AND SURVEYS

Introduction to the Inventories, Questionnaires, and Surveys Section   87

Cornerstones: A Measure of Trust in Work Relationships
Amy M. Birtel, Valerie C. Nellen, and Susan B. Wilkes   89

Successful Consulting Orientation and Readiness Evaluation
(SCORE)
Ralph R. Bates and Phyliss Cooke   103

Systems Thinking Best Practices Instrument
Stephen G. Haines   113

PRESENTATION AND DISCUSSION RESOURCES

Introduction to the Presentation and Discussion Resources Section   129

Appreciative Inquiry: New Thinking at Work
Sherene Zolno   131

The Coaching Styles Advantage
Patrick J. Aspell and Dee Dee Aspell   137

Ethical Issues Surrounding Online Research
Heidi A. Campbell   153

Brainstorming and the Myth of Idea Generation in Groups
Adrian F. Furnham   159

Systems Thinking and Learning: From Chaos and Complexity
to Elegant Simplicity
Stephen G. Haines   173

Being an Agent of Organizational Healing
Beverly J. Nyberg and Roger Harrison   193

The Role of the Executive Coach
Barbara Pate Glacel   229

Twenty-One Ways to Delight Your Customers
Peter R. Garber   237

Influence: Key to the Door of Leadership
Marlene Caroselli   251

Spirituality and Business: Where's the Beef?
Gary Schouborg   261

Contributors   277

Contents of the Companion Volume,
The 2002 Annual: Volume 1, Training   281

GENERAL INTRODUCTION TO THE 2002 ANNUAL

The 2002 Annual: Volume 2, Consulting is the thirty-ninth volume in the *Annual* series, a collection of practical and useful materials for professionals in the broad area described as human resource development (HRD). The materials are written by and for professionals, including trainers, organization-development and organization-effectiveness consultants, performance-improvement technologists, educators, instructional designers, and others.

Each *Annual* has three main sections: experiential learning activities; inventories, questionnaires, and surveys; and presentation and discussion resources. Each published submission is classified in one of the following categories: Individual Development, Communication, Problem Solving, Groups, Teams, Consulting and Facilitating, Leadership, and Organizations. Within each category, pieces are further classified into logical subcategories, which are identified in the introductions to the three sections.

This year we have added a new subcategory to the "Organizations" category, which first appeared in the 1999 *Annual*. "Change Management" joins "Communication" and "Vision, Mission, Values, Strategy" as the third subcategory in "Organizations." Although these topics have been addressed in the past, it may have been difficult to locate them in the former structure. Appropriate past submissions will be cross-referenced in the next update to the *Reference Guide to Handbooks and Annuals*, which indexes all the materials by key words.

A new subcategory, "Technology," was added in the 1999 *Annual*. Much has changed for the HRD professional in recent years, and technology has lead much of that change. Given the important role technology plays, we will continue to publish material that relates technology to the HRD field and how the HRD professional can use technology as a tool.

We continue to identify "cutting edge" topics in this *Annual*. This designation highlights topics that present information, concepts, tools, or perspectives that may be recent additions to the profession or that have not previously appeared in the *Annual*.

The series continues to provide an opportunity for HRD professionals who wish to share their experiences, their viewpoints, and their processes with their colleagues. To that end, Jossey-Bass/Pfeiffer publishes guidelines for potential authors. These guidelines are available from the Pfeiffer editorial department at Jossey-Bass, Inc., in San Francisco, California.

Materials are selected for the *Annuals* based on the quality of the ideas, applicability to real-world concerns, relevance to current HRD issues, clarity of presentation, and ability to enhance our readers' professional development. In addition, we choose experiential learning activities that will create a high degree of enthusiasm among the participants and add enjoyment to the learning process. As in the past several years, the contents of each *Annual* span a wide range of subject matter, reflecting the range of interests of our readers.

Our contributor list includes a wide selection of experts in the field: in-house practitioners, consultants, and academically based professionals. A list of contributors to the *Annual* can be found at the end of the volume, including their names, affiliations, addresses, telephone numbers, facsimile numbers, and email addresses. Readers will find this list useful if they wish to locate the authors of specific pieces for feedback, comments, or questions. Further information is presented in a brief biographical sketch of each contributor that appears at the conclusion of each article. We publish this information to encourage "networking," which continues to be a valuable mainstay in the field of human resource development.

We are pleased with the high quality of material that is submitted for publication each year and often regret that we have page limitations. In addition, just as we cannot publish every manuscript we receive, you may find that not all published works are equally useful to you. Therefore, we encourage and invite ideas, materials, and suggestions that will help us to make subsequent *Annuals* as useful as possible to all of our readers.

Introduction

to the Experiential Learning Activities Section

Experiential learning activities ensure that lasting learning occurs. They should be selected with a specific learning objective in mind. These objectives are based on the participants' needs and on the facilitator's skills. Although the experiential learning activities presented here all vary in goals, group size, time required, and process,[1] they all incorporate one important element: questions that ensure learning has occurred. This discussion, lead by the facilitator, assists participants to process the activity, to internalize the learning, and to relate it to their day-to-day situations. It is this element that creates the unique experience and learning opportunity that only an experiential learning activity can bring to the group process.

Readers have used the *Annuals'* experiential learning activities for years to enhance their training and consulting events. Each learning experience is complete and includes all lecturettes, handout content, and other written material necessary to facilitate the activity. In addition, many include variations of the design that the facilitator might find useful. If the activity does not fit perfectly with your objective, within your time frame, or to your group size, we encourage you to adapt the activity by adding your own variations. You will find additional experiential learning activities listed in the "Experiential Learning Activities Categories" chart that immediately follows this introduction.

The 2002 Annual: Volume 2, Consulting includes thirteen activities, in the following categories:

Individual Development: Self-Disclosure

710. Internet Impressions: Responding to Different Levels of Self-Disclosure, by Lori Silverman and Karen Ostrov

---

[1]It would be redundant to print here a caveat for the use of experiential learning activities, but HRD professionals who are not experienced in the use of this training technology are strongly urged to read the "Introduction" to the *Reference Guide to Handbooks and Annuals* (1999 Edition). This article presents the theory behind the experiential-learning cycle and explains the necessity of adequately completing each phase of the cycle to allow effective learning to occur.

Problem Solving: Generating Alternatives

711. Ask Everyone: Generating Solutions,
by Yvette Delemos Robinson

Problem Solving: Consensus/Synergy

712. Successful Leadership Traits: Reaching Consensus,
by Robert Alan Black

Groups: How Groups Work

713. Construction Project: Task vs. People Orientation in Teams,
by Edward L. Harrison and Paul H. Pietri

Groups: Competition/Collaboration

714. Team Traps: Learning to Take Risks, by Lynn A. Baker, Sr.

Teams: Roles

715. Island Survival: Choosing Roles in a Group, by Nancy Jackson

Teams: Problem Solving/Decision Making

716. Scrambled Words: A Problem-Solving Task,
by Phyliss Cooke and Ralph R. Bates

Consulting and Facilitating: Facilitating: Opening

717. Me in a Bag: Breaking the Ice in an Intact Work Team,
by Steve Sphar

Consulting and Facilitating: Facilitating: Skills

718. What's Next? Building an Agenda, by Kristin J. Arnold

Consulting and Facilitating: Facilitating: Closing

719. Billboard Sentiments: Saying Goodbye,
by Niki Nichols and Ed Werland

Leadership: Diversity/Stereotyping

720. Supervisory Success: Balancing Followership with What Seems
Right, by Bob Shaver

Organizations: Vision, Mission, Values, Strategy

721. Futures: Planning Creatively, by Kevin J. Pokorny

Organizations: Change Management

722. Pink Slip: Dealing with Organizational Change, by M.K. Key

Locate other activities in these and other categories in the "Experiential Learning Activities Categories" chart that follows, or by using the comprehensive *Reference Guide to Handbooks and Annuals*. This book, which is updated regularly, indexes all of the *Annuals* and all of the *Handbooks of Structured Experiences* that we have published to date. With each revision, the *Reference Guide* becomes a complete, up-to-date, and easy-to-use resource for selecting appropriate materials from all of the *Annuals* and *Handbooks*.

EXPERIENTIAL LEARNING ACTIVITIES CATEGORIES

1–24	Volume I, *Handbook*	377–388	1985 *Annual*	581–592	1997 *Annual:* Volume 2, Consulting
25–48	Volume II, *Handbook*	389–412	Volume X, *Handbook*	593–604	1998 *Annual:* Volume 1, Training
49–74	Volume III, *Handbook*	413–424	1986 *Annual*		
75–86	1972 *Annual*	425–436	1987 *Annual*	605–616	1998 *Annual:* Volume 2, Consulting
87–100	1973 *Annual*	437–448	1988 *Annual*		
101–124	Volume IV, *Handbook*	449–460	1989 *Annual*	617–630	1999 *Annual:* Volume 1, Training
125–136	1974 *Annual*	461–472	1990 *Annual*		
137–148	1975 *Annual*	473–484	1991 *Annual*	631–642	1999 *Annual:* Volume 2, Consulting
149–172	Volume V, *Handbook*	485–496	1992 *Annual*		
173–184	1976 *Annual*	497–508	1993 *Annual*	643–656	2000 *Annual:* Volume 1, Training
185–196	1977 *Annual*	509–520	1994 *Annual*		
197–220	Volume VI, *Handbook*	521–532	1995 *Annual:* Volume 1, Training	657–669	2000 *Annual:* Volume 2, Consulting
221–232	1978 *Annual*				
233–244	1979 *Annual*	533–544	1995 *Annual:* Volume 2, Consulting	670–681	2001 *Annual:* Volume 1, Training
245–268	Volume VII, *Handbook*				
269–280	1980 *Annual*	545–556	1996 *Annual:* Volume 1, Training	682–694	2001 *Annual:* Volume 2, Consulting
281–292	1981 *Annual*				
293–316	Volume VIII, *Handbook*	557–568	1996 *Annual:* Volume 2, Consulting	696–709	2002 *Annual:* Volume 1, Training
317–328	1982 *Annual*				
329–340	1983 *Annual*	569–580	1997 *Annual:* Volume 1, Training	710–722	2002 *Annual:* Volume 2, Consulting
341–364	Volume IX, *Handbook*				
365–376	1984 *Annual*				

Vol. Page   *Vol. Page*   *Vol. Page*

INDIVIDUAL DEVELOPMENT

Sensory Awareness

	Vol.	Page
Feelings & Defenses (56)	III	31
Lemons (71)	III	94
Growth & Name Fantasy (85)	'72	59
Group Exploration (119)	IV	92
Relaxation & Perceptual Awareness (136)	'74	84
T'ai Chi Chuan (199)	VI	10
Roles Impact Feelings (214)	VI	102
Projections (300)	VIII	30
Mastering the Deadline Demon (593)	'98–1	9
Learning Shifts (643)	'00–1	11
Secret Sponsors (657)	'00–2	11
Spirituality at Work (670)	'01–1	11

Self-Disclosure

	Vol.	Page
Johari Window (13)	I	65
Graphics (20)	I	88
Personal Journal (74)	III	109
Make Your Own Bag (90)	'73	13
Growth Cards (109)	IV	30
Expressing Anger (122)	IV	104
Stretching (123)	IV	107
Forced-Choice Identity (129)	'74	20
Boasting (181)	'76	49
The Other You (182)	'76	51
Praise (306)	VIII	61
Introjection (321)	'82	29
Personality Traits (349)	IX	158
Understanding the Need for Approval (438)	'88	21
The Golden Egg Award (448)	'88	89
Adventures at Work (521)	'95–1	9
That's Me (522)	'95–1	17
Knowledge Is Power (631)	'99–2	13
Spirituality at Work (658)	'00–2	15
The Imposter Syndrome (696)	'02–1	11
Internet Impressions (710)	'02–2	11

Sex Roles

	Vol.	Page
Polarization (62)	III	57
Sex-Role Stereotyping (95)	'73	26
Sex-Role Attributes (184)	'76	63
Who Gets Hired? (215)	VI	106
Sexual Assessment (226)	'78	36
Alpha II (248)	VII	19
Sexual Values (249)	VII	24
Sex-Role Attitudes (258)	VII	85
Sexual Values in Organizations (268)	VII	146
Sexual Attraction (272)	'80	26
Sexism in Advertisements (305)	VIII	58
The Promotion (362)	IX	152
Raising Elizabeth (415)	'86	21
The Problem with Men/Women Is .. (437)	'88	9
The Girl and the Sailor (450)	'89	17
Tina Carlan (466)	'90	45

Diversity

	Vol.	Page
Status-Interaction Study (41)	II	85
Peer Perceptions (58)	III	41
Discrimination (63)	III	62
Traditional American Values (94)	'73	23
Growth Group Values (113)	IV	45
The In-Group (124)	IV	112
Leadership Characteristics (127)	'74	13
Group Composition (172)	V	139
Headbands (203)	VI	25
Sherlock (213)	VI	92
Negotiating Differences (217)	VI	114
Young/Old Woman (227)	'78	40
Pygmalion (229)	'78	51
Race from Outer Space (239)	'79	38
Prejudice (247)	VII	15
Physical Characteristics (262)	VII	108
Whom To Choose (267)	VII	141
Data Survey (292)	'81	57

	Vol.	Page
Lifeline (298)	VIII	21
Four Cultures (338)	'83	72
All Iowans Are Naive (344)	IX	14
AIRSOPAC (364)	IX	172
Doctor, Lawyer, Indian Chief (427)	'87	21
Life Raft (462)	'90	17
Zenoland (492)	'92	69
First Impressions (509)	'94	9
Parole Board (510)	'94	17
Fourteen Dimensions (557)	'96–2	9
Adoption (569)	'97–1	9
Globalization (570)	'97–1	19
Generational Pyramids (571)	'97–1	33
People with Disabilities (594)	'98–1	15
Expanding the Scope of Diversity Programs (617)	'99–1	13
Tortuga Place and Your Place (644)	'00–1	15
Unearned Privilege (659)	'00–2	25
What's Your Generation X IQ? (682)	'01–2	11
Cultural Triangle (697)	'02–1	19

Life/Career Planning

	Vol.	Page
Life Planning (46)	II	101
Banners (233)	'79	9
Wants Bombardment (261)	VII	105
Career Renewal (332)	'83	27
Life Assessment and Planning (378)	'85	15
Work-Needs Assessment (393)	X	31
The Ego-Radius Model (394)	X	41
Dropping Out (414)	'86	15
Roles (416)	'86	27
Creating Ideal Personal Futures (439)	'88	31
Pie in the Sky (461)	'90	9
What's in It for Me? (463)	'90	21
Affirmations (473)	'91	9

	Vol.	Page
Supporting Cast (486)	'92	15
Career Visioning (498)	'93	13
The Hand You're Dealt (523)	'95–1	23
Living Our Values (548)	'96–1	25
Career Roads (549)	'96–1	35
Collaborating for Success (572)	'97–1	45
High Jump (573)	'97–1	57
Issues, Trends, and Goals (595)	'98–1	21
Bouncing Back (596)	'98–1	35
Work Activities (597)	'98–1	43
From Good Intentions to Results (645)	'00–1	27
What Works Best? (671)	'01–1	21
Passion and Purpose (672)	'01–1	35

COMMUNICATION

Awareness

	Vol.	Page
One-Way, Two-Way (4)	I	13
Think-Feel (65)	III	70
Ball Game (108)	IV	27
Re-Owning (128)	'74	18
Helping Relationships (152)	V	13
Babel (153)	V	16
Blindfolds (175)	'76	13
Letter Exchange (190)	'77	28
Dominoes (202)	VI	21
Blivet (241)	'79	46
Meanings Are in People (250)	VII	28
Mixed Messages (251)	VII	34
Gestures (286)	'81	28
Maze (307)	VIII	64
Feelings (330)	'83	14
Synonyms (341)	IX	5
In Other Words (396)	X	55
Taking Responsibility (397)	X	62
Pass It On (398)	X	68
Shades of Difference (417)	'86	35
E-Prime (440)	'88	39
Words Apart (464)	'90	29
Supportive Versus Defensive Climates (474)	'91	15
Let Me (511)	'94	31
Bugs (553)	'96–1	73
Red Light/Green Light (598)	'98–1	53
Supreme Court (660)	'00–2	33
Music While You Work (683)	'01–2	23
Speed Up! (698)	'02–1	29

Building Trust

	Vol.	Page
Dyadic Encounter (21)	I	90
Nonverbal Communication I (22)	I	101
Intimacy Program (70)	III	89
Dialog (116)	IV	66
Dimensions of Trust (120)	IV	96
Dyadic Renewal (169)	V	116
Disclosing & Predicting (180)	'76	46
Current Status (196)	'77	57
Dyadic Risk Taking (220)	VI	130
Work Dialogue (524)	'95–1	27
Coal to Diamonds (533)	'95–2	9
Alter Ego (599)	'98–1	59
Building Trust in Pairs (632)	'99–2	19
What to Say (661)	'00–2	37

Conflict

	Vol.	Page
Frustrations & Tensions (75)	72	5
Conflict Fantasy (130)	'74	22
Escalation (219)	VI	127

	Vol.	Page
Defensive & Supportive Communication (238)	'79	28
Conflict Management (242)	'79	54
Resistance (309)	VIII	75
Conflict Role Play (340)	'83	80
The Company Task Force (352)	IX	84
The Decent but Pesky Co-Worker (400)	X	80
VMX Productions, Inc. (441)	'88	43
Quality Customer Service (475)	'91	27
The Parking Space (476)	'91	35
Time Flies (499)	'93	19
Alpha/Beta (512)	'94	37
Common Ground (539)	'95–2	51
Thumbs Up, Thumbs Down (574)	'97–1	65
The M&M® Game (618)	'99–1	19
Retaliatory Cycle (662)	'00–2	45

Feedback

	Vol.	Page
Group-on-Group (6)	I	22
Coins (23)	I	104
Behavior Description Triads (50)	III	6
Psychomat (84)	'72	58
Puzzlement (97)	'73	30
Analyzing & Increasing Open Behavior (99)	'73	38
The Gift of Happiness (104)	IV	15
Sculpturing (106)	IV	21
The Portrait Game (107)	IV	24
Party Conversations (138)	'75	10
Adjectives (168)	V	114
Introspection (209)	V	157
Cards (225)	'78	34
Developing Trust (303)	VIII	45
Giving and Receiving Feedback (315)	VIII	125
Feedback (355)	IX	107
Pin Spotter (377)	'85	11
Feedback on Nonverbal and Verbal Behaviors (379)	'85	35
Gaining Support (380)	'85	39
I Am, Don't You Think? (390)	X	8
Two Bags Full (391)	X	22
Seeing Ourselves as Others See Us (426)	'87	17
The Art of Feedback (449)	'89	9
Feedback Awareness (487)	'92	29
A Note to My Teammate (497)	'93	9
Lines (551)	'96–1	59
Coloring Book (646)	'00–1	37
I Appreciate (673)	'01–1	63

Listening

	Vol.	Page
Listening Triads (8)	I	31
Rumor Clinic (28)	II	12
Not-Listening (52)	III	10
Peter-Paul (87)	'73	7
Active Listening (252)	VII	39
I'm All Ears (395)	X	46
Poor Listening Habits (428)	'87	25
In Reply (465)	'90	35
Needs, Features, and Benefits (513)	'94	47
Levels of Dialogue (525)	'95–1	45

Styles

	Vol.	Page
Building Open & Closed Relationships (93)	'73	20

	Vol.	Page
Submission/Aggression/ Assertion (206)	V	136
Organizational TA (310)	VIII	83
The Human Bank Account (399)	X	76
The Candy Bar (457)	'89	73
Stating the Issue (503)	'93	43
Enhancing Communication (550)	'96–1	51
Go Left, Go Right (575)	'97–1	69
Memories (699)	'02–1	51

Technology

	Vol.	Page
Virtual Scavenger Hunt (619)	'99–1	27
Mediated Message Exchange (647)	'00–1	43
Telephone Conference (648)	'00–1	51

PROBLEM SOLVING

Generating Alternatives

	Vol.	Page
Broken Squares (7)	I	25
Brainstorming (53)	III	14
Quaker Meeting (76)	'72	11
Nominal Group Technique (141)	'75	35
Poems (185)	'77	13
Package Tour (192)	'77	35
Numbers (221)	'78	9
Puzzle Cards (240)	'79	41
Analytical or Creative? (285)	'81	24
Vacation Schedule (312)	VIII	100
Pebbles (335)	'83	45
Bricks (343)	IX	10
Departmental Dilemma (350)	IX	66
QC Agenda (370)	'84	44
Water Jars (392)	X	26
Marzilli's Fine Italian Foods (454)	'89	55
Cooperative Inventions (467)	'90	61
Greenback Financial Services (470)	'90	83
Puzzling Encounters (481)	'91	97
The Real Meaning (502)	'93	39
PBJ Corporation (568)	'96–2	131
Broken Triangles (576)	'97–1	73
Deck of Cards (663)	'00–2	51
Decision, Decisions (684)	'01–2	33
Ask Everyone (711)	'02–2	21

Information Sharing

	Vol.	Page
Energy International (80)	'72	25
Pine County (117)	IV	75
Farm E-Z (133)	'74	44
Sales Puzzle (155)	V	34
Room 703 (156)	V	39
Al Kohbari (178)	'76	26
Murder One (212)	VI	75
Farmers (284)	'81	16
The Sales Manager's Journey (359)	IX	125
The Welsh Boothouse (383)	'85	67
Society of Taos (432)	'87	57
Dust Pan Case (482)	'91	107
Diversity Quiz (514)	'94	55
Bean Counters (552)	'96–1	67
Systems Redesign (633)	'99–2	31

Consensus/Synergy

	Vol.	Page
Top Problems (11)	I	49
Residence Halls (15)	I	72
NORC (30)	II	18

	Vol.	Page
Kerner Report (64)	III	64
Supervisory Behavior/Aims of		
Education (69)	III	84
Shoe Store (102)	IV	5
Consensus-Seeking (115)	IV	51
Hung Jury (134)	'74	64
Kidney Machine (135)	'74	78
Lost at Sea (140)	'75	28
Cash Register (151)	V	10
Letter Occurrence/Health		
Professions Prestige (157)	V	44
Wilderness Survival (177)	'76	19
Pyramids (187)	'77	20
Admissions Committee (223)	'78	15
Alphabet Names (236)	'79	19
What's Important on My Job?		
(244)	'79	71
Lists (255)	VII	57
Values for the 1980s (271)	'80	20
Ranking Characteristics (429)	'87	31
People Are Electric (501)	'93	35
The Lottery (526)	'95–1	53
Councils to the President		
(605)	'98–2	9
New-Member Welcome		
(606)	'98–2	19
The Affinity Diagram (620)	'99–1	39
Shift Happens (664)	'00–2	57
Electric Company (700)	'02–1	55
Successful Leadership		
Traits (712)	'02–2	25

Action Planning

	Vol.	Page
Force-Field Analysis (40)	II	79
Wahoo City (73)	III	100
Dhabi Fehru (259)	VII	91
Island Commission (260)	VII	99
Missiles (275)	'80	43
Robbery (334)	'83	40
The Impact Wheel (458)	'89	83
Coping Strategies (485)	'92	9
Wreck Survivors (515)	'94	67
Values, Visions, and		
Missions (527)	'95–1	59
River of Change (555)	'96–1	93
Ideal Work Place (561)	'96–2	45
Award Ceremony (581)	'97–2	9
Inputs, Process, Outputs		
(582)	'97–2	17
Diametrically Opposed		
(649)	'00–1	57
Make a Mark (665)	'00–2	63
New Owners (674)	'01–1	75

GROUPS

How Groups Work

	Vol.	Page
Committee Meeting (9)	I	36
Process Observation (10)	I	45
Group Tasks (29)	II	16
Self-Interaction Task (37)	II	68
Towers (54)	III	17
What To Look for in Groups		
(79)	'72	19
Greeting Cards (82)	'72	44
Cog's Ladder (126)	'74	8
Faculty Meeting (139)	'75	15
Tinkertoy Bridge (160)	V	60
LEGO Bridge (161)	V	73
Word-Letter (200)	VI	15
Spy (218)	VI	117
Homesell (228)	'78	46
Line of Four (237)	'79	21

	Vol.	Page
Slingshots (256)	VII	69
Four-Letter Words (287)	'81	34
Dynasell (290)	'81	50
Structures (308)	VIII	69
Team Planning (351)	IX	74
Group Sell (357)	IX	114
Four Corners (442)	'88	51
Orientations (443)	'88	57
Whirlybird (491)	'92	63
Let's Come to Order (528)	'95–1	73
Airplanes (534)	'95–2	13
Rope Trick (577)	'97–1	81
Lincoln Decision Com-		
mittee (578)	'97–1	89
Web of Yarn (583)	'97–2	25
Innovative Meetings (607)	'98–2	23
No Strings Attached (608)	'98–2	31
Crime-Fighting Task Force		
(634)	'99–2	35
Piccadilly Manor (650)	'00–1	65
Logos (675)	'01–1	81
Neutral Corner (685)	'01–2	37
Construction Project (713)	'02–2	31

Competition/Collaboration

	Vol.	Page
Model Building (32)	II	29
Prisoners' Dilemma (61)	III	52
Decisions (83)	'72	51
Wooden Blocks (105)	IV	18
World Bank (147)	'75	56
Testing (164)	V	91
X-Y (179)	'76	41
Blue/Green (189)	'77	24
Circle in the Square (205)	VI	32
Balance of Power (231)	'78	63
Paper Box (243)	'79	60
Trading Cards (263)	VII	112
War Gaming (264)	VII	117
Move to Newtown (278)	'80	60
High Iron (280)	'80	78
Cross-Group Negotiation		
and Cooperation (302)	VIII	41
Risk Game (311)	VIII	93
Intertwine (319)	'82	20
Block Buster (320)	'82	24
Stock Exchange (384)	'85	75
Assignment Flexibility (516)	'94	75
Property Game (554)	'96–1	77
Egg Drop (564)	'96–2	77
Allied Circuits (609)	'98–2	39
The Forest vs. the Trees		
(610)	'98–2	53
Powerful Exercise (666)	'00–2	67
Power Poker (701)	'02–1	69
Team Traps (714)	'02–2	37

Conflict

	Vol.	Page
Conflict Resolution (14)	I	70
Lindell-Billings Corporation		
(144)	'75	46
Conflict Styles (186)	'77	15
Controversial Issues (224)	'78	28
Budget Cutting (323)	'82	35
Trouble in Manufacturing		
(374)	'84	67
Datatrak (375)	'84	74
Winterset High School (435)	'87	79

Negotiating/Bargaining

	Vol.	Page
Unequal Resources (78)	'72	17
Monetary Investment (265)	VII	124
Creative Products (279)	'80	69
Territory (314)	VIII	120

	Vol.	Page
Bargaining, United Nations		
Style (471)	'90	95
Merger Mania (584)	'97–2	29

TEAMS

How Groups Work

	Vol.	Page
System Problems (111)	IV	38
Top Secret Contract (194)	'77	47
Team Development (208)	VI	54
Slogans (276)	'80	51
Project Colossus (288)	'81	43
Group Identity (299)	VIII	25
Chips (322)	'82	31
Meetings Audit (325)	'82	49
Work-Group Review (327)	'82	60
Healthy or Unhealthy? (404)	X	96
Sticky Wickets (405)	X	99
Bean Bags (419)	'86	45
Instant Survey (434)	'87	75
Team Interventions (558)	'96–2	19
Take Note of Yourself		
(621)	'99–1	43
Team Troubles (635)	'99–2	49
Share the Load (667)	'00–2	73
When Shall We Meet		
Again? (676)	'01–1	85
Sweet Tooth (702)	'02–1	85

Roles

	Vol.	Page
Role Nominations (38)	II	72
Line-Up & Power Inversion		
(59)	III	46
Role Clarification (171)	V	136
Baseball Game (270)	'80	14
The Car (326)	'82	55
The Seven Pieces (366)	'84	16
Role Power (368)	'84	26
Kaleidoscope (408)	X	122
Position Power (420)	'86	51
America's Favorite Pastime		
(455)	'89	61
Symbols (469)	'90	73
Multiple Roles (480)	'91	85
Yours, Mine, and Ours (500)	'93	31
Tasks, Skill, and Commit-		
ments (546)	'96–1	15
Risky Business (636)	'99–2	67
Appreciative Introductions		
(668)	'00–2	85
Island Survival (715)	'02–2	41

Problem Solving/Decision Making

	Vol.	Page
Lutts & Mipps (31)	II	24
Joe Doodlebug (103)	IV	8
Planning Recommendations		
or Action (132)	'74	32
The Lawn (337)	'83	65
Threats to the Project (373)	'84	62
Unscrambling the Bank		
Accounts (431)	'87	51
Control or Surrender (453)	'89	47
Fishing for "Why?" (535)	'95–2	21
Team Checkup (547)	'96–1	19
Turbo Affinity Technique		
(585)	'97–2	47
Hit the Target Fast (586)	'97–2	53
Scope of Control (600)	'98–1	63
News Room (611)	'98–2	59
Risk Tolerance (677)	'01–1	89
Jet Away (686)	'01–2	45
Puzzles (703)	'02–1	91
Scrambled Words (716)	'02–2	45

	Vol.	Page

Feedback

Leveling (17) — I — 79
Dependency-Intimacy (18) — I — 82
Group Development (39) — II — 76
Group Self-Evaluations (55) — III — 22
Nominations (57) — III — 33
Dividing the Loot (60) — III — 49
Team Building (66) — III — 73
Organizational Mirror (67) — III — 78
Team Identity (77) — '72 — 13
Twenty-Five Questions (118) — IV — 88
Agenda Setting (166) — V — 108
Cups (167) — V — 111
Person Perception (170) — V — 131
Affirmation of Trust (216) — VI — 110
Stones, Bands, & Circle (254) — VII — 53
I Hear That You.. (291) — '81 — 54
Group Effectiveness (297) — VIII — 18
Group Sociogram (316) — VIII — 131
Constructive Criticism (345) — IX — 28
Messages (356) — IX — 110
Sharing and Supporting
Goals (386) — '85 — 87
Smackers (388) — '85 — 95
Power and Affection
Exchange (402) — X — 88
Yearbook (403) — X — 92
Group Sociogram II (418) — '86 — 41
The Advertising Firm (444) — '88 — 69
Images (445) — '88 — 73
It's in the Cards (456) — '89 — 67
The Genie's Wish (468) — '90 — 67
Bases of Power (477) — '91 — 43
Group Calendar (489) — '92 — 47
Strengths and Needs (490) — '92 — 51
The Helping Hand (529) — '95–1 — 87
Comfort Zones (536) — '95–2 — 29
This and That (587) — '97–2 — 59
TeamScores (588) — '97–2 — 63
Enablers and Barriers (612) — '98–2 — 63
Jigsaw Puzzles (622) — '99–1 — 47
Nicknames (678) — '01–1 — 97

Conflict and Intergroup Issues

Conflict

Ajax Appliance Corporation
(406) — X — 106
Sharing Perspectives (409) — X — 126
Conflict Management (483) — '91 — 119
Performance Unlimited
(566) — '96–2 — 113

Intergroup Issues

Win as Much as You Can (36) — II — 62
Intergroup Meeting (68) — III — 81
Intergroup Model Building (81) — '72 — 36
Win What, Lose What? (145) — '75 — 51
Riddles (150) — V — 5
Intergroup Clearing (289) — '81 — 48
The Value Profile (407) — X — 118
They Said, We Said (530) — '95–1 — 91
Group Sculptures (637) — '99–2 — 75

CONSULTING & FACILITATING

Consulting: Awareness

Strategies of Changing (98) — '73 — 32
Organization Structures (110) — IV — 34
Coloring Book (163) — V — 85
Marbles (165) — V — 98
Tug O'War (188) — '77 — 22
MANDOERS (232) — '78 — 71
Organizational Blasphemies
(339) — '83 — 77

Matrix (360) — IX — 136
The Shoe-Distribution Com-
pany (372) — '84 — 55
The People of Trion (410) — X — 132
Dos and Don'ts (446) — '88 — 77
Prairie General Hospital (479) — '91 — 65
The Hundredth Monkey (505) — '93 — 75
Hats "R" Us (517) — '94 — 93
Exploring Our Cultural
History (537) — '95–2 — 41
Straws and Pins (538) — '95–2 — 45
By the Numbers (589) — '97–2 — 71
Focus Groups (590) — '97–2 — 89
System Review (613) — '98–2 — 69
Koosh(r) Ball Company
(623) — '99–1 — 53
Press Conference (638) — '99–2 — 81

Consulting: Diagnosing/Skills

Roxboro Electric Company
(131) — '74 — 24
Consulting Triads (183) — '76 — 53
Tri-State (193) — '77 — 39
HELPCO (211) — VI — 66
Willington (230) — '78 — 55
Elm Street Community
Church (347) — IX — 34
Inquiries (348) — IX — 48
Measuring Excellence (385) — '85 — 81
Client Concerns (412) — X — 148
The Client-Consultant
Questionnaire (424) — '86 — 79
City of Buffington (460) — '89 — 101
Metaphors (484) — '91 — 125
Working at Our Company
(493) — '92 — 79
Help Wanted (494) — '92 — 87
International Equity Claims
Department (506) — '93 — 85
Operational Definitions
(540) — '95–2 — 63
Wooden Towers (541) — '95–2 — 69
Walking the Talk (559) — '96–2 — 27
The MPM Scale (563) — '96–2 — 67
U.S. National Healthcare
Commission (591) — '97–2 — 95
Business Cards (601) — '98–1 — 71
Collecting Diagnostic Data
(639) — '99–2 — 89
Interrogatories (704) — '02–1 — 95

Facilitating: Opening

Listening & Inferring (1) — I — 3
Two-Four-Eight (2) — I — 5
Who Am I? (5) — I — 19
Group Conversation (25) — II — 3
Jigsaw (27) — II — 10
First Names, First Impressions
(42) — II — 88
"Who Am I?" Variations (49) — III — 3
"Cold" Introductions (88) — '73 — 9
Getting Acquainted (101) — IV — 3
Hum-Dinger (125) — '74 — 7
Energizers (149) — V — 3
Limericks (173) — '76 — 7
Labeling (174) — '76 — 10
Best Friend (197) — V — 13
Choose an Object (198) — V — 17
Tea Party (245) — VII — 5
Autographs (269) — '80 — 11
Alliterative Names (281) — '81 — 9
Birth Signs (282) — '81 — 11
Name Tags (293) — VIII — 5

Learning Exchange (294) — VIII — 7
Rebus Names (317) — '82 — 9
Just the Facts (329) — '83 — 11
News Bulletin (342) — IX — 8
Group Savings Bank (376) — '84 — 92
Daffodil (387) — '85 — 91
Getting To Know You (413) — '86 — 11
I Represent (436) — '87 — 87
Color Me (507) — '93 — 93
Parsley, Garlic, Ginger,
Pepper (518) — '94 — 107
Your Book Jacket (531) — '95–1 — 97
Bingo (545) — '96–1 — 9
I Have an Opinion (602) — '98–1 — 75
Openers (624) — '99–1 — 59
A New Twist (640) — '99–2 — 101
Alpha "Bets" (651) — '00–1 — 81
Age Barometer (679) — '01–1 — 101
Who Says What? (687) — '01–2 — 49
Me in a Bag (717) — '02–2 — 51

Facilitating: Blocks to Learning

Gunnysack (89) — '73 — 11
Perception of Task (91) — '73 — 15
The "T" Test (112) — IV — 41
Communication Analysis
(191) — '77 — 32
Buttermilk (234) — '79 — 13
Resistance to Learning
(301) — VIII — 37
Needs, Expectations, and
Resources (324) — '82 — 46
Taking Your Creative Pulse
(567) — '96–2 — 119
Benefits and Barriers (652) — '00–1 — 87
Crochet Hook (705) — '02–1 — 99

Facilitating: Skills

Fantasies (16) — I — 75
Awareness Expansion (19) — I — 86
Assumptions About Human
Relations Training (24) — I — 107
Miniversity (26) — I — 17
Verbal Activities Within Groups
(43) — II — 91
Nonverbal Communication II
(44) — II — 94
Helping Pairs (45) — II — 97
Microlab (47) — II — 113
Process Intervention (48) — II — 115
Empty Chair (51) — III — 8
Nonverbal Communication III
(72) — III — 97
Medial Feedback (92) — '73 — 17
Participant-Staff Expecta-
tions (96) — '73 — 29
Group Leadership Functions
(148) — '75 — 63
Training Philosophies (363) — IX — 159
Good Workshops Don't Just
Happen (495) — '92 — 97
Up Close and Personal with
Dr. Maslow (496) — '92 — 111
Zodiac for Trainers (508) — '93 — 97
Disability Awareness (519) — '94 — 115
Seaside Towers (532) — '95–1 — 101
Eight Training Competen-
cies (579) — '97–1 — 105
Word Game (603) — '98–1 — 79
Your Voice, Your Self (625) — '99–1 — 63
Building Blocks (626) — '99–1 — 69
Continuum (669) — '00–2 — 89
Trade Fair (680) — '01–1 — 105

	Vol.	Page
Rotating Facilitators (688)	'01–2	53
What's Next? (718)	'02–2	55
Facilitating: Closing		
Symbolic Closing Exercise (86)	'72	61
Closure (114)	IV	49
Payday (146)	'75	54
Symbolic Toast (176)	'76	17
Bread Making (201)	VI	19
Golden Awards (222)	'78	12
Kia Ora (318)	'82	12
Aloha (389)	X	5
Feedback Letters (556)	'96–1	99
Tool Box (627)	'99–1	73
Management Wizards (653)	'00–1	93
Wrap-Up (689)	'01–2	59
Certificates (706)	'02–1	111
Billboard Sentiments (719)	'02–2	59

LEADERSHIP

Ethics

	Vol.	Page
What Do You See? (137)	'75	7
Ideal Cards (143)	'75	43
Who Killed John Doe? (235)	'79	15
Personal Identity (246)	VII	11
Louisa's Problem (283)	'81	13
Values and Decisions (361)	IX	146
The Gold Watch (411)	X	142
Living Ethics (580)	'97–1	127
Global Service Provider (592)	'97–2	105
Ethics in Action (614)	'98–2	75

Interviewing/Appraisal

	Vol.	Page
Live Case (142)	'75	40
Sunglow (257)	VII	73
Assistant Wanted (333)	'83	31
Interviewing (358)	IX	122
Inquiries and Discoveries (365)	'84	9
Constructive Discipline (371)	'84	49
BARS (423)	'86	73
Performance Appraisal (425)	'87	11
What's Legal? (451)	'89	23
Consultant's Report (542)	'95–2	89
Precision Bicycle Components (543)	'95–2	97

	Vol.	Page
Calloway Power Station (562)	'96–2	57
Sign Here (615)	'98–2	81
Apple of Your Eye (628)	'99–1	75
Communication Games		
Selection Interview (707)	'00–1	97
	'02–1	115

Motivation

	Vol.	Page
Motivation (100)	'73	43
Motivation (204)	VI	28
Darts (210)	VI	61
Penny Pitch (253)	VII	46
People on the Job (295)	VIII	10
The Manager's Guidebook (354)	IX	102
MACE (367)	'84	22
There's Never Time To Do It Right (430)	'87	45
Four Factors (452)	'89	39
Master and Apprentice (544)	'95–2	117
The Flip-It Company (560)	'96–2	39
Managerial Perceptions (616)	'98–2	87
Management-HR Partnering (629)	'99–1	81
If You Think You Can (641)	'99–2	105
Millennium Mobile (655)	'00–1	119
The Stephanie Syndrome (690)	'01–2	63

Diversity/Stereotyping

	Vol.	Page
Hollow Square (33)	II	32
Hampshire In-Basket (34)	II	41
Absentee (158)	V	49
When To Delegate (304)	VIII	52
Reviewing Objectives and Strategies (328)	'82	65
Vice President's In-Basket (336)	'83	49
Meeting Management (421)	'86	55
Raises (422)	'86	65
Delegation (447)	'88	81
The Robotics Decision (459)	'89	89
Termination (472)	'90	103
The Employment Case (520)	'94	123
Under Pressure (565)	'96–2	87
Leadership History (691)	'01–2	71
Supervisory Success (720)	'02–2	63

Styles

	Vol.	Page
T-P Leadership Questionnaire (3)	I	7
Choosing a Color (12)	I	56
Auction (35)	II	58
Toothpicks (121)	IV	99
Styles of Leadership (154)	V	19
Fork-Labyrinth (159)	V	53
Pins & Straws (162)	V	78
Executive Pie (195)	'77	54
Staff Meeting (207)	VI	39
Power Personalities (266)	VII	127
Managerial Characteristics (273)	'80	31
Choosing an Apartment (274)	'80	37
Power & Affiliation (277)	'80	54
Boss Wanted (296)	VIII	15
Tangram (313)	VIII	108
Manager's Dilemma (331)	'83	19
Power Caucus (346)	IX	31
Management Skills (353)	IX	93
Follow the Leader (369)	'84	38
Management Perspectives (381)	'85	45
Chipping In (384)	'85	57
Choose Me (401)	X	85
Quantity Versus Quality (433)	'87	69
Rhetoric and Behavior (478)	'91	51
The Good Leader (488)	'92	37
Organizational Structures (504)	'93	63
Today and Tomorrow (604)	'98–1	87
Rope-a-Leader (630)	'99–1	87
Leadership Style (656)	'00–1	125
Show and Tell (681)	'01–1	109
Second to None (708)	'02–1	127

ORGANIZATIONS

Communication

	Vol.	Page
If We Only Knew (642)	'99–2	121
Story Weaving (692)	'01–2	77
Knowledge Is Good (693)	'01–2	85

Vision, Mission, Values, Strategy

	Vol.	Page
It's in the Bag (694)	'01–2	97
Futures (721)	'02–2	71

Change Management

	Vol.	Page
The Alphabet Game (709)	'02–1	137
Pink Slip (722)	'02–2	79

710. INTERNET IMPRESSIONS: RESPONDING TO DIFFERENT LEVELS OF SELF-DISCLOSURE

Goals

- To explore the impact of self-disclosure on first impressions we have of another person.
- To develop awareness of how stereotyping, bias, and jumping to conclusions affect our first impressions of others.

Group Size

Eight to thirty participants, in groups of four or five.

Time Required

One hour and ten to fifteen minutes.

Materials

- One copy of Internet Impressions Female Personals Ad A for half the participants and Internet Impressions Female Personals Ad B for the other half.
- One copy of Internet Impressions Male Personals Ad A for half the participants and Internet Impressions Male Personals Ad B for the other half.
- Two copies of the Internet Impressions Worksheet for each participant.
- Pens or pencils for each participant.
- A flip chart and felt-tipped markers for each subgroup.
- Masking tape.

Physical Setting

A room that has tables where subgroups of four or five members can complete their assignments without disturbing one another as they work.

Process

1. Have participants divide into groups of four or five members each, using any method you wish, and be seated at separate tables.

2. Introduce the activity to the group.

   "There are many different types of work situations in which we meet people for the first time through their written communications. This occurs when a job is advertised and resumes are sent in reply, when information from customers or suppliers is received, when correspondence is sent to us from co-workers in another part of the organization or at a different locale, and when notes are left for us in our work areas. These communications often give us different types of information about the person who sent them. Knowingly or unknowingly, we use this information to form an impression or opinion of the other individual. In this activity, we will explore these first impressions and how they are formed using Internet dating personal ads as examples."

   (Five minutes.)

3. Distribute one Internet Impressions Female Personals Ad A (or B) and one Internet Impressions Male Personals Ad A (or B) and two Internet Impressions Worksheets and a pen or pencil to each participant. Give out both A and B ads within each subgroup.

4. Ask participants to read the Female Personals Ad they have received and to individually answer the questions on the worksheet. Tell them that when it appears that everyone at their table has completed the worksheet that they are to share their responses to each question. Have each table select one member of its group to record individual member responses on the flip chart. (Ten minutes.)

5. Instruct participants to follow the same steps for the Male Personals Ad. (Ten minutes.)

6. After everyone has finished, facilitate a discussion with the entire group using the following questions:

   ■ In general, what sorts of topics came up in your group? How similar or different were the discussions between the male and female ads? Between ads A and B?

- What kinds of conclusions did you draw about each person who placed an ad, based on the information in the ad?

- Why did you arrive at these conclusions?

(Fifteen minutes.)

7. Summarize the participants' comments and share your own observations. (Five minutes.)

8. Draw a continuum on a flip chart. Label the left side of the continuum "low self-disclosure" and the right side of the continuum "high self-disclosure." Explain that low self-disclosure includes small talk, such as the weather or sports, and is typically guarded in nature, not revealing anything personal. On the other hand, high self-disclosure communicates a lot of personal information, going beyond physical characteristics, and includes topics such as philosophy of life; personal aspirations, wishes, hopes or dreams; traumatic incidents; and pet peeves. Lead a concluding discussion using the following information and questions.

- What does level of self-disclosure have to do with the first impressions that we formulate about other people?

- How much self-disclosure is in each of the personal ads?

- How do we stereotype others based on what they write?

- How do our personal biases make us jump to conclusions about other people, either negatively or positively?

- What causes us to stereotype and/or jump to conclusions based on our first impressions?

(Fifteen minutes.)

9. Explain that we form opinions and judgments very quickly based on limited information. Our brains are wired so that we learn to do this. Our skill in sorting people into categories is rooted in the survival of the species, as it is necessary to distinguish friend from foe. Filtering information received through the senses and intuition—and making decisions based on that information—is a strength in the human species. However, a strength overused can become a weakness. For example, sometimes we make snap judgments that we learn later were errors. Jumping to conclusions could lead to things like the wrong person being reprimanded for an error or our not confronting the person who is actually responsible and holding him or her accountable. This may create ill will among staff. However, the reverse is true as well. Taking too long to form an opinion

about someone else can mean that we lose an opportunity to hire some-one or that we don't form a relationship that could be advantageous. (Ten minutes.)

Variations

- Give half of the subgroups Female Ad A and Male Ad A, the other half Female Ad B and Male Ad B. (*Note:* both ads are from the same person in each case). Have them write down their perceptions about the ads and then share with the other subgroups.

- Give half of the subgroups Female Ad A and Female Ad B, the other half Male Ad A and Male Ad B. Then assign each subgroup the task of find-ing the differences between the ads and to share their first perceptions about the ads with the other subgroups.

- Have male only and female only subgroups. Give them the same ads to work on.

- Resumes can be used instead of personal ads as long as identifying infor-mation is removed from them.

Submitted by Lori Silverman and Karen Ostrov.

Lori Silverman, M.S., M.B.A., is the author of Critical SHIFT: The Future of Quality in Organizational Performance *and the owner of Partners for Prog-ress, a management consulting firm that helps organizations achieve and main-tain a sustainable competitive advantage in their marketplace. She has a wide range of public- and private-sector consulting experience in strategic management, enterprise-wide change, and performance improvement. Ms. Silverman is also a faculty associate with the Fluno Center for Executive Education at the University of Wisconsin-Madison.*

Karen Ostrov, Ph.D., is the president of KONECT, an executive and management coaching and training company. Dr. Ostrov is a practicing psychologist, working with decision makers in private and public sector corporations. She brings a fresh psychological perspective to demonstrating effective human communications in the workplace. Her training programs focus on learning the intra- and interpersonal skills required of today's leaders. She also serves as adjunct faculty with the Fluno Center for Executive Education at the University of Wisconsin-Madison.*

INTERNET IMPRESSIONS FEMALE PERSONALS AD A

- Age 35 ~ Taurus
- Average body
- 5' 7"
- Caucasian (white)
- College graduate
- Christian
- Nonsmoker
- Drinks occasionally
- Divorced

Investing in a new relationship is mentally, emotionally, and financially exhausting. I have found that most men don't like change any more than I do. Lucky for you I've found a solution that will work for both of us. Not only do I already have Smith as a last name, but everything in, on, and around the house already has the name stenciled or decoratively burned in, saving you from all the backbreaking work of scraping, filling, and repainting. Your towels (monogrammed BS) are already hanging in your bathroom, and your collection of BOB coffee mugs hangs on the tree next to the automatic drip coffee pot—the one with a timer so you can set it yourself before retiring to bed. On the butler next to our matching twin beds is your favorite bowling shirt silk-screened with your league nickname, "The Big B.S.er". Don't worry if your Christian name isn't really Robert. Many men use Bob as a nickname to cover up embarrassing or complicated names containing more than three characters. I wouldn't even worry about your last name not being Smith. A name change won't cost you all that much. My other Bobs eventually got used to their new names, and you will too. Please respond before Tuesday, which is garbage day and league night.

Internet Impressions Female Personals Ad B

- Age 35 ~ Taurus
- Average body
- 5' 7"
- Caucasian (white)
- College graduate
- Christian
- Nonsmoker
- Drinks occasionally
- Divorced

Never Be Penniless. This expression is something that flows easily from my pen, my keyboard, my lips. My heart is BIG. It has to be to hold all the dreams I passionately create on rainy afternoons and in the early evening as the sun sets. The wind's howling cry carries my plea for companionship into the deep woods, winding rivers, and back streets of cities and villages on quiet, snowy nights. And I sit on my balcony awaiting the echoed return of my plea—hoping, praying that its voice is not merely a copy of my own. Adversity is my companion, although I never allow him to lead. He follows me about like a lost puppy in search of things I cannot allow him. I never look behind, for if I did I'd see the pillar of salt from the tears I have shed standing as a looming monument to the life I have not only survived but have determinedly seized a hold on and dared to live. The Lord is my compass. The warmth of his brilliance guides my days; on cold, quiet nights his heavenly angels illuminate my shattered dreams across the darkened sky, daring me to continue to dream; and in the interim a childlike spirit finger paints the sky in swirling colors of adoration. I have traveled the length of the earth being careful not to ignore my own back yard—a back yard full of family barbecues, friendly gatherings, and neighbors whose identities are more than names on a mailbox. I have loved and I have lost—borne and buried—risen and fallen—been rich and poor—but through it all I have never been penniless. The keys to unlocking my heart lie at your fingertips. Win me with words.

Internet Impressions Male Personals Ad A

- Age 42 ~ Sagittarius
- Average body
- 5' 10"
- Caucasian (white)
- Some college courses
- Other religion
- Nonsmoker
- Doesn't drink
- Divorced

Hi there! Thanks for checking me out! I'm a bit shy at first, especially when I find myself attracted to a person. It's a curse I've had since I was a boy. Anyway, I wish to find a life mate who has warmth and tenderness in her heart. A woman who can communicate that warmth through a soft touch, a gentle glance, or a tender kiss. These are the desires that drive my dreams. I enjoy being a kind, caring, and considerate person. I like listening and communicating on an intimate level when in a relationship. My nature is to play and to have fun with life. I seek to create excitement and adventure. Although I have dated off and on since my divorce, I realize that I need to put my shyness aside and become more aggressive in finding the woman of my dreams. I'm down-to-earth, spiritual in many ways. I do not play mind games. I put importance on self-respect and respect of others before material things. I do enjoy and believe in having nice things, insofar as creating beauty in one's life. I believe in simplicity versus complexity. I love music, art, nature. I believe in the importance of family and children. I like to spend quality time with my 14-year-old son; we are very close. One of my favorite movies is *Dances with Wolves*. I identify a lot of myself with the principles in that movie. As far as music, I love the mood that captures me when listening to jazz and world music on the program "Echoes" (Public Radio International-PRI). If you share some of these qualities/interests and would like to find out more about me, take a chance and touch those keys gently my way! Have a wonderful day!!:)

Internet Impressions Male Personals Ad B

- Age 42 ~ Sagittarius
- Average body
- 5' 10"
- Caucasian (white)
- Some college courses
- Other religion
- Nonsmoker
- Doesn't drink
- Divorced

Please wait a minute. Okay, I'm looking in the mirror. I'll describe what I see. I see an average-looking man, good looking in some respects. He seems kind and gentle, yet there's a sense of fun and excitement. Okay, I don't want to be too weird. I'm a down-to-earth guy, spiritual in nature—meaning I am trying to make sense of this experience we call life. I am for the woman who will make the puzzle of life make beautiful sense. I love the outdoors, nature, art. I enjoy indoor decorating and outdoor landscaping, although I haven't had much time for a while. (Busy with work and all!) I enjoy going to movies and having nice conversations. I like to communicate on an intimate level with the one I'm interested in. I have a 14-year-old son who is a wonderful gift. We hang out and have as much fun as is humanly possible. If any of this is of interest to you, please take a chance and give me a jingle. I'll be waiting!:)

Internet Impressions Worksheet

Instructions: Use one worksheet for each personal ad you have received. First, read through the personal ad on your own. Then individually answer the following questions about the ad. When your entire group has finished, compare your responses and have someone write them on the flip chart so that you have a record of your group's observations and perceptions.

1. What facts do you know about this person?

2. What positive qualities does this person seem to possess?

3. What concerns do you have about this person?

4. What is your overall first impression of this person?

5. If you could choose a nickname for this person, what would it be?

6. Would you be interested in meeting him or her? Why or why not?

711. Ask Everyone: Generating Solutions*

Goals

- To identify organizational problems in a structured manner.

- To increase understanding of the impact of certain organizational problems.

- To examine possible solutions to organizational problems that have been previously identified and to identify benefits of those solutions.

- To identify and prioritize action steps quickly.

- To involve participants in problem solving and provide a forum for candid discussion.

Group Size

Six to eight participants from one organizational work group.

Time Required

Approximately ninety minutes.

Materials

- Two flip charts on stands.

- One flip-chart page for each problem statement posted on the wall.

- Masking tape.

- Assorted felt-tipped markers, at least one per participant.

- Note paper and pencils for all participants.

---

*We provide this piece as a service for newer group leaders. It is not, strictly speaking, an experiential learning activity as it does not use all of the steps of the Experiential Learning Cycle. However, we believe it to be a highly useful technique for uncovering organizational issues and their solutions.

Physical Setting

A room large enough to seat participants comfortably is required, with sufficient space to hang seven to fifteen flip-chart sheets on the wall where they can be seen by all participants.

Process

1. Explain to the group that the purpose of the session is to gather their input on problem(s) previously identified within the organization or work group. These problems could have been found by an employee survey or be problems that the group itself has previously brought up. Post the problem statement(s) on the flip-chart sheets and use masking tape to affix them to a wall where everyone can see them.

2. Say to the group, "We will be spending the next ninety minutes gathering information and your recommendations with regard to the posted problem(s). To make the best use of time, we will follow a standardized process.

3. Hand out paper and pencils and explain the process: "I will ask each person, going around the group, to state very clearly what you think the central *cause* of the problem is, the *impact* of each issue or cause, and how you would *solve* the problem if money and resources were not a concern. Last, I want to know what the *benefit* is to employees and to the organization if we are able to solve the problem." (*Note:* The key is to help the group members to channel their emotions, to craft their input in a way that all can understand, and to gather information very quickly. By completing one chart for each issue and by capturing potential solutions and benefits on the same chart, it is easy to summarize and prioritize later in the session.)

4. Write the letter "A" in the upper left-hand corner of a flip-chart sheet containing a problem statement and circle the letter. Write the word "Cause" on the next line. Then list the causes that each participant verbalizes on the flip chart. If anything is unclear, ask the person to clarify before continuing. (Two minutes.)

5. Next, ask each participant in turn, "What impact has this issue had on you (or others)?" Write the word "Impact" on the flip chart and note what each participant says. Again the goal is to write a clear and concise statement of the impact of the problem on others. (Two minutes.)

6. Now seek each participant's input on how the issue should be addressed. First write the letters "IWBNI" on the flip chart to stand for "It would be nice if. . . ." Again, write what each participant suggests. (Two minutes.)

7. Write the word "Benefits" on the flip chart; then write the participants' responses to the question, "What are the benefits to individuals (or to the organization) if we were to implement this solution?" (Two minutes.)

8. Post the completed flip-chart sheet on the wall with masking tape.

9. Repeat Steps 4 through 9, asking the participants in turn to respond to each of the problem statements previously posted, giving each the next letter of the alphabet, "B" for the second chart, "C" for the third chart, etc. Keep the pace moving. The average number of charts for a ninety-minute session with six to eight participants is twelve. Remember that any participant may have knowledge about any issue. Encourage open dialogue, but keep the group on track. (Eight minutes per problem statement.)

10. Now help the group to prioritize the issues that you have posted. Place the flip-chart pages in order around the room and direct the participants to decide on their priority on a piece of scratch paper, from 1 through [the number of issues].

11. Briefly review each of the charts. Provide everyone with felt-tipped markers. Then ask participants to write their priority ranking for each of the topics on the appropriate flip-chart sheets. (Five minutes.)

12. While the participants are completing Step 11, draw a matrix on a flip chart by first listing all of the letters used for the issues vertically. Then create rows equal to the number of participants plus one, to create columns horizontally.

13. Fill in the matrix after examining the rankings given by participants. Then total each row and write the total in the last column.

14. With a different color marker, circle the three *lowest* scores. These are the issues, noted by the letter, that participants have indicated are of greatest importance. Solicit participant observations on the score and the process. (Five minutes.)

15. Thank the participants for their time in contributing to improving the organization. Advise all about the organization's next steps with regard to implementing solutions.

Variations

- The same process can be used with multiple focus groups on the same problem. For example, five focus groups can be held at different times. Utilizing the same format and problem statement will allow you to identify trends across a larger sample size. Like issues should be combined when creating a report on aggregate results.

- Subgroups may be formed if there are too many issues for the entire group to handle within the time frame.

Submitted by Yvette Delemos Robinson.

Yvette Delemos Robinson is a director at PricewaterhouseCoopers LLP Management Consulting Services in Fairfax, Virginia. A skilled facilitator, Ms. Robinson has helped both private- and public-sector organizations implement major learning and organizational change initiatives. She has successfully led projects at Nortel Networks, ETS, Amtrak, and Avon. Ms. Robinson holds a B.S. degree from Drexel University and an M.B.A. from Pennsylvania State University.

712. Successful Leadership Traits: Reaching Consensus

Goals

- To examine the traits, behaviors, and skills of highly successful leaders.

- To discuss learnable traits, behaviors, and skills associated with leadership.

- To identify skills and attributes required for reaching consensus.

Group Size

Any size in subgroups of five.

Time Required

Fifty to sixty minutes.

Materials

- A copy of the Successful Leadership Traits Listing for each participant.

- A Successful Leadership Traits Collage of current leaders' photos on one sheet as a handout, prepared by the facilitator prior to the session.

- A feature photo from a magazine or newspaper of each of the leaders to be discussed, prepared in advance by the facilitator. The photos may be posted on the wall.

- A copy of the Successful Leadership Traits Sample List of Successful Leaders for the facilitator.

- Paper and pencils for participants.

- Two flip charts and felt-tipped markers.

Physical Setting

A room arranged with tables that will accommodate five people.

Process

1. Lead a short discussion about traits, skills, and behaviors of highly successful leaders. Post the participants' ideas about them on the flip chart. (Five minutes.)

2. Give everyone copies of the Successful Leadership Traits Listing and compare it with the list generated by the participants. (Five minutes.)

3. Distribute the prepared Successful Leadership Traits Collage with photos of ten to twelve well-known contemporary leaders on it. Also distribute paper and pencils.

4. Explain to the group that they are to answer the first two questions that you write on the flip chart individually. Write the following on a flip chart.

   - Which individual traits stand out for you in the leaders shown on the handout?

   - Which traits do all the leaders have in common?

   (Five minutes.)

5. When everyone has finished, form subgroups of five at tables and ask them to reach consensus on the next two questions after you post them on the flip chart:

   - Which of the leadership traits you listed earlier can be taught?

   - Which traits are most needed in today's workplaces?

   (Ten minutes.)

6. When the time is up, ask for two volunteer scribes to record the traits that *can be taught* and the traits that *are most needed* on two separate flip charts at the front of the room. Have the scribes capture the responses from the groups one at a time. Facilitate the capturing of the answers while they record. (Ten minutes.)

7. Bring closure with the following discussion questions:

   - What are the most common traits listed?

   - What are the most significant ones in today's workplaces?

- How easy was it to reach consensus on the most desirable traits required in today's workplace?

- Which ones can be taught easily?

- Given what you believe are the most necessary, how easy will it be for leaders to learn those particular behaviors and traits?

- What behaviors hindered your group reaching consensus?

- What behaviors/skills helped you reach consensus?

- How can you use what you have learned through this activity to work in groups in the future?

- To reach consensus in the future?

- To select leaders in your organizations?

(Twenty minutes.)

Variations

- Warm up the group with a list of leaders from the past representing different nationalities, races, cultures, professions (governmental, military, business, educational). (See the sample listing.)

- Include leaders from an occupation or profession that is familiar to group members.

Submitted by Robert Alan Black.

Robert Alan Black, Ph.D., CSP, founder and president of Cre8ng People, Places & Possibilities, is a creative thinking consultant and award-winning professional speaker who specializes in the S.P.R.E.A.D.ng™ of Cre8ng™ and creative thinking throughout workplaces around the world. Each year he speaks at many executive development institutes, conferences, and conventions in the United States, Canada, Turkey, and South Africa. He has written eleven books and over two hundred articles that have been published throughout the United States, Canada, Malaysia, Turkey, and South Africa.

SUCCESSFUL LEADERSHIP TRAITS LISTING

Adventurous

Boundless energy

Committed

Creative

Curious

Dedicated

Encouraging

Focused

Goal-oriented

Headstrong

Intelligent

Jewels (finds them in people)

Kaleidoscopic, willing to try anything

Loyal

Measures the odds of risk

Negotiates when necessary

Organized for success

Passionate about their cause

People-focused

Praises others

Quick to act when necessary

Reduces wasted effort

Secure in his/her thinking

Supportive

Task-focused

Tough

Unwilling to give up

Valiant

Willing to work hard

X-ray vision of problems

Zealous

Successful Leadership Traits Sample List of Successful Leaders

Adolf Hitler

Alexander the Great

Anita Roderick (The Body Shop)

Attila the Hun

Ben and Jerry

Betty Friedan

Bill Gates

Billie Jean King

Caesar Chavez

Chang Kai-shek

Colin Powell

Confucius

Dwight D. Eisenhower

Eleanor Roosevelt

Fidel Castro

General Norman Schwartzkoff

Gloria Steinem

Harry S. Truman

Henry Ford

Henry Kissinger

Joseph Stalin

Julius Caesar

Karl Marx

Malcolm Baldrige

Margaret Sanger

Margaret Thatcher

Martin Luther

Martin Luther King, Jr.

Mohandas Gandhi

Mother Teresa

Napoleon Bonaparte

Nelson Mandela

Pearl Buck

Rosa Parks

Teddy Roosevelt

The Dalai Lama

Walt Disney

William Safire

William Shakespeare

Winston Churchill

713. Construction Project: Task vs. People Orientation in Teams

Goals

- To highlight the importance of planning for task completion.
- To demonstrate group affinity for addressing task-related issues versus people-related issues.
- To experience difficulties involved in changing work teams from a task-oriented culture to a task-*and*-people oriented culture.
- To demonstrate the influence of involvement and work role on job satisfaction.

Group Size

Up to thirty-two in subgroups of five to eight members. Especially powerful with intact work teams.

Time Required

Approximately ninety minutes.

Materials

- Construction Project Instructions prepared in advance and posted on newsprint by the facilitator.
- Rating scale prepared in advance on newsprint by the facilitator (see explanation in Step 10).
- One large set of Tinkertoys® per subgroup.
- Paper and a pen or pencil for each participant.
- Newsprint and felt-tipped markers.

- Retractable tape measure.
- A calculator.

Physical Setting

One room that will accommodate the total group plus small breakout rooms if desired. Otherwise, a room sufficiently large so that subgroups can work without distracting one another. (*Note:* it is preferable that subgroups not see one another's output.)

Process

1. Explain that the activity will be focused on team orientation when working on a task. Form teams A, B, C, etc., of five to eight participants each with equal numbers of members and assign breakout rooms (or if in a single room, the separate work areas) or put intact work groups together. (Three minutes.)

2. Display on newsprint (prepared in advance) the following Construction Project Instructions:

   "Your team objective is to construct the tallest freestanding structure you can, using only materials found within the resource canister that your team receives. Your structure must stand by itself for at least ten seconds to qualify and will be measured from base to top. Total construction time will be ten minutes."

   Explain that "freestanding" means they may not wedge structures into the ceiling, lean them against a wall, hold onto them, or use other means to keep them from falling. Although the structure may be placed on a table or desk, this added height will not be counted when measuring the results. Clarify the instructions if necessary, and then hand out construction materials (the Tinkertoy canisters) to teams in their work areas. (Five minutes.)

3. Tell everyone to begin construction. Circulate among the groups to observe and to be available for questions. (Five minutes.)

4. After five minutes, call a temporary time out and have all participants return to their seats in the main room. Give everyone paper and pens or pencils and ask them to write their team letters (A, B, C, etc.) on half of a sheet of paper and to rate themselves on the following question (post on newsprint if desired) on a scale of 0 to 10, 10 being high and 0 being low. Say, "On a scale of 0 to 10, indicate your degree of satisfaction with

the part you have played *thus far* as a team member in building the structure. Do not let anyone see your score." (Five minutes.)

5. Collect the sheets of paper and record each score on a newsprint sheet as shown in the sample below:

Team A	Team B	Team C
5 9 8 5 8 6 2	3 7 6 4 7 5 1	9 4 7 9 6 8 5
ave: 6.14	4.71	6.71

Remind the group that they are not to reveal which number they gave, and then lead a general discussion of some factors that may have caused individuals to give high or low scores. (Five minutes.)

6. Lead a discussion with the entire group, asking the following questions:

- Did any of you actively attempt to involve less participative team members? What was the result?

- Was there a link between the scores and your team's actual effectiveness in working on the task? What was it?

- If this same question were asked of you in your actual organizations, would results have been similar? How so?

- What conclusions can be drawn about on-the-job behaviors of high scorers and low scorers, if any?

(Fifteen minutes.)

7. Announce that the following two changes will be in effect when the construction process resumes:

- · First, each team will have a five-minute planning period before resuming construction; however, no materials are to be touched during the planning period.

- Second, team performance will be based on height of structure (task) *and* team member satisfaction (people), with each factor weighted as 50 percent. Team member satisfaction will be based on a second survey of member satisfaction with their contributions.

(Three minutes.)

8. Send teams back to their areas and have them begin the planning period. (Three minutes.)

9. Announce the re-start of the construction period and that five minutes of construction time remains. (Five minutes.)

10. Call time and ask everyone to return to the meeting area. Allow participants to take a break while you use a tape measure to measure the height of each structure. Write the heights down on a sheet of paper—not publicly on the flip chart—and assign team task scores on a 10-point basis, for example, tallest structure = 10 points, next tallest (if within a few inches) = 9.7, etc. Structures will typically be within a few to twelve to fifteen inches of each other. (*Note:* The authors typically assign scores ranging from 9.8 to 8.0, with a score of 7.0 to a team whose structure fails to stand freely.) (Ten minutes.)

11. Call everyone back to the primary meeting room and ask participants to again respond to the team member satisfaction rating. (*Note:* Remind participants to be totally honest in giving their scores.) Collect, record, and average the scores. (Five minutes.)

12. Draw a grid on newsprint, as shown in the sample below, and post each team's Task, People, and Total scores. Recognize the teams with the highest scores (the winner) and the greatest change between scores. (Two minutes.)

Team	A	B	C	D	etc.
Task Score					
People Score					
Average (from Step 11)					
Total Score					

13. Lead a discussion of the results and the entire experience. Key discussion issues should include:

- What were the major changes discussed in your team's planning session?

- Did the five-minute planning period significantly impact your Task score? Why or why not?

- Which factor, Task or People, did your team primarily address in its five-minute planning period? Why was this so? (*Note:* many groups only superficially, if at all, devote attention to the best way to achieve high member satisfaction.)

- If teams knew before starting the first construction phase that team member satisfaction (People) was to count 50 percent, would this have made a difference?

- What parallels do you see between this activity and what is happening in organizations today?

(Ten to fifteen minutes.)

14. Conclude by saying that this activity highlights the importance of using an approach that includes both Task and People factors to achieve superior performance. The rationale underlying many current organizational culture change efforts is the belief that enhanced performance on the Task elements will more likely come from units with highly committed team members who feel that they play important roles in their teams. (Ten minutes.)

Submitted by Edward L. Harrison and Paul H. Pietri.

Edward L. Harrison, Ph.D., is chair of the Department of Management at the University of South Alabama. He has been an active trainer and consultant for over thirty years for organizations such as International Paper Company, Champion International, U.S. Army Corps of Engineers, Baldor Electric, and Teledyne. Dr. Harrison's articles have appeared in journals such as Organization Development Journal, National Productivity Review, Training & Development, and others.

Paul H. Pietri is a professor of management at the University of South Alabama in Mobile, Alabama. He has been a consultant and trainer for over thirty years. Mr. Pietri is author of ten books, including the current Management: Leadership in Action and Supervisory Management.

714. Team Traps: Learning to Take Risks

Goals

- To help teams learn to plan for and adapt to high-risk situations.
- To demonstrate less than effective ways that groups may deal with intense competition.
- To sharpen team members' skills for generating options under competitive conditions.

Group Size

Eight to twenty participants divided into subgroups of four each.

Time Required

Approximately one hour.

Materials

- For each team
  - One spring-set, no-bait-needed, mouse trap (one and three-fourths by two and seven-eighths inches).
  - One table-tennis ball.
  - Three unsharpened, wooden pencils with erasers (each seven and one-half inches long).
- A timing device for the facilitator and for each observer.

Physical Setting

Any room large enough to allow the group to work in subgroups, each with a separate work table.

Process

1. Introduce the activity by stating the goals and some precautions about the mouse traps. Say that you, the facilitator, will set or reset all traps for safety!

2. Before distributing materials, show the group at large all the materials to be used. Set one of the mouse traps and, using a pencil, spring the trap for all to see and hear. Remind everyone to KEEP FINGERS CLEAR.

3. Explain that each team of three (plus an observer) is to use one pencil per player and, working together, is to lift the ball, transport it to the trap, and position it on the bait pad without tripping the trap; then they are to retrieve the ball in the same manner, again without tripping the trap. At no time during the exercise may any member of a team touch the ball with his or her fingers. Any player touching the ball or any player using more than one pencil will result in disqualification of the whole team.

4. Distribute materials, be sure all subgroups are ready to go, and then shout "Go." The first team to complete the task successfully wins. Observers time their respective teams and make sure that the rules are followed.

5. When a winner has been declared, have everyone sit down again and lead a discussion, which may include the following questions:

   - What were your feelings as you worked in this simulated high-risk situation?

   - How did it affect your behavior to know that you were in competition with other teams?

   - Did your team make plans before attempting the task? What options did your team members generate? How did the team select the best option?

   - Did your team practice before trying the task? Why or why not?

   - Based on what you observed here, what changes would you suggest to improve your team's performance if you were to repeat the activity?

   - What lessons can you take away for future work on teams in "high-risk" situations? In intense competitive situations?

(Twenty minutes.)

Variations

- The traps have two possible settings. Use the more sensitive, rather than the less challenging, setting.

- Distribute play money. Have each team invest its funds according to how successful members believe they will be in each of three timed runs. The team that affects the greatest return on its investment wins.

- Stage a cooperative event among teams. The goal would be for *all* teams to finish successfully within a given time frame. In this case, encourage inter-team collaboration.

Submitted by Lynn A. Baker, Sr.

Lynn A. Baker, Sr., is an associate professor at the University of Oklahoma. He also serves as an independent consultant, specializing in leadership, team building, and designing simulations. He is an examiner for the Oklahoma Quality Foundation, a Toastmaster, and a published author.

715. Island Survival:
Choosing Roles in a Group

Goals

- To allow participants to discuss the importance of roles in a group.

- To allow participants the opportunity to choose roles in an unstructured situation.

- To allow participants to acknowledge their responsibility and the affect of their choices on the whole group.

- To give a team the opportunity to recognize its role patterns—its strengths and areas to improve.

Group Size

From five to thirty participants. Most effective with from twelve to twenty.

Time Required

One hour: ten minutes for introduction, twenty minutes for the role play, and thirty minutes for the debriefing and discussion.

Materials

- A flip chart and felt-tipped markers.

Physical Setting

Chairs set in a circle so that participants can see one another.

Process

1. (*Note:* In this simulation, participants are given minimal instructions and are expected to decide what to do and how to do it on their own.) Explain that the participants will be using a simulation created to help them experience the process of taking on roles and role identification in an ambiguous group situation. Explain that effective communicators and effective team players are able to take a variety of roles and perform whatever role functions are needed within a group. (Five minutes.)

2. Have participants move their chairs into a circle and give the following introduction (*Note:* Form two or more groups if there are more than ten participants):

   "You are on a deserted island. All you have is what you have with you now. There is a fresh water stream and a mountain in the distance."

   (Two minutes.)

3. Stop talking and answer any questions people may have by repeating what you have just said. (Three minutes.)

4. Observe the group process but do not intervene. After twenty minutes stop the process. (Twenty minutes.)

5. Give participants a few minutes to discuss their overall observations from the experience within small groups. Many will express frustration with the lack of structure in the activity. If so, ask the participants whether, in their experience, life comes already structured or whether it is created. (Ten minutes.)

6. Now take more formal control of the discussion by asking participants to return to the large circle and respond one by one around the circle as you ask the questions. As participants reply, some will become aware of their own responsibility for choosing their roles during the simulation and their contribution to the group and others will rationalize their actions. Point this out only through questioning. Basically, stay on the topic of what a team needs to survive and which roles people must take.

   - What roles did members of your group choose and why?

   - What roles were missing or caused conflict in the group?

   - Whose responsibility is it to fill the roles needed in a group?

   - If you were able to continue the role play at this time, would you do anything differently?

- How was this situation similar to your work life?

- What roles are missing in your workplace group? How do you think they should be filled?

- What can you do about this back on the job?

(Twenty minutes.)

Variation

- Special tasks may be added to challenge the group. For example, the group may be given a puzzle to solve.

Submitted by Nancy Jackson.

Nancy Jackson, Ph.D., is the lead coordinator (staff and faculty developer) for Red Rocks Community College, Aurora, Colorado, and a past contributor to training activity collections. She also teaches communication, conflict and negotiation, and business courses as an adjunct faculty member. Dr. Jackson conducts workshops on communication for Nancy Jackson and Associates and has published a number of articles.

716. Scrambled Words: A Problem-Solving Task

Goals

- To develop participants' awareness of the importance of planning to the problem-solving process.

- To highlight the importance of utilizing individual talents in team or group problem-solving tasks.

- To provide a structure for participants to begin the team-building process by working collaboratively to solve a problem.

Group Size

Any number of small groups with three to five members each.

Time Required

Eighty to ninety minutes, depending on the number of words given and the processing issues desired.

Materials

- A Scrambled Words List for each participant.
- A Scrambled Words Answer Key for each participant.
- Small token prizes, such as candy bars, for members of the winning subgroup.
- A flip chart and felt-tipped markers.
- Pens or pencils for participants.

Physical Setting

A room large enough to permit subgroups to work on the task without being overheard.

Process

1. Create subgroups of three to five members each. Depending on the overall training objectives of the program, you can create subgroups to highlight various issues to bring to the trainees' attention through the processing of the activity.

2. Explain the task: Each subgroup will be given a list of words with the letters scrambled. (*Note:* The number of words to be unscrambled should be determined based on time available for this type of activity and the processing focus intended.) Announce that a total of [specific amount of time (also to be determined by time available for this activity)] will be allowed to unscramble the words. The subgroup unscrambling the most words in the least amount of time will be declared the winners.

3. Explain two possible strategies for earning the highest score: (a) Each correctly unscrambled word can earn one point credit or (b) bonus credit of one-fourth point for each correct word can be earned for each minute of the allowed time *not* used. In the latter case, the maximum amount of time can be utilized, or subgroup members can turn in their results before the end of the formal task completion time and earn bonus credits for each correctly unscrambled word.

4. Ensure that the task directions and the scoring procedure are clearly understood. (Ten minutes.)

5. Prior to distributing the Scrambled Words List, tell each subgroup to decide on its strategy for working on the task. (Ten to fifteen minutes.)

6. Distribute the lists and have subgroups begin the task.

7. At the end of the formal timed task, distribute the Scrambled Words Answer Key and have each subgroup compute and then report its score. Post the scores on a flip chart. (Ten to fifteen minutes.)

8. If a subgroup turns in its results before the end of the time allowed, compute the time bonus (one-fourth point for each minute early for each correct word) and score their results. (*Note:* Do not report these results to the subgroup until the end of the activity when all other subgroups are computing their scores.)

9. Following the reporting of results (and awarding of prizes, if used), have participants discuss results within their subgroups, touching on the following topics:

- Factors that helped or hindered the process.

- Especially valuable contributions made by individuals.

- The importance of planning an approach for problem-solving tasks.

- Whether subgroups actually utilized their plans. If not, why not, and what influenced their decision to switch strategies?

(Fifteen to twenty minutes.)

10. Ask subgroups to report significant insights and learning to the large group. (Fifteen to twenty minutes.)

11. Conclude the activity by relating the learnings reported to the goals of the training session. (Ten minutes.)

Variations

- Cross-group competition can be emphasized by increasing the value of the prizes or privileges earned through winning and by reporting scores aloud as subgroups complete the task.

- Subgroup leaders can be selected and made responsible for determining the strategy that is to be used.

Submitted by Phyliss Cooke and Ralph R. Bates

Phyliss Cooke, Ph.D., is an independent consultant working with clients in the United States, including government agencies and Native American enterprises, and with clients based in Pacific Rim countries. She typically works with clients to develop strategies for improved management development training, incorporating the organization's traditional practices into daily business activities; to design staff development interventions to improve morale and productivity; to train, coach, assess, and select trainers; to customize training designs; and to facilitate strategic HRD planning.

Ralph R. Bates, M.A., M.HRD., *is president of Bates & Associates, located in the Washington, D.C., area. He has alliances with five small consulting firms specializing in executive coaching, executive team building, and organizational transformation. For nearly half of his thirty-five-year career, he has been a leader responsible for people, budgets, results, and the bottom line. For the other half of his career, Mr. Bates has been a successful organization development and change management consultant. In addition, he has extensive experience designing and developing leadership, management, and supervisory courses for business, associations, and government in the United States and abroad, as well as for Georgetown, Johns Hopkins, and American Universities, where he was an adjunct faculty member. He co-founded the Chesapeake Bay OD Network and was its first president. He is an active member of the NTL Institute for the Applied Behavioral Sciences.*

SCRAMBLED WORDS LIST

Instructions: Unscramble each of the words below and write your answer on the blank beside it.

TEAQUE _____   BEFLAD _____

WEFTES _____   DEAGAN _____

RYBUL _____   TAWNUL _____

TEARRY _____   TONOCY _____

JOUMB _____   APITOE _____

CEHEN _____   NYGERT _____

BLAURT _____   SWEDIT _____

RITTA _____   BEATA _____

CANIP _____   COAZID _____

DAGNIE _____   FRIDAT _____

PIDAUN _____   AYGITE _____

SMACH _____   DEXENP _____

FLERBY _____   LIMPE _____

PHOSUT _____   DEMUGS _____

CALPEA _____   NORBOC _____

ROUPAR _____   THINEW _____

YETID _____   ADGRU _____

TOOPH _____   BOMERY _____

MYLOD _____   YIPTTS _____

SCRAMBLED WORDS ANSWER KEY

EQUATE	FABLED
FEWEST	AGENDA
BURLY	WALNUT
ARTERY	TYCOON
JUMBO	OPIATE
HENCE	GENTRY
BRUTAL	WIDEST
TRAIT	ABATE
PANIC	ZODIAC
GAINED	ADRIFT
UNPAID	GAIETY
CHASM	EXPEND
BELFRY	IMPEL
UPSHOT	SMUDGE
PALACE	BRONCO
UPROAR	WHITEN
DIETY	GUARD
PHOTO	EMBRYO
MOLDY	TYPIST

The 2002 Annual: Volume 2, Consulting/© 2002 John Wiley & Sons, Inc.

717. Me in a Bag:
Breaking the Ice in an Intact Work Team

Goals

- To strengthen relationships within a work unit.
- To deepen understanding of teammates within a work unit.
- To increase listening skills.
- To prepare and focus participants for an upcoming training session.

Group Size

Ten or fewer members of an intact work team. If more participants are present, divide people into two or more subgroups.

Time Required

Thirty to sixty minutes, depending on the number of people in the group (about three minutes per presentation, plus discussion).

Materials

None, other than what the participants bring.

Physical Setting

Chairs arranged in a circle. If there is more than one group, allow enough room so that the groups will not disturb each other.

Process

1. A day or two prior to a training session, instruct all participants that they are to bring one item from home that tells something about themselves *that their team members do not already know*. It can be something from their personal history, something about a hobby or interest they enjoy, or any other object that reveals some aspect of their personal lives. Tell them to bring the item inside a brown paper bag so it is hidden from the view of the other participants.

2. When you are ready to begin, have participants form into their intact work groups and then explain the following sequence of events for the activity:

   "Each participant will take a brief turn and show his or her item to the others. The participant will take the object out of the bag, tell what it is, and say why it is meaningful to him or her. During each presenta-tion, the other participants will give their full attention to the person speaking, but will listen silently and refrain from making comments, giving compliments, or talking—both during and between sharings. After everyone has finished, we will discuss the experience as a group."

3. Ask for a volunteer to begin. When the first person has finished, succes-sive turns can be taken by going in one direction around the circle, by choice of the person who last shared, or by waiting until the spirit moves another volunteer to begin. (*Note:* Explain which method will be used before the first participant begins.)

4. When all participants have finished, ask for comments about what people have shared. People will usually begin the group discussion by making specific comments about the items and complimenting the persons who brought them. Sample questions to deepen the discussion can include:

   - What values did you see revealed by a particular item?

   - What did you notice about people as they described their items?

   - Was it hard to sit silently and listen? Why?

   - What did it feel like to talk about something meaningful to you, know-ing that other people would not speak or interrupt?

   - What did you notice about the group as people listened silently?

   - What purpose does silent listening serve in a group discussion?

- Now that you know something new about your teammates and they know something new about you, will you work with them in different ways? In what new ways?

(Fifteen minutes.)

5. End the activity by commenting on the value of listening to one another carefully throughout the day's events.

Variations

- This activity can be used at the end of a session instead of as an icebreaker. In this case, after the group discussion described in Step 4 above, go around the circle and have each participant, in turn, tell the person to his or her right what he or she liked about the item and what value it symbolizes about that person. In this case, the activity serves as an appreciation exercise and closing.

- If time is limited, act as a timekeeper, giving people a signal when three minutes of presentation time have elapsed.

Submitted by Steve Sphar.

Steve Sphar, J.D., *is an internal organization development consultant for the California State Teachers' Retirement System. He has counseled managers and employees in both the private and public sectors for over fifteen years. He is a past contributor to professional publications, including the* Annual *and the* McGraw-Hill Training and Performance SourceBook.

718. What's Next? Building an Agenda*

Goal

- To learn how to build a group agenda prior to a meeting.

Group Size

Three or more people who work together regularly.

Time Required

Ten to fifteen minutes.

Materials

- Flip chart and felt-tipped markers.

Physical Setting

The group's regular meeting room.

Process

1. Either plan a meeting without an agenda or use this activity when a group habitually has no agenda prior to meeting. Ask the group for permission to "build an agenda."

2. Ask: "What do we need to accomplish at this meeting?" Legibly write each idea on a flip chart along with the name of the person who suggested it.

3. As you list topics, make sure to phrase them as outcomes or expected results. Make sure the group understands each outcome and clarify if necessary.

---

*We provide this piece as a service for newer group leaders. It is not, strictly speaking, an experiential learning activity as no learning is involved. However, we believe it to be a useful technique.

4. Once you have the list, ask the group to combine similar topics. If any dissent occurs, assume that the topics are distinct and leave them separate.

5. Ask the person who suggested each topic how long it will take to achieve the desired outcome. If necessary, allow the group to discuss the item for a few seconds. Next to the topic, write down the agreed-on time (e.g., ten minutes). Also ask the person who suggested the topic whether he or she would like to lead the discussion. If not, ask for a volunteer from the rest of the group. Beware of asking only one or two people to lead the discussion of all the items. Rather, make the meeting as participative as possible.

6. Now that you have a list of topics, a time frame, and the leader for each topic, add up the times. If the amount of time needed is less than the amount of time allotted for the meeting, simply start at the top and move down through the list. However, if the estimated time needed is *more* than the time allotted, the group will need to prioritize the list. Depending on your preference, the team may prioritize the list using the 1–2–3 method or the A-B-C method:

   ■ *1–2–3 Method:* Agree on the most important topic to discuss and place a one (1) beside it, two (2) as next important, etc. Colored dots may also be used to vote, with each team member being given the same number of dots to place beside preferred items. The items receiving the most dots are highest in priority for the group.

   ■ *A-B-C Method:* Agree that the group will use the "loudest voice wins" to assign the priorities with "A" as vital, that is, "We must accomplish this outcome at this meeting"; B as important, that is, "We should accomplish this outcome"; and C as trivial, "We could do this, but the world won't come to an end if we don't accomplish it today." Quickly go through the list and ask "Is this an A, B, or C?" and write down the most agreed-on letter for each.

7. Assign a timekeeper to keep the team on schedule, then start with the most important items on the list (the 1's or the A's) and move through the agenda for a more effective meeting.

Submitted by Kristin J. Arnold

Kristin J. Arnold, M.B.A., *specializes in coaching executives and their leadership, management, and employee teams, particularly in the areas of strategic and business planning, process improvement, decision making, and collaborative problem solving. An accomplished author and editor of several professional articles and books, as well as a featured columnist in* The Daily Press, *a Tribune Publishing newspaper, Ms. Arnold is regarded as an expert in team development and process improvement techniques. With building extraordinary teams as her signature service, she has provided process facilitation, training, and coaching support to both public- and private-sector initiatives.*

719. Billboard Sentiments: Saying Goodbye

Goals

- To close a team-building session or an extended training event on a positive note.
- To reinforce learning points.
- To validate the contributions of the participants.

Group Size

Twenty to eighty participants in subgroups of five to seven.

Time Required

Forty-five minutes to one hour.

Materials

- One flip-chart sheet for each subgroup or enough newsprint paper for the length of two walls in the meeting room.
- Masking tape.
- One dark colored felt-tipped marker for each participant or several for each subgroup.

Physical Setting

A meeting room with wall space for posting flip-chart pages or enough floor space for placing flip-chart easels and pads for each subgroup.

Process

1. At the end of an extended training session on any topic, affix paper to the walls or distribute flip-chart easels and pads around the room with enough space to allow several participants to stand around each area.

2. Ask participants to reflect for a couple of minutes on what they have learned and/or experienced during the training session. (Five minutes.)

3. Give the participants markers and tell them to write, on the flip-chart paper, a short, positive message that communicates the significance of the work accomplished or points learned during the course. Ask them to be sure that their messages are easy to read from a distance. Tell them to sign their work and then to post it on the wall with masking tape. (Fifteen minutes.)

4. When everyone has had an opportunity to write a statement, ask the participants to wander around the room and read the others' statements and to pick others that show special insight or have specific impact for them and to sign underneath the person's signature in agreement. (Ten minutes.)

5. After ample time for participants to read and sign one another's statements, ask them to return to their seats.

6. Ask for volunteers to share their favorite statements that other participants wrote. Be sure to cover all the learning points that have been written. (Fifteen minutes.)

Variations

- Have small groups work at specific flip charts and assign a reporter to share the group's insights with the other participants.

- In smaller groups, simply go around the group asking each participant to read another's statement until all have been heard.

Submitted by Niki Nichols and Ed Werland.

Niki Nichols, M.A., is a training specialist with Texas Parks and Wildlife in Austin, Texas. She has over ten years' experience in management and as a consultant and trainer, with a focus on improving the effectiveness of the organization by improving the effectiveness of the managers and employees. Ms. Nichols has published several articles on management development and change management.

Ed Werland, M.S., has over twenty-seven years of professional management/supervisory experience in the public and private sectors: teaching at the university level, on special assignment to the State of Texas Governor's Center for Management Development, as a training specialist for Texas Parks and Wildlife, as an umpire staff development instructor, as a registered architect, and in recreation/construction management. Mr. Werland has done considerable work in the organization development arena.

720. SUPERVISORY SUCCESS: BALANCING FOLLOWERSHIP WITH WHAT SEEMS RIGHT

Goals

- To examine followership as a supervisory value.

- To recognize different philosophies about supervision.

- To introduce and explore topics such as corporate culture, ethical decision making, loyalty, organizational politics, personal courage, responsibility, and the role of new supervisors.

- To encourage a supervisory team to uncover and discuss differences that may exist within the group.

Group Size

Any group of supervisors or managers who work together on a regular basis.

Time Required

Approximately one hour.

Materials

- One Supervisory Success Survey for each participant.
- A copy of the Supervisory Success Discussion Guide for the facilitator.
- A flip chart and felt-tipped markers.
- Pencils or pens for participants.

Physical Setting

A room with sufficient open space for people to stand and gather in three distinct groups.

Process

1. Distribute the Supervisory Success Survey and pencils. Give the participants three to five minutes to complete the survey, telling them not to spend too much time on any one item. (Five minutes.)

2. Ask participants who said "Agree" with Question 1 to walk to the *front* of the room. Participants who said "Disagree" should walk to the *back* of the room. Participants who said "Don't know" or "It depends" should go to the *middle* of the room. Ask participants to carry the survey with them.

3. Set the stage by saying:

   "This activity is designed to help each of us understand the hidden assumptions and values that we bring to our jobs as supervisors. There are no right or wrong answers. However, some people may feel very strongly on any of these issues. We are not here to change anyone's mind. However, it will be helpful if we discover some of the differences that exist within the group and some of the effects these differences have on how we work together. I encourage you to share how these differences might influence: the organization as a whole, employee morale, performance evaluations, teamwork, respect for supervisors, or task accomplishment."

4. Start with the smallest of the three groups, working to the largest group. Ask whether anyone wants to explain why he or she took that position on the first question. List their answers on the flip chart. Proceed to the next group and so on. Once the key issues for all three responses to a question have been identified, move the group to the next question. (Two minutes per group.)

5. With each question, ask the participants to "vote with your feet." The movement energizes the participants and makes the commitment to a position feel more real.

6. Repeat the process each time. As participants share their views, insert follow-up questions to explore important issues raised during the activity. For example:

- Are you expected to be a "company man" to be successful in this company?

- How much of your "voice" (what you really believe) must you check at the door?

- How do we distinguish followership from blind obedience?

- Does the organizational culture reward or punish those who challenge company policies?

(Fifteen minutes.)

7. Upon completion of the process for the last question, remind the participants of the purpose of the exercise—not to change minds, but to recognize the differences that exist and some of the effects of these differences. Use the Supervisory Success Discussion Guide to sum up the discussion, with a reminder to use what they have learned about one another when they return to the job. (Fifteen minutes.)

Variations

- Ask those who "agreed" with *all five* statements to stand; count them and post their scores on the flip chart. Ask those who "disagreed" with all five statements to stand; count them and post their scores on the flip chart. Draw attention to the two extreme positions and note that most participants have differing views.

- Assign one question to each subgroup. Give them five to seven minutes to explore their differences and identify how these differences might influence: the organization, employee morale, performance evaluations, organizational rewards, teamwork, respect for supervisors, or task accomplishment.

- Request a brief report from each group.

- Discuss the Supervisory Success Discussion Guide of past results in detail.

Readings

Chaleff, I. (1998). *The courageous follower: Standing up to and for our leaders.* San Francisco, CA: Berrett-Koehler.

Kelly, R. (1992). *The power of followership.* New York: Doubleday Currency.

Ryan, K.D., Oestreich, D.K., & Orr, G.A., III. (1996). *The courageous messenger: How to successfully speak up at work.* San Francisco, CA: Jossey-Bass.

Submitted by Bob Shaver.

Bob Shaver, M.B.A., *is a faculty associate and director of the Basic Management Certificate program at the University of Wisconsin-Madison School of Business. He has twenty years of industry and military experience, including ten years in managerial positions as a first-line supervisor, middle manager, and senior manager. For more than ten years, Mr. Shaver has designed and facilitated seminars on the future, instructional skills, leadership, management of change, motivation, problem solving, and survey design.*

Supervisory Success Survey

One of the difficult choices new supervisors face is that of advocating, supporting, implementing, and enforcing new management policies and practices—particularly those that they might not agree with.

Instructions: For each of the following questions, indicate whether you agree, would have to decide under the circumstances, disagree, or don't know whether you agree or not. Circle the answer and write any comments for each question without discussing it with others. Your answer should be indicative of what you believe and what is expected of you.

1. It is weak supervision to refer to management as "they"; when talking with employees or fellow supervisors, management is the inclusive "we."

   agree   it depends   disagree   don't know

   Comments:

2. To be successful in this organization, you must be considered a "company man."

   agree   it depends   disagree   don't know

   Comments:

3. By taking a supervisory position, a person automatically accepts the obligation to support and advocate all of management's philosophies, policies, and procedures.

agree   it depends   disagree   don't know

Comments:

4. If a supervisor finds himself or herself in such conflict with the organization's philosophies and practices that he or she cannot enthusiastically support those practices, he or she should resign from the position.

agree   it depends   disagree   don't know

Comments:

5. As a supervisor/manager/leader, my first responsibility is to serve those whom the organization exists to serve, its customers, and second, the leaders of the company.

agree   it depends   disagree   don't know

Comments:

Supervisory Success Discussion Guide

Author's Note: In four years of administering this survey to nearly five hundred team leaders and first-line supervisors, the following outcomes have been charted:

Question	Agree	Disagree	DK/It Depends
1	72%	9%	19%
2	31%	46%	23%
3	55%	23%	22%
4	33%	37%	30%
5	59%	27%	14%

Discussion

Question 1: One of the challenges all supervisors face is the need to introduce and enforce new policies and practices that are almost certain to be objected to by their direct reports. The language the supervisor uses during the presentation of a new policy or procedure can strongly influence his or her perceived credibility and employees' belief that the supervisor will enforce the new policy.

The generally accepted rule is that management should be referred to globally as "we" when announcing policy changes. Respondents will usually think of many qualifiers on the use of the term "we." Ask participants to reflect on a time when they, as supervisors, had to make a decision on a difficult issue that was important to their boss. Did they support their direct reports or their manager? What were the outcomes? How did they present the issue to the employees?

Question 2: Younger employees may not know all of the "baggage" associated with the term "company man," but they will have opinions. Discuss unreasonable expectations, changes in work ethic, Generation X versus Baby Boomers, life/work balance, and blind obedience for purposes of self-preservation.

Question 3: The issue here is whether we are expected to be lemmings, blindly following management over a cliff. Some participants will object to the word "automatically." Others will believe that supervisors have a responsibility to support management policy publicly but think that it is okay to privately express concerns to other members of the management team (avoiding group think) and collaborate with other managers who seek to change a policy.

Question 4: You may notice significant differences between age groups (younger workers may say they would leave, but older workers may feel that "golden handcuffs" or family responsibilities prevent them from leaving). Some will argue that they can only influence change by being willing to work within the organization. Others will take the view that blind obedience to company policy is what permits unethical behaviors to continue.

Question 5: The question is how long an organization can survive if it exists only to serve the shareholders. Discussion of this question leads to spirited debates about quality, customer service, safety, and responsibility to the employees.

After discussions on these five questions, it is easy to transition to other management topics, such as leadership, motivation, the role of organizations in society, corporate responsibility, employability, or life/work balance.

721. Futures: Planning Creatively

Goals

- To learn a creative thinking process to develop strategic ideas and direction for an organization.
- To practice storytelling when presenting strategic ideas.
- To build on an organization's strategic planning process.

Group Size

Any size group participating in an organization's strategic planning process, divided into subgroups of five to seven. (*Note:* This activity works best as an introduction to the strategic planning process involving only managers or for a future search involving all employees of an organization. It also can be used for planning the future of a single division or department.)

Time Required

Two to three hours, depending on the number of participants.

Materials

- Copies of the organization's mission and values statement posted for easy viewing.
- A copy of the Futures Instruction Sheet, Chapter One: Changes, for one third of the participants.
- A copy of the Futures Instruction Sheet, Chapter Two: Benefits, for one third of the participants.
- A copy of the Futures Instruction Sheet, Chapter Three: Obstacles, for one third of the participants.
- A flip chart and felt-tipped markers or writing paper and pencils for each subgroup.

- Colored dots (for Variation).
- Other visual aids specific to the organization, as needed.

Physical Setting

A room large enough to allow subgroups to be separated by at least fifteen feet or one large room and breakout rooms for subgroups.

Process

1. Prior to the activity, post the organization's mission and values in a prominent place. When everyone has gathered, explain to the participants that they will be generating ideas and strategic direction for the future growth of their organization or department. Tell them that the ideas and direction that they come up with must be in line with their organization's mission and philosophy. Provide copies of the mission and values if desired. (Two minutes.)

2. Ask everyone to sit back and relax, closing their eyes, if desired. Say to the group, "I want each of you to visualize what life is like in your organization five years from now. . . . Imagine that you are now in that time period. . . . Now reflect back five years to the present time. Think about the changes the organization [or department] has made over the last five years. . . . Think how well you have managed the changes. . . . Imagine that a group of prospective clients wants to know what happened in your organization. . . . They wonder what has changed over that period of time and how you have achieved what you have. . . . Think what your organization and its employees are doing strategically that is different from what was happening five years ago."

3. Tell the participants that their task is to tell the story of how their organization has changed strategically over the five-year period. Explain that they will be assigned to small groups, each of which will prepare one chapter of their organization's story and then share that story with the large group.

4. Have participants form three subgroups of five to seven members each and give them writing paper and pencils or a flip chart and felt-tipped markers, as well as a space in which to work. (*Note:* If there are more than twenty-one participants, form additional subgroups and assign other logical chapter topics, such as "Needs," or assign time periods for the chapters.)

5. Give each subgroup enough copies of one of the three Futures Instruction Sheets for every member. Read through the General Instructions, which are the same on each Instruction Sheet. Clarify if necessary, emphasizing the following points:

   - Pay attention to which chapter you are creating: Changes, Benefits, or Obstacles.

   - Involve everyone in the subgroup in writing the story.

   - Use creative methods, such as putting the story to music, using mind mapping, acting out the story, and so forth, so that you can make a more memorable presentation to the large group.

   (Five minutes.)

6. Remind everyone that they will have one hour to complete the task. Keep track of the time and check in with each small group occasionally to make sure they are on task. (Sixty minutes.)

7. When the time is up and the subgroups have written their stories, reconvene as a large group. Create a central place in the room so everyone can clearly see and hear each chapter of the story. Invite subgroups to tell their stories, in order of the chapters assigned. Encourage creative presentations with all members of each group participating. (Twenty minutes for three groups.)

8. Make notes for use during the debriefing. At the end of each presentation, encourage everyone in the large group to ask questions about the changes that were presented in that story. Then give a round of applause for the subgroup, have them answer questions from the other participants (the recorder writes down these questions and their answers), and move on to the next story.

9. After all the subgroups have presented their stories and answered questions, facilitate a discussion with the large group to identify common strategic changes that were suggested, as well as strategic changes mentioned only once. Write the suggested changes on a flip chart. (Fifteen minutes.)

10. Facilitate a discussion about what is missing now that would be needed if their future plans were to come to fruition and any actions that must be taken at this point in their strategic planning process. Connect ideas that are similar or that are different cuts on the same topic. (Fifteen minutes.)

11. Ask the recorder from each small group to present his or her summary of their responses to the key questions that were asked in the Futures Instructions Sheet. Collect their summaries, along with the changes identified

from the large group discussion, for further action and distribution as required in the organization. (Fifteen minutes.)

Variations

- After the large group identifies the strategic changes that will need to be made, list two to three strategic changes per flip-chart page and post them around the room. Then allow subgroups to discuss the strategic changes, their benefits, and obstacles for about fifteen minutes.

- At the end of the small group discussion time, give each subgroup five colored dots to place next to the suggested strategic changes they believe are most achievable. They can place all five dots on one change or place their dots next to several changes. Facilitate a discussion about their observations and what action should be taken next.

- Subgroups can be given time to rewrite their stories after the question-and-answer period.

Submitted by Kevin J. Pokorny.

Kevin J. Pokorny, owner of Management Training and Consulting Services, is a management consultant who offers multiple consulting services in helping organizations meet their business needs. He provides services as a facilitator, legal and training expert in EEO laws, management and employee trainer, and one-on-one coach. For the last several years, Mr. Pokorny has used live drama in sexual harassment training and creative thinking processes in his facilitation work.

FUTURES INSTRUCTION SHEET, CHAPTER ONE: CHANGES

General Instructions

Before you begin: Choose a recorder and a moderator. The recorder will record your answers to the specific questions below as well as record the questions asked by members of other subgroups after your presentation. This can be done on flip-chart paper or on a notepad. Your group's responses will be collected for further strategic planning sessions. The moderator is to keep the group on task.

Your group has one hour to piece together your story and to prepare how you want to tell your story to the large group. Your story should last no more than five to seven minutes. Remember:

- You must involve everyone from your group in the writing and telling of your story.

- Use any visual aids you wish and other creative ways to tell your story, put your story to music, use mind mapping, act out the story, etc.

- Concentrate on the highlights; do not get bogged down in details.

Specific Instructions

Your task as a small group is to create and then tell the story of how your organization made strategic changes over the last five years.

- What are the changes your organization made in the last five years, e.g., hired staff, added new services or products, improved services or products, remodeled or built new facilities, etc.?

- How did you manage these changes so well? What happened?

- What has changed over that period of time?

- How did your organization get to where it is now?

- What is your organization doing differently now than it was five years ago in the area of strategic planning?

Have fun and enjoy!!

Futures Instruction Sheet, Chapter Two: Benefits

General Instructions

Before you begin: Choose a recorder and a moderator. The recorder will record your answers to the specific questions below as well as record the questions asked by members of other subgroups after your presentation. This can be done on flip-chart paper or on a notepad. Your group's responses will be collected for further strategic planning sessions. The moderator is to keep the group on task.

Your group has one hour to piece together your story and to prepare how you want to tell your story to the large group. Your story should last no more than five to seven minutes. Remember:

- You must involve everyone from your group in the writing and telling of your story.

- Use any visual aids you wish and other creative ways to tell your story, put your story to music, use mind mapping, act out the story, etc.

- Concentrate on the highlights; do not get bogged down in details.

Specific Instructions

Your task as a small group is to create and then tell the story of how changes that your organization has made over the last five years have affected your customers, clients, and stakeholders.

- How have your clients benefited as a result of the changes?

- How did the changes impact the services or products of your organization?

- How are these changes fulfilling your organization's mission and business philosophy?

Have fun and enjoy!!

FUTURES INSTRUCTION SHEET, CHAPTER THREE: OBSTACLES

General Instructions

Before you begin: Choose a recorder and a moderator. The recorder will record your answers to the specific questions below as well as record the questions asked by members of other subgroups after your presentation. This can be done on flip-chart paper or on a notepad. Your group's responses will be collected for further strategic planning sessions. The moderator is to keep the group on task.

Your group has one hour to piece together your story and to prepare how you want to tell your story to the large group. Your story should last no more than five to seven minutes. Remember:

- You must involve everyone from your group in the writing and telling of your story.

- Use any visual aids you wish and other creative ways to tell your story, put your story to music, use mind mapping, act out the story, etc.

- Concentrate on the highlights; do not get bogged down in details.

Specific Instructions

Your task as a small group is to create and then tell the story of the obstacles your organization has had to overcome in the last five years as you made changes.

- What were the obstacles—financial, policies, equipment, management, organizational culture, etc.—that your organization had to contend with?

- How was success achieved in spite of the obstacles?

- Tell some of the ways you were able to overcome obstacles.

Have fun and enjoy!!

722. Pink Slip:
Dealing with Organizational Change

Goals

- To demonstrate the ill effects of poor organizational change strategies on human motivation.

- To heighten awareness of human needs in times of organizational change.

- To help organization leaders plan healthy strategies for change.

Group Size

Four to one hundred participants from an organization that has undergone or is contemplating change of any kind.

Time Required

Forty-five minutes to one hour.

Materials

- Red Pink Slip Memos* for one fourth the number of participants. (*Note:* For best effect, the memos can be printed on four different colors of paper.)

- Blue Pink Slip Memos* for one fourth the number of participants.

- Pink Pink Slip Memos* for one fourth the number of participants.

- Green Pink Slip Memos* for one fourth the number of participants.

- A flip chart easel in each of four corners of the room, one for each color of Pink Slip Memo.

---

*Special thanks to Mark Medlin of empactHealth.com for help in crafting these very typical memos.

- Blank overhead transparencies or a flip chart for the facilitator.
- An overhead projector (if using transparencies).
- Felt-tipped markers at each easel.

Physical Setting

A room large enough to comfortably house the four groups, one in each corner. Chairs that can be rearranged.

Process

1. Prior to the session, place flip charts in the four corners of the room, one identified with each of the colors of the handouts, either with words or by a splash of color.

2. Briefly explain the goals of the activity and then randomly distribute the four different Pink Slip Memos after participants have entered the room. (Five minutes.)

3. Instruct participants to go to the place in the room where the flip chart with their color is indicated. Have them move their chairs for the activity.

4. After they have settled in at their locations, ask participants to read the memo they received to themselves (or you could embellish the memos by reading them aloud in a dramatic fashion to each group). Request that the subgroups not confer with other subgroups. (Five minutes.)

5. Ask the subgroups to caucus and record (on their flip charts) their responses to the following questions:

   - What are you feeling right now, having read your memo?

   - What do you need from others in your organization in order to process the information you have received and to move on?

   Circulate among the groups while they work. (Ten minutes.)

6. When the participants seem to be running out of ideas, request that the subgroups report back to the large group and share what they have written. Help everyone to see the common themes. (Fifteen minutes.)

7. Lead the entire group in a discussion of smarter ways to plan for change in order to avoid the ill effects that were brought up during the discussion and to provide what people need in times of change. Ask "What could an organization put in place to prevent the type of demotivation

that occurred here?" and "How could an actual cutback have been done differently?" List their suggestions on a flip chart or overhead projector. (Fifteen minutes.)

8. Bring the activity to a close with a brief discussion of what is happening in their own organization, if this is appropriate. See that organizational leaders are given the suggestions that came up.

Variations

- Tailor the activity and memo to real circumstances facing the organization. Design the ideal way to carry out an actual organizational change, after hearing what each group needs and wants. (Clearly, this would take more than one meeting with more than one group.)

- With a smaller group, the memos could be the basis for a role play activity. Observers could be assigned to record the process as it unfolds, with role players in a position to lay one another off and to help arrange new work procedures.

Submitted by M.K. Key.

M.K. Key, Ph.D., founding principal of Key Associates, LLC, is a clinical-community psychologist. Dr. Key has over thirty years' experience in the healthcare industry—as a provider, researcher, administrator, and consultant/teacher. She has published widely and is a nationally recognized speaker on topics such as leadership, systems thinking, customer-mindedness, releasing the creative spirit, mediation as a method of healing differences, collective visioning, and working through change. Her newest book is Managing Change in Healthcare: Innovative Solutions for People-Based Organizations *(McGraw-Hill). Another recent book is* Corporate Celebration: Play, Purpose and Profit at Work, *with Terry Deal.*

PINK SLIP MEMO (RED)

To all employees:

Due to recent changes in our financial status, the
senior management team of this corporation will begin
a restructuring process, effective immediately, that will
include all divisions of the organization. We regret that
some positions will be eliminated in an overall workforce
reduction. *You will have some new responsibilities added
to your workload,* and you will be asked to absorb some
or all of the duties and tasks now being performed by
people who will be leaving the organization. You must also
prepare to move to a new work location and perhaps to
assist management in the restructuring process itself.

We appreciate your commitment to the company
in the past and hope that you will continue to strive for
excellence within our fine organizational family.

PINK SLIP MEMO (BLUE)

To all employees:

Due to recent changes in our financial status, the
senior management team of our corporation will begin
a restructuring process, effective immediately, that will
include all divisions of the organization. *Your future with
the organization is undetermined at this time.* Upper
management has asked that your group wait quietly
in this place to await further announcements as they
determine how you will be affected by the change.

Some possibilities include that you *may* be asked
to take on additional responsibilities, move your work
location, or assist in the restructuring itself. We regret that
some of your positions may be eliminated, but we do not
know which at this time.

We appreciate your commitment to the company
in the past and hope that you will continue to strive for
excellence within our fine organizational family.

Pink Slip Memo (Pink)

To all employees:

Due to recent changes in our financial status, the senior management team of our corporation will begin a restructuring process, effective immediately, that will include all divisions of the organization. Unfortunately, *we have had to eliminate your job.* You have been asked to meet here so that we can process the paperwork for your layoff in an orderly fashion.

Others have been asked to take on additional responsibilities, move into your work location, or assist in restructuring itself. We regret that your position had to be eliminated. We appreciate your commitment to the company in the past and hope that we may be able to rehire you in the future.

Pink Slip Memo (Green)

To all employees:

Due to recent changes in our financial status, the senior management team of our corporation will begin a restructuring process, effective immediately, that will include all divisions of the organization. *You have been named to serve on the Restructuring Team.* You will all move into a special work area, where you will plan the rollout of this particular organizational change, which will include asking some employees to take on additional responsibilities, move to new work locations, or assist your team in the restructuring itself. We regret that some positions were eliminated, but we count on you to help break the news to those employees and to process the paperwork for laying them off.

We know that you have shown commitment to the company in the past and hope that you will continue to strive for excellence within our fine organizational family.

Introduction
to the Inventories, Questionnaires, and Surveys Section

Inventories, questionnaires, and surveys are valuable tools to the HRD professional. These feedback tools help respondents take an objective look at themselves and their organizations. These tools also help to explain how a particular theory applies to them or to their situations.

Inventories, questionnaires, and surveys are useful in a number of training and consulting situations: privately for self-diagnosis; one-on-one to plan individual development; in a small group to open discussion; in a work team to help the team to focus on its highest priorities; or in an organization to gather data to achieve progress.

You will find that the use of inventories, questionnaires, and surveys enriches, personalizes, and deepens training, development, and intervention designs. Many can be combined with other experiential learning activities or articles in this or other *Annuals* to design an exciting, involving, practical, and well-rounded intervention.

Each instrument includes the background necessary for understanding, presenting, and using it. Interpretive information, scales, and scoring sheets are also provided. In addition, we include the reliability and validity data contributed by the authors. If you wish additional information on any of these instruments, contact the authors directly. You will find their addresses and telephone numbers in the "Contributors" listing near the end of this volume.

Other assessment tools that address a wider variety of topics can be found in our comprehensive *Reference Guide to Handbooks and Annuals*. This guide indexes all the instruments that we have published to date in the *Annuals*. You will find this complete, up-to-date, and easy-to-use resource valuable for locating other instruments, as well as for locating experiential learning activities and articles.

This year we have added a new category—Organizations. This category will include questionaires and surveys that evaluate organizations as a whole.

The 2002 Annual: Volume 2, Consulting includes three assessment tools in the following categories:

Communication

Cornerstones: A Measure of Trust in Work Relationships, by Amy M. Birtel, Valerie C. Nellen, and Susan B. Wilkes

Consulting and Facilitating

Successful Consulting Orientation and Readiness Evaluation (SCORE), by Ralph R. Bates and Phyliss Cooke

Organizations

Systems Thinking Best Practices Instrument, by Stephen G. Haines

CORNERSTONES: A MEASURE OF TRUST IN WORK RELATIONSHIPS

Amy M. Birtel, Valerie C. Nellen, and Susan B. Wilkes

Abstract: Trust between co-workers in the workplace has been demonstrated to be a key component of effective management, organizational commitment, and job satisfaction. The Cornerstones Trust Survey can be used to assess the level of trust between individuals in organizational life and in work relationships. It measures three dimensions of trust: *competence* (the person's perceived ability to do the work), *credibility* (the person's consistency and predictability), and *care* (the other person's valuing of the respondent's needs and concerns).

Respondents answer fifteen questions regarding their level of trust for an identified colleague. Composite scores are obtained on the three dimensions. Instructions are included for using this instrument as a basis for personal feedback and action planning.

INTRODUCTION

The Cornerstones Trust Survey is designed to assist the professional in assessing the level of interpersonal trust among respondents who work together. The reasons for wanting to measure interpersonal trust are many and are supported by research emphasizing the importance of trust between individuals in the workplace. McAllister (1995) suggests that it is especially important for managers to be able to build trust with employees, as much of their work function involves acting as a conduit between people and/or systems. Mishra and Morrissey's (1990) study of employee/employer relationships found six main advantages for an organization when workers trusted their leaders: improved communication; greater predictability, dependability, and confidence; a reduction in employee turnover; openness and willingness to listen and accept criticism non-defensively; repeat business; and a reduction of friction between employees. Posner and Kouzes (1988), two highly regarded scholars of leadership, cite research in which the degree to which employees trusted their management directly affected their organizational commitment, job satisfaction, role clarity, and perceptions of organizational effectiveness. It thus seems evident that the ability to inspire interpersonal trust is an invaluable asset in the workplace and that evaluating it and finding ways to improve it are important in today's organizations.

There is a great deal of research on the situational antecedents of trust, and many of the findings are similar or related. For purposes of this instrument, many of the researchers' suggested antecedents were subsumed into three major categories: *competence, credibility,* and *care.* A similar grouping is seen in the work of Mayer, Davis, and Schoorman (1995). *Competence* refers to the ability of the individual in question to perform the task or activity on which the assessment of trust is being based. For example, if a person is thinking about allowing a doctor to perform heart surgery on him or her, the person must trust in the doctor's skill as a cardiac surgeon. In the same way, an employee must trust his or her co-worker or manager to carry out assigned duties in a highly effective way. *Credibility* is defined as a measure of the individual's consistency across situations. For example, one person's trust in another is strongly influenced by the degree to which that person's word matches his or her deeds, as well as by the predictability of the person's behaviors based on previous behaviors or statements. Finally, the construct of *care* provides an assessment of how much the individual in question has demonstrated a willingness to value the needs and concerns of the person who is thinking about trusting him or her. People are more likely to trust others if they have evidence to suggest that the others will consider their interests when taking actions that may affect them, especially important in employer/employee relationships.

DESCRIPTION OF THE INSTRUMENT

The Cornerstones Trust Survey is a self-scoring instrument with fifteen items, five on each of the three dimensions described above. Respondents use a seven-point Likert scale to rate the trust they hold in an identified colleague, co-worker, or supervisor. The instrument takes approximately five minutes to complete.

Respondents can calculate their own scores on this survey, using the Cornerstones Trust Survey Self-Scoring Sheet. After scores have been tabulated, they are plotted onto a grid provided on the scoring sheet. There are a number of potential uses for the results, described in the "Using the Results" section.

ADMINISTERING THE SURVEY

Explain to respondents that they will complete a brief survey to determine the level of trust they feel for an identified colleague. If the results will not be shared with the other person, assure the respondents that they do not need to write the person's name on the survey and that you will not be "sharing" their results with others or requiring them to do so. In this case, mention that some people do find it helpful to use the survey simply as a way to get in touch with their own feelings about another.

If the survey *is* being used as a feedback tool, remind them to be especially conscientious, as they will be sharing their answers with the persons they rated. Remind them that the purpose of the instrument is not only to help them learn about trust and its component parts but to provide feedback to their colleagues in order to improve their working relationships.

Distribute copies of the survey. Instruct participants to think of only one colleague and to use the full range of responses from 1 to 7 when answering each of the questions about that particular colleague. (It is possible to use this survey in a team-building workshop, in which case a small work group fills out surveys on each of their co-workers and their manager and then spends time sharing with one another one-to-one and in a facilitated group discussion.)

After respondents have finished filling out the survey, but prior to scoring it, give a brief explanation about the importance of interpersonal trust in the workplace. Explain the three components of trust that have been identified in the research and distribute a copy of the Cornerstones Trust Survey Handout to each respondent.

Explain that it is important for colleagues to build trust in order to work together effectively and to maximize job satisfaction and organizational commitment. Show the participants the key components of trust, as seen on the diagram on the handout; then read through the handout with them. *Competence* refers to the ability of the individual in question to perform the task or activity on which the assessment of trust is being based. For example, if a person is thinking about allowing a doctor to perform heart surgery on him or her, the person must trust in the doctor's skill as a cardiac surgeon. In the same way, an employee must trust his or her co-worker or manager to carry out assigned duties in a highly effective way. *Credibility* is defined as a measure of the individual's consistency across situations. For example, one person's trust in another is strongly influenced by the degree to which that person's word matches his or her deeds, as well as by the predictability of the person's behaviors based on previous behaviors or statements. Finally, the construct of *care* provides an assessment of how much the individual in question has demonstrated a willingness to value the needs and concerns of the person who is thinking about trusting him or her. People are more likely to trust others if they have evidence to suggest that the others will consider their interests when taking actions that may affect them, especially important in employer/employee relationships.

SCORING THE SURVEY

Hand out copies of the Cornerstones Trust Survey Self-Scoring Sheet. Instruct respondents to transfer their answers to the scoring sheet and to follow the instructions for calculating their scores. Offer assistance to any participants who may need help.

Once respondents have scored their surveys, have them plot their scores to create a visual representation of the levels of trust experienced on the three dimensions using the diagram on the second page of the scoring sheet. The center of the triangle represents 0 and each point of the triangle represents a score of 35 on that dimension. After participants have plotted their scores, tell them to connect the three points to create a "trust triangle" that can be used as a basis for discussion, if desired. If the survey is being used as the focus of a team-building session, repeat the process for each member of the team before continuing.

INTERPRETING THE RESULTS

Next, help the respondents interpret their results. Draw a sample triangle on a piece of flip-chart paper with scores of 10, 23, and 15 on care, competence, and credibility, respectively. Note how, in this case, the respondent feels that the person is skilled, but the respondent is not confident that the individual being rated cares about him or her personally or would be truthful under all circumstances. On the other hand, if the scores were high on care, high on credibility, and low on competence, the interpretation might be that the respondent thinks the person is open, honest, and can be trusted, but that he or she needs to improve his or her overall competence in doing the work. Finally, tell respondents that the overall size of the triangle can be interpreted as a measure of general trust, with a small but balanced triangle suggesting that improving trust on all three dimensions might be useful. Suggest that examining individual items to detect particular areas of strength or weakness in their level of trust for the other person can also be beneficial. They should mark items that they want to discuss one-on-one.

USING THE RESULTS

Following are a number of ways that the Cornerstones Trust Survey can be used.

1. The survey can be included as an activity in a workshop module on trust, leadership, or team building. The focus would be on understanding the components of trust and on learning more about the implications of levels of trust in work relationships. Additional discussion topics might include ways of building trust in work relationships.

2. The survey can provide a basis for intervention in dyads offering one another one-on-one feedback. Participants can provide feedback to one another in pairs, using their survey results. In some cases, it may be useful for this discussion to be facilitated by a skilled consultant. In preparation for giving one another feedback, the participants may want to review specific items with particularly high or low scores. As with any form of feedback, remind participants to provide examples and to focus on actual behavior rather than on personal characteristics or on supposition about another's motives.

3. The survey can be employed in 360-degree feedback sessions by aggregating a number of respondents' scores for one individual and providing the scores to that person with accompanying qualitative feedback.

4. The survey may be adopted on a team or organization-wide basis to assess general levels of trust within the organization by compiling a number of individual results.

In all of these cases, an action plan should be created to assist the individual(s) to apply what each has learned. Generally speaking, an action plan would include goals, specific action steps leading to the achievement of the goals, and a time frame for accomplishing each step.

PSYCHOMETRIC PROPERTIES OF THE INSTRUMENT

Demographics of the Sample

In order to test reliability of the instrument, 118 employees from a variety of organizations completed the Cornerstones Trust Survey. Of those completing the survey, 69.8 percent were female and 30.2 percent were male. The large majority of the respondents were working adults, 88.7 percent of whom were twenty-six or older (61.7 percent were thirty-six or older). Racial breakdowns were as follows: 82.8 percent Caucasian, 9.5 percent African-American, 3.4 percent Asian-American, 3.4 percent Latino, and .9 percent "other."

Reliability

Internal consistency for the overall scale and each of the three subscales was calculated using Cronbach's alpha for the full sample of 118 participants. The internal consistency score for the overall scale of fifteen items was very high, with an alpha of .96. Alpha coefficients for the subscales of competence, caring, and credibility were .95, .92, and .92, respectively.

Validity

Validity of the instrument as a measure of trust in a work relationship was assessed by examining the relationship between scores on the scales and a separate item about trust. The item was "This is a person I trust." Correlations between the item and the scales are noted in Table 1. All correlations were significant at the p<.01 level.

Table 1. Correlations for General Item

	General Trust Item
Competence Score	.617
Care Score	.860
Credibility Score	.853

References

Mayer, R.C., Davis, J.H., & Schoorman, F.D. (1995). An integrative model of organizational trust. *Academy of Management Review, 20*(3), 709–734.

McAllister, D.J. (1995). Affect- and cognition-based trust as foundations for interpersonal cooperation in organization. *Academy of Management Journal, 38*(1), 24–59.

Mishra, J., & Morrisey, M.A. (1990). Trust in employee/employer relationships: A survey of West Michigan managers. *Public Personnel Management, 19*(4), 443–486.

Posner, B., & Kouzes, J. (1988). Relating leadership and credibility. *Psychological Reports, 63*(2), 527–530.

Amy M. Birtel, M.S., is a program designer and trainer with the Workplace Initiatives Program, a training and consulting unit in the Department of Psychology at Virginia Commonwealth University. She is a doctoral student in VCU's APA-accredited counseling psychology program. Her professional interests include group processes, organization development, and effective communication. She has designed and led training programs on these and other topics. She has also taught introductory psychology as an adjunct faculty member at VCU.

Valerie C. Nellen, Ph.D., *is a leadership and team development consultant with Conexant Systems, Inc., in Newport Beach, California. She received her doctorate in counseling psychology from Virginia Commonwealth University and her undergraduate degree from Harvard University. Dr. Nellen's areas of interest include the study of trust, the application of psychodynamic principles in the workplace setting, and the interrelationship between physical and psychological health.*

Susan B. Wilkes, Ph.D., *manages the Workplace Initiatives Program, a training and consulting unit in the Department of Psychology at Virginia Commonwealth University. She is an organizational psychologist and a frequent workshop leader, consultant, and executive coach. Her areas of expertise include the effective use of 360-degree feedback, leadership, team performance, and stress management. Dr. Wilkes is a Licensed Professional Counselor and a highly rated classroom instructor who has taught courses in group dynamics, industrial/organizational psychology, career counseling, and social psychology.*

CORNERSTONES TRUST SURVEY

Amy M. Birtel, Valerie C. Nellen, and Susan B. Wilkes

Instructions: Think of the individual for whom you are filling out this survey and, using the seven-point scale below, respond to the following with only that person in mind. Circle the numbers that correspond to your level of agreement. If you will be sharing your feedback with this person, write his or her name at the top of the page.

1 = Very strongly disagree	2 = Strongly disagree	3 = Disagree	4 = Neutral	5 = Agree	6 = Strongly agree	7 = Very strongly agree

This is a person . . .

1. who effectively completes the tasks on which he or she works.	1	2	3	4	5	6	7
2. who tells me the truth.	1	2	3	4	5	6	7
3. who considers my needs and interests when making decisions that impact me.	1	2	3	4	5	6	7
4. to whom I would delegate important tasks, if I had the opportunity.	1	2	3	4	5	6	7
5. who keeps confidential any information that he or she has promised not to share.	1	2	3	4	5	6	7
6. who does things to help me out when I need help.	1	2	3	4	5	6	7
7. who demonstrates an appropriate level of skill in completing tasks.	1	2	3	4	5	6	7
8. who honors his or her commitments.	1	2	3	4	5	6	7
9. who demonstrates concern for my well-being.	1	2	3	4	5	6	7
10. who produces work that is useful to others.	1	2	3	4	5	6	7

1 = Very strongly disagree	2 = Strongly disagree	3 = Disagree	4 = Neutral	5 = Agree	6 = Strongly agree	7 = Very strongly agree

11. who is honest about his or her own ability to get things done.
    1   2   3   4   5   6   7

12. who has expectations of me that challenge me, but who provides the support I need to live up to those expectations.
    1   2   3   4   5   6   7

13. who demonstrates competence in his or her work.
    1   2   3   4   5   6   7

14. who makes statements that are credible.
    1   2   3   4   5   6   7

15. who knows some personal details of my life outside of work because I've felt comfortable sharing that information.
    1   2   3   4   5   6   7

Cornerstones Trust Survey Self-Scoring Sheet

Instructions: Transfer your responses for each question to this page. Add the numbers in each column to obtain a total score for each dimension of trust.

1. _____   2. _____   3. _____

4. _____   5. _____   6. _____

7. _____   8. _____   9. _____

10. _____   11. _____   12. _____

13. _____   14. _____   15. _____

Totals: _____   _____   _____

Competence   Credibility   Care

What Your Scores Mean

29 through 35: You have a great deal of trust in this individual on this dimension.

20 through 28: You have a reasonable amount of trust in this individual on this dimension, but would like to feel more comfortable trusting the individual.

11 through 19: You are somewhat wary of this individual on this dimension, and your relationship would likely benefit from increased trust.

5 through 10: You have very little trust in this individual on this dimension, and it is imperative that this be improved in order for you to work well together.

Now, plot your scores on the following diagram, with the middle of the triangle representing a score of 0 and each end point representing a score of 35 on the dimension identified. Finally, connect the plotted points to create a "trust triangle" representing your overall level of trust in the identified individual.

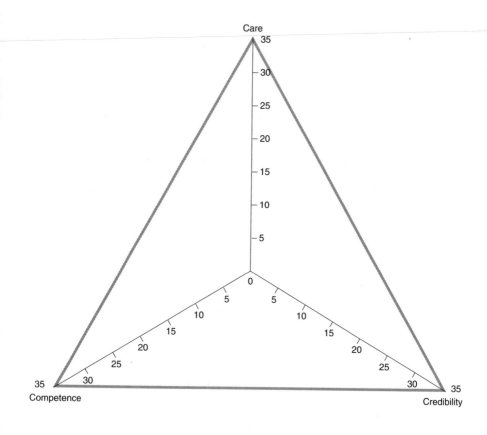

CORNERSTONES TRUST SURVEY HANDOUT

Competence refers to the ability of the individual in question to perform the task or activity on which the assessment of trust is being based. For example, if a person is thinking about allowing a doctor to perform heart surgery on him or her, the person must trust in the doctor's skill as a cardiac surgeon. In the same way, an employee must trust his or her co-worker or manager to carry out assigned duties in a highly effective way.

Credibility is defined as a measure of the individual's consistency across situations. For example, one person's trust in another is strongly influenced by the degree to which that person's word matches his or her deeds, as well as by the predictability of the person's behaviors based on previous behaviors or statements.

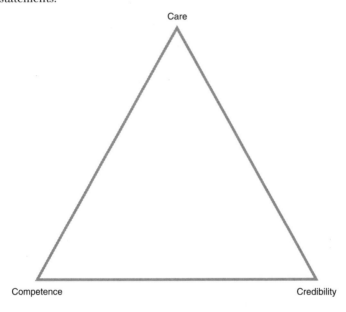

Finally, the construct of *care* provides an assessment of how much the individual in question has demonstrated a willingness to value the needs and concerns of the person who is thinking about trusting him or her. People are more likely to trust others if they have evidence to suggest that the other will consider their interests when taking actions that may affect them, especially important in employer/employee relationships.

Successful Consulting Orientation and Readiness Evaluation (SCORE)

Ralph R. Bates and Phyliss Cooke

Abstract: There is an increasing trend among HRD professionals today to take on the role of external consultant. The allure of "becoming one's own boss" and having control over the types of assignments one works on, rather than struggling with assignments that are handed to one by others, can seem irresistible. Some see external consultants solely in terms of their career perks: being able to say yes or no to assignments, setting their own fees and schedules, traveling to exotic locations at a client's expense, and being able to "walk away" from a client system. The authors' contention is that, even when HRD professionals seem to possess the necessary skills and experience to succeed as external consultants, other not so apparent "success indicators" can spell the difference between their success and failure.

INTRODUCTION

The Successful Consulting Orientation and Readiness Evaluation (SCORE) inventory was designed to help the respondent to clarify his or her attitude toward taking on the role of an external consultant and knowledge of the requirements for success in that role. The inventory provides an excellent start to a discussion of external consulting as a career in a program on training for HRD careers, or for someone considering switching to that role from another position in the field.

The inventory takes about twenty minutes to complete; respondents score their own results; and a simple scoring format allows respondents to interpret their own comparative strengths and areas of weakness.

There is no certification or licensing process to authorize one to offer services as a consultant; the ethics, fees, philosophies, academic credentials, experience, style, and personal agenda of consultants are open questions. *Virtually anyone* can be a consultant. The implications of assuming such a role may not be considered; nor do most people think in depth about what external consultants do for whom, or how they do it.

Assuming the role of a professional consultant is a serious undertaking. Therefore, before one decides to earn a living and base his or her professional reputation on the results of his or her consulting efforts, it is important to assess both one's readiness and one's ability to provide value-added services, not just one's willingness. Readiness, for purposes of the survey, is seen not only in terms of persona and relevant experience, but in readiness to assume responsibility for the consequences of the "help" provided. The SCORE inventory allows respondents to assess some of the realities for entry into the field. The survey is meant only to serve as an introductory means to assess "readiness" and to highlight areas that might need to be strengthened. The scores do not predict success or failure, but simply help respondents to see areas for additional self-motivated preparation.

THE INSTRUMENT

The SCORE inventory provides respondents with a vehicle for assessing their suitability for the role of external consultant and their potential for success, based on their answers to thirty-two questions that describe a variety of the realities facing one who undertakes the life of an external consultant.

For each of the thirty-two questions, the respondent rates his or her probable readiness or willingness using a ten-point scale (1 is low; 10 is high).

Two self-scoring sheets are provided. Scoring Sheet A provides an overall score. Scoring Sheet B allows respondents to sort their scores into four categories of readiness: Knowledge/Technique, Ability to Self-Manage, Nature of Work Experience, and Personal Qualities so that they can quickly note which category is potentially the most challenging for them and see items within each category that were rated significantly lower or higher.

The SCORE inventory is based on the authors' observations and experiences as external consultants, as well as on suggestions from colleagues of factors affecting success as external consultants. The preferred answer for each question is one that represents:

- Understanding the theoretical basis from which effective techniques derive;

- Assuming the responsibility for becoming an independent businessperson;

- Taking responsibility for one's opinions and actions within the workplace; and

- Possessing the personal qualities to succeed in the role.

VALIDITY AND RELIABILITY

No validity or reliability data are available for this inventory. However, in the limited number of situations in which it has been used, respondents have reported that it had face validity and that it served its intended purpose of helping them become more aware of their potential suitability and readiness for success in the role of an external consultant.

USES OF THE INSTRUMENT

SCORE was developed as a training aid to be included in a much more comprehensive program designed to introduce participants to the concepts and skills necessary to succeed as HRD/OD consultants. While the scope of the inventory is very narrow, it stimulates a meaningful group discussion of success factors and their relevance for HRD/OD career choices. It can also serve as a

vehicle for structuring professional mentoring programs and/or for self-initi-
ated ongoing professional development.

ADMINISTERING AND SCORING THE INVENTORY

Make enough copies of the inventory for all respondents. Review the information; the intended purpose of the activity; how the inventory is to be completed; and how the scoring is structured. Answer any procedural questions
and ensure that the appropriate climate exists for meaningful self-assessment.
Then distribute a copy of the inventory and a pencil to each participant. Allow
approximately twenty minutes for them to complete the assessment, although
additional time may be needed depending on the group size and their famil-
iarity with self-assessment instruments.

After all respondents have finished, tell them that they will score their
own inventories. Then distribute Scoring Sheet A and ensure that participants
are clear about how to transfer their scores to the correct lines.

INTERPRETING THE RESULTS

When all respondents have transferred their scores to Scoring Sheet A, structure appropriate subgroups for processing the results and review the suggested
guidelines for interpreting overall scores.

A group profile may be posted for further processing and discussion
of implications after participants have had sufficient time to discuss their
personal scores and you have sufficiently reviewed the general rationale for
the interpretations that have been suggested. A group profile should *not* be
undertaken prematurely, as it may distract individuals from the implications
of their personal profiles.

New subgroups may be formed prior to the distribution and completion of Scoring Sheet B, or participants may remain in the original groupings.

The B scoring procedure is optional, depending on the training objective, sophistication of the participants, and other factors. Similarly, you may
delay using Scoring Sheet B until later in a training program when participants
are engaging in "next steps" planning.

Remind participants that their scores simply reflect their current responses to the items presented and cannot be used to predict future success.

The general interpretive scoring guidelines are provided as a means of stimulating discussion and introspection, not for accurately assessing suitability or determining readiness for a consulting career. Once this point has been made, the balance of the training can take one of several directions, depending on the overall objectives. For example:

- The concept of professional "readiness" can be linked to specific content or skill modules in the overall training program;

- Participants can expand on the scope of the items that have been included in the inventory;

- Specific developmental activities and/or resource material can be provided for supporting professional development in each of the four proposed areas; or

- Follow-up sessions can be arranged for post-assessments.

Ralph R. Bates, M.A., M.HRD, is president of Bates & Associates, located in the Washington, D.C., area. He has alliances with five small consulting firms specializing in executive coaching, executive team building, and organizational transformation. For nearly half of his thirty-five-year career, he has been a leader responsible for people, budgets, results, and the bottom line. For the other half of his career, Mr. Bates has been a successful organization development and change management consultant. In addition, he has extensive experience designing and developing leadership, management, and supervisory courses for business, associations, and government in the United States and abroad, as well as for Georgetown, Johns Hopkins, and American Universities, where he was an adjunct faculty member. He co-founded the Chesapeake Bay OD Network and was its first president. He is an active member of the NTL Institute for the Applied Behavioral Sciences.

Phyliss Cooke, Ph.D., is an independent consultant working with clients in the United States, including government agencies and Native American enterprises, and with clients based in Pacific Rim countries. She typically works with clients to develop strategies for improved management development training, incorporating the organization's traditional practices into daily business activities; to design staff development interventions to improve morale and productivity; to train, coach, assess, and select trainers; to customize training designs; and to facilitate strategic HRD planning.

SUCCESSFUL CONSULTING ORIENTATION AND READINESS EVALUATION (SCORE)*

Ralph R. Bates and Phyliss Cooke

Instructions: The purpose of this instrument is to aid you in assessing your readiness to become an independent HRD/OD consultant and businessperson. The questions cover a wide range of issues related to establishing a successful independent practice.

For each item, circle the number that seems best to describe you (1 being low and 10 high). Through this means, you will obtain a composite view from which to answer the question: "Am I ready to establish my own practice?"

1. How *effective* am I in establishing trust and rapport early in a relationship?   1 2 3 4 5 6 7 8 9 10

2. How *positive* is the first impression I usually make on others?   1 2 3 4 5 6 7 8 9 10

3. How *high* is my tolerance for ambiguity or uncertainty?   1 2 3 4 5 6 7 8 9 10

4. How *willing* would I be to work for clients with whom my values were congruent, but whom I perceived to have goals that were different from mine?   1 2 3 4 5 6 7 8 9 10

5. How *comfortable* would I be if I had simultaneous responsibilities for serving five to seven clients?   1 2 3 4 5 6 7 8 9 10

6. How *high* is my tolerance for working alone, without a close colleague or team, for long periods of time?   1 2 3 4 5 6 7 8 9 10

7. How *much* of a risk taker am I?   1 2 3 4 5 6 7 8 9 10

---

*This questionnaire assumes that you already possess sufficient skills and experience in HRD/OD to consider becoming an independent consultant. Thus, there are no specific questions about your knowledge of the theories or concepts that underlie the work of successful practitioners.

8. How willing am I to sell my services or products?

    1 2 3 4 5 6 7 8 9 10

9. How willing am I to NOT be in charge of the outcomes of my consulting services?

    1 2 3 4 5 6 7 8 9 10

10. How effective do I think I would be at selling my own services or products?

    1 2 3 4 5 6 7 8 9 10

11. How broad is the range of consulting roles I could fill (expert, catalyst, process observer, advocate, problem solver, facilitator, mediator, etc.)?

    1 2 3 4 5 6 7 8 9 10

12. How adaptable am I when situations require that I change roles?

    1 2 3 4 5 6 7 8 9 10

13. How able am I to withhold my personal opinions about others' behaviors, decisions, opinions, etc.?

    1 2 3 4 5 6 7 8 9 10

14. How skilled am I in pacing my current work to avoid burnout?

    1 2 3 4 5 6 7 8 9 10

15. How comfortable would I be with being turned down by potential clients?

    1 2 3 4 5 6 7 8 9 10

16. How patient am I when dealing with people whom I want to influence but over whom I have no direct control?

    1 2 3 4 5 6 7 8 9 10

17. How quickly do I "size things up" when facing new and demanding situations?

    1 2 3 4 5 6 7 8 9 10

18. How skilled am I in "managing myself" (emotions, reactions, behaviors) when I am in conflict with others?

    1 2 3 4 5 6 7 8 9 10

19. How skilled am I in helping others to manage conflict?

    1 2 3 4 5 6 7 8 9 10

20. How effective am I at strategic or long-term planning? 1 2 3 4 5 6 7 8 9 10

21. How effectively would I model my HRD/OD values with my clients? 1 2 3 4 5 6 7 8 9 10

22. How comfortable am I with how much I know about HRD/OD? 1 2 3 4 5 6 7 8 9 10

23. How clear am I about the market value of the type of services I will be offering? 1 2 3 4 5 6 7 8 9 10

24. How confident am I of my ability to negotiate the value of my services with prospective clients? 1 2 3 4 5 6 7 8 9 10

25. How able am I to NOT view my mistakes as personal failures or signs of general incompetence? 1 2 3 4 5 6 7 8 9 10

26. How willing am I to do without tangible proof or validation of success from clients? 1 2 3 4 5 6 7 8 9 10

27. How successful am I in balancing my personal and professional lives? 1 2 3 4 5 6 7 8 9 10

28. How successful have I been in the past in managing my finances? 1 2 3 4 5 6 7 8 9 10

29. How flexible am I in my style of relating to others? 1 2 3 4 5 6 7 8 9 10

30. How often do others comment positively on my sense of humor? 1 2 3 4 5 6 7 8 9 10

31. How effectively do I communicate verbally with others (express my ideas and feelings, listen and respond, challenge and confront differences of opinion, collaborate through dialogue, initiate verbal interactions, etc.)? 1 2 3 4 5 6 7 8 9 10

32. How skilled am I in learning from my own experiences as well as from the experiences of others? 1 2 3 4 5 6 7 8 9 10

SUCCESSFUL CONSULTING ORIENTATION AND READINESS (SCORE): SCORING SHEET A

Instructions: Use the following procedure for scoring and interpreting your answers:

1. Add the numbers you assigned to determine your total raw score and transfer that score to the blank below. Then read the possible interpretations below.

   Total raw score: _____
   (The range for the total raw score is between 32–320)

Interpreting Your Scores

- A score between 32 and 100 suggests that this business may not be right for you.

- A score between 101 and 200 suggests that you should explore opportunities to gain experience and develop strengths in your weakest areas before leaving your current position.

- A score significantly over 200 suggests that you possess sufficient confidence and self-assessed competence to succeed as an independent consultant and businessperson. The next step should be to discuss your self-ratings with others whose feedback and advice you value and "go for it!"

Successful Consulting Orientation and Readiness Evaluation (SCORE): Scoring Sheet B

Instructions: To interpret the meanings of your answers in further detail, transfer your scores for each question to the appropriate blank below.

Knowledge/Technique

11 _____   12 _____   16 _____   17 _____

19 _____   20 _____   22 _____   31 _____

Ability to Self-Manage

13 _____   14 _____   18 _____   21 _____

25 _____   27 _____   28 _____   32 _____

Nature of Work Experience

5 _____   6 _____   8 _____   10 _____

15 _____   23 _____   24 _____   26 _____

Personal Qualities

1 _____   2 _____   3 _____   4 _____

7 _____   9 _____   29 _____   30 _____

Review your "profile" of scores in each category above. Double-check any item(s) that are scored lower than 4 or those that are significantly lower than the answers given for the other items in the category.

Look for patterns and significant factors in your low and high scoring responses. Use your results as the basis for self-exploration or share your insights with others, as instructed by your facilitator.

SYSTEMS THINKING BEST PRACTICES INSTRUMENT

Stephen G. Haines

Abstract: The premise behind systems thinking is that changing the way you think changes the way you act. Collectively, better results are almost guaranteed for an organization that can switch from piecemeal and analytical thinking to systems thinking. "Strategic thinking" is a first cousin to this concept, as they both focus first on the environment and on the desired results—and only then on the strategies needed to get there.

The purpose of this instrument is to assess an organization's practices against the best practices of organizations that use systems thinking. These best practices have been proven to be key contributors to organizational success. Thus, it is useful for almost any "system" or entity, including all public, private, and not-for-profit organizations. The information obtained assists organizations in planning for improvement. The instrument was developed using the author's interpretation of systems thinking principles and research as applied in his consulting and training practice over the past eleven years.

INTRODUCTION

The background for the Systems Thinking Best Practices Instrument comes from almost fifty years of research generated by the Society for General Systems Research, founded in 1954 by Ludwig Von Bertalanffy, along with three other distinguished scientists from economics, physics, and physiology.

They and their colleagues published an annual report for a number of years on the Society's research results and eventually identified the "Twelve Characteristics of Living Systems" (Vickers, 1972). These characteristics have been shown to be relevant to organizational learning worldwide through research by over twenty-three chapters of the Society, dating back to the 1950s. The current-day successor to this Society is the International Society for Systems Sciences (ISSS).

In addition to the Society's research, James G. Miller's (1995) classic book, *Living Systems,* shows how we are one of seven levels of living systems on earth, all of which follow the same twelve characteristics.

The list used here is the most comprehensive best practices listing to date from the literature. These best practices have been tested with clients around the world. The results are consistent: Organizations achieve better results when they use these particular systems thinking best practices and are less effective when they do not understand and apply them.

DESCRIPTION OF THE INSTRUMENT

The instrument is split into seven sections, representing seven key areas of best practices research. They include the following:

1. Systems thinking basics,

2. Six levels of organizational systems,

3. ABCs of a yearly strategic management cycle,

4. Organization as an open system,

5. The Rollercoaster of Change^{SM},

6. The learning organization, and

7. A strategic management system overall.

The Scoring Sheet reflects the respondent's assessment of his or her organization for each of these seven sections and also provides an overall score.

ADMINISTRATION OF THE INSTRUMENT

To administer the survey, follow the steps below:

1. Define the entity to be assessed, a particular organization or unit of an organization. All respondents must be members of the same organization or unit. Fill out the blanks at the beginning of the survey saying where to send the completed survey if you will not be collecting the data yourself.

2. Select respondents from among management, professional (exempt) employees, or, if appropriate, non-exempt blue collar workers. A team outside the organization, such as consultants who are experts in the systems thinking approach, could also be asked to assess the organization by completing the survey.

3. Bring the people who will be responding and senior management together to complete the survey simultaneously. Then distribute the article "Systems Thinking and Learning" from this *Annual* both to those who will be completing the survey and to the senior management of the organization. Ask that everyone read the article silently and then lead a discussion of the principles presented. This should take ten to twenty minutes and serve as an executive briefing on systems thinking as well as an opportunity to answer any questions the respondents may have. Although the survey has been field-tested to ensure that it can be used generically, there may be those who do not understand certain items, so be prepared to answer questions.

4. Give everyone copies of the survey. Be sure that everyone understands which entity they are assessing and that they are evaluating the entity's *current* practices. Ask participants to fill out the survey by giving their initial response in each case, rather than trying to read anything into the questions. Have everyone begin. Allow about ten minutes.

5. When everyone has finished, ask them to total and average their scores for each section and for the questionnaire as a whole. This usually take five or ten more minutes.

6. Have the completed surveys returned to you for data collation and report preparation.

7. Set up a meeting with senior management to review the survey results and report back to the participants on their organization's strengths and weaknesses against the best practices in systems thinking and learning.

8. Build an action plan to leverage improvement in the areas that require it.

THE SCORING PROCESS

The instrument is self-scoring. Respondents add and average their scores within each of seven sections and place those numbers in the spaces provided within each section. They then transfer those numbers to the "Scoring by Section" area of the Scoring Sheet. Here they can rank order their scores from 1 to 7 and see how they have rated the overall organization compared with best practices of other organizations.

The "Overall Organizational Profile" section, an examination and assessment of the overall total score, is followed by an "Analysis" section, whereby participants can identify specific areas in which their organization needs improvement as well as those in which it is performing well. A more comprehensive analysis of the results can be achieved by reviewing the data with a trained systems thinking consultant.

DATA POSTING

Data can be broken down by levels within the organization or by departments in order to see whether the scores are consistent organization-wide.

The key to future action planning is having a facilitator who is knowledgeable about systems thinking and who can help the group talk openly about the results. It is best to prepare CEOs ahead of time to ensure they are comfortable with open dialogue and honest differences of opinion about the organization. Allowing CEOs to see the data results first reduces the likelihood of their responding defensively in front of others.

RELIABILITY AND VALIDITY

Although the items are based on many years of research in general systems theory (Bertalanffy, 1968; Forrester, 1971a, b; Miller & Rice, 1967; and Vickers, 1972) and proven best practices reported in numerous research studies examined over the past eleven years by the Centre for Strategic Management, this instrument can best be viewed as having only face validity and operational validity at the present time. The Centre has begun further validity studies.

SUGGESTED USES

This survey can be used as either a pre- or post-workshop instrument when teaching systems thinking or strategic management. As an executive or management development tool, it is quite useful and eye opening to most participants.

References

Ackoff, R. (1974). *Redesigning the future: A systems approach to societal problems.* New York: John Wiley & Sons.

Ackoff, R. (1991). *Ackoff's fables: Irreverent reflections on business and bureaucracy.* New York: John Wiley & Sons.

Bertalanffy, L. (1968). *General systems theory.* New York: Brazille.

Forrester, J.W. (1969). *Urban dynamics.* Norwalk, CT: Productivity Press.

Forrester, J.W. (1971a). *Principles of systems.* Norwalk CT: Productivity Press.

Forrester, J.W. (1971b). *World dynamics* (2nd ed.). Norwalk, CT: Productivity Press.

Miller, J.G. (1995). *Living systems.* Boulder, CO: University Press of Colorado.

Miller, E.J., & Rice, A.K. (1967). *Systems of organization.* London: Tavistock.

Naisbitt, J. (1982). *Megatrends: Ten new directions transforming our lives.* New York: Warner.

Naisbitt, J. (1994). *Global paradox: The bigger the world economy, the more powerful its smallest players.* New York: William Morrow.

Naisbitt, J., & Aburdene, P. (1990). *Megatrends 2000: Ten new directions for the 1990s.* New York: William Morrow.

Vickers, G. (Ed.). (1972). A classification of systems. In *Yearbook of the Society for General Systems Research/Academy of Management Research*. Washington, DC: Author.

Stephen G. Haines is a CEO, entrepreneur, and strategist. As a premier systems thinker, facilitator, and prolific author, he is recognized internationally as a leader in strategic management and in leading planning and change efforts. He is president and founder of both the International Centre for Strategic Management and its sister company, Systems Thinking Press.

SYSTEMS THINKING BEST PRACTICES INSTRUMENT

Stephen G. Haines

Systems thinking is an absolute necessity to make sense of and succeed in today's complex world. If life on earth is governed by the natural laws of living systems, then a successful person must learn the rules. If you leverage the way you think and act, you will achieve better results more naturally.

Instructions for Use

Fill in the blanks below before turning the page:

Today's date: _____

Organization: _____

Return confidentially and anonymously to the person listed below.

Name: _____

Address or Unit: _____

By (date): _____

Demographic Data (circle the appropriate level below)

      Management   Non-management (exempt)

      Non-exempt   Not in the organization

Your scores will be combined with others to find an organizational average for each question. You will not be identified. However, if you want this instrument back for discussion purposes, either put your name or some other code only you know here:

SYSTEMS THINKING BEST PRACTICES INSTRUMENT

Instructions: This survey will help others to determine what level of improvement your organization needs in each of seven areas. Simply complete the following form, circling the number that applies in each case according to the scale below. Do not ponder over the questions; answer with your first instincts.

No need	Low need	Average need	Important need	Critical need
5	4	3	2	1

1. Systems Thinking Basics

This organization:

1. Needs to better understand and apply six natural and usual internal organizational dynamics to our work.   5   4   3   2   1

2. Needs to better understand and apply the properties and principles of organizations as open systems.   5   4   3   2   1

3. Needs to better understand the Key Systems Questions and how to use them (especially Question 1: What are our desired outcomes?)   5   4   3   2   1

4. Needs a better fit and integration of relationships between parts/departments of the organization to support the whole vision.   5   4   3   2   1

5. Needs better decision-making and problem-solving methods and skills to solve customer issues.   5   4   3   2   1

Section 1 Total Score = _____ **/5 =** _____ **(Average Score)**

No need	Low need	Average need	Important need	Critical need
5	4	3	2	1

2. Six Levels of Organizational Systems

This organization:

6. Needs to roll strategic planning down to other levels and tie it in at the departmental level, specifically in a "strategic consistency/operational flexibility" way to build operational plans and budgets.

      5   4   3   2   1

7. Needs to tie the strategic plan to performance and rewards systems.

      5   4   3   2   1

8. Needs a leadership development system for all management levels.

      5   4   3   2   1

9. Needs to identify and develop the six natural leadership competency levels for the collective management team.

      5   4   3   2   1

10. Needs succession planning with individual leadership development plans.

       5   4   3   2   1

11. Needs to create a systems approach to management's people/HR practices as a competitive business advantage.

       5   4   3   2   1

This organization needs better team effectiveness for the following:

	No need	Low need	Average need	Important need	Critical need
12. Senior management team.	5	4	3	2	1
13. Departmental management teams.	5	4	3	2	1
14. Cross-functional teams.	5	4	3	2	1
15. External alliances/partnerships.	5	4	3	2	1

Section 2 Total Score = _____ **/10 =** _____ **(Average Score)**

No need	Low need	Average need	Important need	Critical need
5	4	3	2	1

3. ABCs of a Yearly Strategic Management Cycle

This organization:

16. Needs a strategic plan for the overall organization.	5	4	3	2	1
17. Needs to define the organization's position in the marketplace clearly, vis-a-vis its competition.	5	4	3	2	1
18. Needs to create a more measurable, high performance, results-oriented atmosphere (clear outcome vs. effort-focused).	5	4	3	2	1
19. Needs to be more market/customer-focused.	5	4	3	2	1
20. Needs to provide better customer service, especially in the area of error recovery.	5	4	3	2	1
21. Has three-year business plans for all strategic business units/lines of business and all major support departments.	5	4	3	2	1
22. Needs to improve efficiency and/or effectiveness of its key business processes and eliminate some bureaucracy.	5	4	3	2	1
23. Needs to learn better project management skills.	5	4	3	2	1
24. Needs strategic life plans for senior management so that they will learn to better balance their lives.	5	4	3	2	1
25. Needs an annual strategic review and update on its strategic plan.	5	4	3	2	1

Section 3 Total Score = _____ /10 = _____ (Average Score)

No need	Low need	Average need	Important need	Critical need
5	4	3	2	1

4. Organization as an Open System

This organization:

26. Needs a clear model and a description of itself as an open system (that is, the same framework).	5	4	3	2	1
27. Needs overall improvement in its strategic business design and organizational structure for better "watertight integrity," fit, integration, and collaboration.	5	4	3	2	1
28. Needs improvement or change in its values and/or culture.	5	4	3	2	1
29. Needs an overall organizational assessment to find ways to improve.	5	4	3	2	1
30. Needs a specific strategic HR management practices assessment.	5	4	3	2	1

Section 4 Total Score = _____ **/5 =** _____ **(Average Score)**

5. Rollercoaster of Change℠

This organization:

31. Has a change leadership steering committee in place, led by the CEO and top management team, that meets regularly (quarterly at a minimum).	5	4	3	2	1
32. Needs the understanding of and skills to use proven change management principles (for example, the Rollercoaster of Change Model) on major change projects.	5	4	3	2	1
33. Needs a better understanding and additional skills to use the structures/hierarchies of effective change management.	5	4	3	2	1

No need	Low need	Average need	Important need	Critical need
5	4	3	2	1

34. Needs organizational strategies/actions
for a turnaround and/or for cutting costs.   5   4   3   2   1

35. Needs organizational strategies/actions
for renewal and/or growth.   5   4   3   2   1

36. Needs to improve skills in anticipating
and leading change management to a
higher level of excellence.   5   4   3   2   1

37. Needs to analyze further to find root
causes (not symptoms) of problems and
leverage points for change.   5   4   3   2   1

38. Needs creative ways to increase employee
empowerment, flexibility, and other new
initiatives in support of desired changes.   5   4   3   2   1

39. Needs a better follow-up, tracking, and
monitoring system to offset lack of employee and/or management buy-in and
stay-in for the desired changes.   5   4   3   2   1

40. Needs to expand its definition and use
of resources significantly, going beyond
the traditional financial ones.   5   4   3   2   1

Section 5 Total Score = _____ /10 = _____ (Average Score)

6. The Learning Organization

This organization:

41. Needs to improve its training and devel-
opment as well as its learning processes.   5   4   3   2   1

42. Needs to make flexibility and speed of
learning competitive advantages.   5   4   3   2   1

43. Needs an intranet system for ongoing electronic knowledge transfer and learning
reinforcement.   5   4   3   2   1

No need	Low need	Average need	Important need	Critical need
5	4	3	2	1

44. Needs to debrief projects in a better way
    and learn from successes and failures.   5   4   3   2   1

45. Needs to make learning a way of life
    at work in the organization at all levels.   5   4   3   2   1

Section 6 Total Score = _____ /5 = _____ (Average Score)

7. Strategic Management System Overall

This organization:

46. Needs a better, more integrated, and
    collaborative way to do business day-to-day.   5   4   3   2   1

47. Needs a better annual strategic manage-
    ment system as the way it runs its business.   5   4   3   2   1

48. Needs a better environmental scanning
    system with accountability built in that is
    used regularly throughout the year.   5   4   3   2   1

49. Needs to have an organization-wide,
    up-to-date, integrated, and linked com-
    puterization/telecommunications system
    (such as EDI, SAP, Data Warehouse).   5   4   3   2   1

50. Needs greater clarity and simplicity in its
    business operations and administration.   5   4   3   2   1

Section 7 Total Score = _____ /5 = _____ (Average Score)

SYSTEMS THINKING BEST PRACTICES INSTRUMENT SCORING SHEET

Instructions: Enter the total score and average score for each section below on the appropriate blank lines. Then rank the sections by what you think is their importance to the organization, 1 though 7, with 1 highest.

	Section Total	Section Average	Ranking
1. Systems Thinking Basics	_____	_____	_____
2. Six Levels of Organizational Systems	_____	_____	_____
3. ABCs of a Yearly Strategic Management Cycle	_____	_____	_____
4. Organization as an Open System	_____	_____	_____
5. Rollercoaster of Change	_____	_____	_____
6. The Learning Organization	_____	_____	_____
7. Strategic Management System Overall	_____	_____	_____

Overall Organizational Profile

Now compute the total score and average for your organization and put them in the blanks below.

Overall Total Score = _____ (250 points possible)
/50 = _____ (average score)

Which of the following fits your beliefs about your organization?

201 to 250 points: The organization is doing excellent work in terms of systems thinking. Congratulations, keep it up!

151 to 200 points: The organization is doing average work in terms of systems thinking. There is room for continuous improvement.

101 to 150 points: An important need for improvement in systems thinking exists within the organization. Make a game plan and get going now.

50 to 100 points: A critical need for improvement in systems thinking exists within the organization. Overhaul your organization immediately!

Analysis

Answer the following questions by looking back at the items you assigned a 2 (important) or 1 (critical).

Where did I see our greatest needs for improvement in systems thinking?

What can we do to begin improving?

Who could lead the effort?

By when?

Where did I think that we are performing best in systems thinking?

Why are we doing so well in these areas?

Introduction
to the Presentation and Discussion Resources Section

The Presentation and Discussion Resources Section is a collection of articles of use to every facilitator. The theories, background information, models, and methods will challenge facilitators' thinking, enrich their professional development, and assist their internal and external clients with productive change. These articles may be used as a basis for lecturettes, as handouts in training sessions, or as background reading material.

This section will provide you with a variety of useful ideas, theoretical opinions, teachable models, practical strategies, and proven intervention methods. The articles will add richness and depth to your training and consulting knowledge and skills. They will challenge you to think differently, explore new concepts, and experiment with new interventions. The articles will continue to add a fresh perspective to your work.

The 2002 Annual: Volume 2, Consulting includes ten articles in the following categories:

Individual Development: Personal Growth

Appreciative Inquiry: New Thinking at Work, by Sherene Zolno

Communication: Coaching and Encouraging

The Coaching Styles Advantage,
by Patrick J. Aspell and Dee Dee Aspell

Communication: Technology

Ethical Issues Surrounding Online Research, by Heidi A. Campbell

Problem Solving: Models, Methods, and Techniques

Brainstorming and the Myth of Idea Generation in Groups,
by Adrian F. Furnham

Consulting: Organizations: Their Characteristics and How They Function

Systems Thinking and Learning: From Chaos and Complexity to Elegant Simplicity, by Stephen G. Haines

Consulting: Consulting Strategies and Techniques

Being an Agent of Organizational Healing, by Beverly J. Nyberg and Roger Harrison

The Role of the Executive Coach, by Barbara Pate Glacel

Consulting: Interface with Clients

Twenty-One Ways to Delight Your Customers, by Peter R. Garber

Leadership: Strategies and Techniques

Influence: Key to the Door of Leadership, by Marlene Caroselli

Leadership: Top-Management Issues and Concerns

Spirituality and Business: Where's the Beef?, by Gary Schouborg

As with previous *Annuals,* this volume covers a wide variety of topics. The range of articles presented encourages thought-provoking discussion about the present and future of HRD. Other articles on specific subjects can be located by using our comprehensive *Reference Guide to Handbooks and Annuals.* The guide is updated regularly and indexes the contents of all the *Annuals* and the *Handbooks of Structured Experiences.* With each revision, the *Reference Guide* becomes a complete, up-to-date, and easy-to-use resource for selecting appropriate materials from the *Annuals* and *Handbooks.*

Here and in the *Reference Guide,* we have done our best to categorize the articles for easy reference; however, many of the articles encompass a range of topics, disciplines, and applications. If you do not find what you are looking for under one category, check a related category. In some cases we may place an article in the "Training" *Annual* that also has implications for "Consulting," and vice versa. As the field of HRD continues to grow and develop, there is more and more crossover between training and consulting. Explore all the contents of both volumes of the *Annual* in order to realize the full potential for learning and development that each offers.

APPRECIATIVE INQUIRY: NEW THINKING AT WORK

Sherene Zolno

Abstract: Many of us have been taught that legitimate knowledge derives from an emphasis on what is rational, objective, empirical, and problematic. This ability to identify and solve problems successfully is viewed in most workplace settings as crucial for organizational effectiveness and change. Other means of understanding reality—"appreciation," "valuing," and "affirming"—are considered Pollyannaish, that is, soft-headed and non-essential.

By legitimizing only the first form of thinking, we shut down an entire mode of learning and severely limit the capacity for innovative approaches to organizing and change. A new and inclusive philosophy and approach, however, legitimizes the second form of thinking and facilitates positive organizational change. By connecting people to the organization's strategy, capturing their imaginations, respecting their contributions, and energizing the change process, this approach, called Appreciative Inquiry, enables organizational members to increase their influence on their organization's structure and nature.

WHAT IS APPRECIATIVE INQUIRY?

David Kolb (1984), in his theory of experiential learning, describes the importance of both *appreciative apprehension* and *critical comprehension* as different processes of knowing. Critical comprehension is based on skepticism and doubt, while appreciative apprehension is based on belief, trust, and conviction.

One mistake we make is to define "appreciative" in a limited way as meaning only "gratitude." Appreciative also includes the meanings "to see" (where you pay attention), "to value," and "to increase in value." When Kolb says, "Appreciation is the process of valuing," he is reminding us that it takes more than just the facts to make effective choices about the world.

> *"Appreciation of an apprehended moment is a judgment of both*
> *value and fact. To appreciate apprehended reality is to embrace it.*
> *And from this affirmative embrace flows a deeper fullness and*
> *richness of experience."*   —David Kolb[1]

David Cooperrider (Srivastva & Cooperrider, 1990), of Case Western Reserve University, who is one of the original developers of Appreciative Inquiry, describes it as engaging people in "an inquiry process that tries to apprehend the factors that give life to a living system." Based on information derived from the inquiry, people would then "seek to articulate those possibilities that can lead to a better future." The Appreciative Inquiry process as he has presented it is about finding successful ways to translate best intentions into reality and values and beliefs into practice.

> *"It is important to recognize that the problem-solving method*
> *of organizational inquiry quite systematically paints a picture of*
> *organizational life in which a whole series of colors are considered*
> *untouchable. In this way, the totality of being is obviously ob*
> *scured, leading to a narrowed conception of human nature and*
> *cultural possibility."* —David Cooperrider and Suresh Srivastva[2]

---

[1]Reprinted from D.A. Kolb, *Experiential Learning: Experience as the Source of Learning and Development,* copyright 1984, with permission from Prentice-Hall.

In other words, the expected outcome of the Appreciative Inquiry is an organization that has affirmed its strengths and fundamental values, used that information to engage in a process to envision a collectively desired future, and moved forward toward enacting that vision in daily work life.

PROBLEM SOLVING VERSUS APPRECIATIVE INQUIRY

Because it is highly counter-intuitive in Western culture, it's difficult to understand how affirming strengths and values can lead to transformational change. In fact, most leaders would feel remiss if they failed to engage in a rational process using problem-solving methods to identify ways to improve the cost effectiveness of internal systems. We need to question, however, whether problem solving has already fixed that which is *solvable*, and begin to focus on what is yet *possible*—the untapped potential beyond fixing what's already in place.

Carl Jung, early 20th Century psychological researcher and therapist, noticed that a person's problems faded when the person was confronted with a new or stronger interest. He asserted that the greatest and most important problems in life were fundamentally unsolvable and could only be outgrown (Jung, 1923).

For Jung, Cooperrider, and others, problem solving appeared inherently conservative, limiting, and slow. The philosophy and approach they sought to introduce instead focused on the future of the system as a whole, on engaging participants in collectively imagining new possibilities for their future, and on bypassing the process of solving yesterday's problems.

Thomas White, president of GTE Telephone Operations, expressed his concerns with the limits of problem solving by asking this question: "Should we demoralize a successful group by concentrating on their failures, or help them over the remaining hurdles by building a bridge with their successes?" He felt that using Appreciative Inquiry helped GTE attain much better results than just trying to fix problems—that by shifting their internal conversation away from a focus on negative problems and toward valuing their capabilities, the re-energized organization improved financial results beyond what was expected with traditional problem solving alone (White, 1996).

---

[2]Reprinted from W.A. Pasmore and R.W. Woodman, *Research in Organizational Change and Development,* copyright 1987, with permission from Elsevier Science.

Table 1 identifies some of the differences between problem solving and Appreciative Inquiry.

As many organizational leaders are far from achieving the results they want, the need to reinvent the tools used in helping them is clear. The choice appears to be to stay in the incremental, problem-based, diagnosis/treatment frame or to move on to a fresh perspective that can simultaneously address the compelling triad of strategy, structure, and culture during change.

The Appreciative Inquiry process makes available a whole new array of alternatives to support organizational learning and expand possibilities for action. Using it, change leaders have an opportunity to reframe their philosophical stance in a fundamental way—that is, during organizational improvement efforts, to be deliberately *appreciative*. They would thus be working with optimism and hope, actively engaged in valuing and celebrating the

Table 1. Problem Solving vs. Appreciative Inquiry

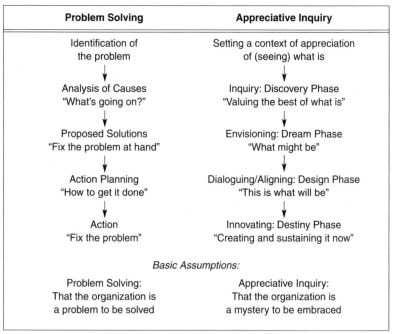

Problem Solving	Appreciative Inquiry
Identification of the problem	Setting a context of appreciation of (seeing) what is
↓	↓
Analysis of Causes "What's going on?"	Inquiry: Discovery Phase "Valuing the best of what is"
↓	↓
Proposed Solutions "Fix the problem at hand"	Envisioning: Dream Phase "What might be"
↓	↓
Action Planning "How to get it done"	Dialoguing/Aligning: Design Phase "This is what will be"
↓	↓
Action "Fix the problem"	Innovating: Destiny Phase "Creating and sustaining it now"

Basic Assumptions:

Problem Solving: That the organization is a problem to be solved	Appreciative Inquiry: That the organization is a mystery to be embraced

human spirit while creating an enspirited environment welcoming to creativity and imagination.

References

Cooperrider, D.L., & Whitney, D. (1999). *Appreciative inquiry*. San Francisco, CA: Berrett-Koehler.

Kolb, D.A. (1984). *Experiential learning: Experience as the source of learning and development*. Englewood Cliffs, NJ: Prentice-Hall.

Jung, C.G. (1923). *Psychological types*. London: Routledge & Kegan Paul.

Srivastva, S., & Cooperrider, D.L. (1987). Appreciative inquiry into organizational life. In W.A. Pasmore and R.W. Woodman (Eds.), *Research in organizational change and development* (Vol. 1). Stamford, CT: JAI Press.

Srivastva, S., & Cooperrider, D.L. (1990). *Appreciative management and leadership*. San Francisco, CA: Jossey-Bass.

White, T.H. (1996). *Vital speeches of the day*. Newark, NJ: City News Publishing Company

Sherene Zolno, RODC, *executive director of The Leading Clinic, is a researcher, educator, and consultant whose expertise includes working with leadership teams to ready them for the future and assisting organizations in identifying strategic intentions, improving operations, and transforming culture. Her research-based New Century Leadership™ program and Timeline for Tomorrow process are the foundation for systems change in several major organizations. Ms. Zolno served on ASTD's OD Professional Practice Area board. Her writing has been published in ASTD's* Research Monograph *and OD Network's* VisionAction Journal, *in Jossey-Bass/Pfeiffer's* 2000 Annual, *and in numerous other professional publications.*

THE COACHING STYLES ADVANTAGE

Patrick J. Aspell and Dee Dee Aspell

Abstract: In this article, the authors explain the need for and benefits of coaching. The authors believe that anyone wanting to be an effective and successful coach must follow a three-phase plan of self-knowledge, self-planning, and self-designed strategies. The authors then describe nine coaching styles—quality performers, supporters, enterprisers, dramatists, insighters, loyalists, strategists, challengers, and mediators—and a two-step process for examining coaching style. In Stage One, the coach examines the nine coaching styles to determine which one most closely describes his or her own style as well as that of his or her clients. Stage Two presents ten steps for effective coaching and gives tips to improve one's coaching skills. The conclusion exhorts coaches to coach others as they would like to be coached.

INTRODUCTION

Have you ever gone to the mall in search of a particular store? Unless you're an adventurous person, where do you start? Right! You go to the map of the mall to see where that store is located. Once you see where it is on the map, what's the next thing you do? Right again! Look for where it says, "You Are Here." Then all you have to do is find out where the store is in relationship to where you are.

That's the way it is with coaching. You need to know where you are, that is, who you are as a coach and what your coaching style is. The next step is to become acquainted with the person you are coaching and what his or her coaching style needs are. Having such knowledge of yourself as a coach and of the other person as the coachee gives you a decisive advantage. Of course, you will need to become familiar with the coachee's life history to appreciate where he or she is now.

There's an old saying, "Nothing willed unless known." In other words, with knowledge of yourself as a coach and the other person(s) as a coachee, you are ready to make some practical, prudent decisions. The material offered in this article will allow you to do the following:

- Learn a three-phase coaching plan;

- Discover the nine coaching styles;

- Grasp three aspects of each of the nine coaching styles: communication, conflict management, and problem solving;

- Follow a ten-step model for effective coaching skills;

- Learn three specific tips for coaching each of the nine styles; and

- Enhance your preferred coaching style.

THREE-PHASE COACHING PLAN

The method described here follows a three-phase coaching plan that progressively unfolds to reveal the riches of your coaching style. The three phases answer three significant questions:

- Who am I as a coach?

- Why am I seeking coaching? Or why is someone coming to me for coaching?

- How can I get what I want from coaching?

The first phase is *self-discovery*. Socrates, the philosopher in ancient Greece, exhorted his listeners with the words, "Know thyself!" One's response to this answers the question, "Who am I as a coach?" Unless you know yourself, how can you know how to coach others, what you want from coaching, or how you're going to get it? Self-knowledge is the foundation of personal coaching.

The second phase is *self-planning*. Why are you coming to a coach, or what goal are you aiming for as you become a better coach? If you don't know where you're going, you may end up some place you don't want to be. You need to stay on the right track. Once you know where you are personally as a coach, you can plan where you want to go.

The third phase is *self-designed strategies*. How are you going to get what you want from coaching?

As a result of working through the three-phase coaching plan, you will gain greater understanding of your own tendencies. In particular, pay attention to how you process information and what motivates you. People typically process information through the head, heart, or gut. These are like your "personal computers." Some coaching styles work through the head and others through the heart or gut. Knowing your preference is helpful in constructing the strategy that will be most effective for you.

Motivation usually stems from one of three instincts: self-preservation of your professional image, networking relationships (one-to-one or in a larger social circle), or personal adaptation.

Knowing the combination of your preferred information-processing style and what motivates you will help you to identify your coaching style. You are invited to look at the nine coaching styles in two stages: Stage One helps you to determine your coaching style, whether you are the one being coached or the actual coach. Stage Two helps you to be more effective as a coach.

STAGE ONE: SELF-KNOWLEDGE AND UNDERSTANDING OTHERS

Each of the nine coaching styles is listed in Table 1, which also includes brief descriptions of how those with each style typically behave in three areas: communication, conflict management, and problem solving. Knowing your coaching style and the preferences of others lays the groundwork for understanding yourself, appreciating how you like to be coached, and recognizing how others like to be coached. To discover more about your coaching style, you may want to take the Aspell Coaching Styles Indicator (Aspell & Aspell, 2000). Imagine how effective you can be if you also possess insights into the coaching styles of other people!

Knowledge of Your Coaching Style

A big mistake we make is trying to know someone else before we know ourselves. People have to develop relationship skills so they can effectively connect with others. It's the same with coaching. First, you need to know *who you are*. Once you know yourself as a coach, then you are in a position to under-

Table 1. Characteristics of Nine Coaching Styles

Coaching Style	Communication Style	Conflict-Management Style	Problem-Solving Style
Quality Performer	Clear, direct, honest	Fair, principled, objective	Stress accurate assessment
Supporter	Listen and speak with feeling	Caring and empathic feeling	Focus on person before task
Enterpriser	Speak persuasively	Deal with problems proactively	See issues as goals to be achieved
Dramatist	Emotional expressions	Disclose genuine feelings	Explore possible solutions
Insighter	Focus on essential	Observe and analyze	Theorize and explain concepts
Loyalist	Careful in speech	Cooperate and conciliate	Coordinate ideas for solutions
Strategist	Talk in lively, humorous manner	Work toward positive outcome	Use innovative alternatives
Challenger	Speak directly and forcefully	Deal with issues proactively	Take action
Mediator	Talk agreeably and calmly	Listen patiently and collaborate	Reconcile differences

stand where others are in the coaching relationship. Knowledge of who you are empowers you to plan those relationships.

Following are descriptions of the nine coaching styles. As you read through them, try to identify which one most closely parallels your own.

Quality Performers

These coaches follow clear standards, have high expectations of clients, and set definite directions in which to proceed. They instinctively process information by dividing results into right or wrong, good or bad. They like to see themselves as correct, conscientious, fair, and honest. Their thinking is orderly and accurate.

Characteristics of Quality Performers

- Are fair in their relationships with clients;
- Aim to be right in their coaching and to avoid criticism;
- Are conscientious about their coaching responsibilities;
- Are well-prepared with a wealth of information;
- Are impatient with poor performance;
- Feel uncomfortable not adhering to standard procedures;
- Focus on order, precision, and discipline;
- Evaluate clients according to high ideals and attention to detail; and
- Can become more effective coaches by adopting a positive, optimistic outlook.

Drawbacks of Quality Performers

- May be inflexible and rigid in their strategy;
- May be so organized that they lack flexibility in relating to different people; and
- May be upset by clients' expressing different viewpoints.

Supporters

Supportive coaches put people first, show they care by their generous giving of self, make clients feel at home, and listen with the heart more than the head. They also are warm and friendly mentors. They like to see themselves as altruistic. Their immediate attraction to people they like enables others to feel right at home with them.

Characteristics of Supporters

- Give priority to people over tasks;
- Like clients to accept them;
- Express empathy toward people with challenges or problems;
- Come across as warm and kindhearted;
- Make sure the client's needs are met;
- Are available to help clients;
- Influence clients by assisting and advising;
- Are influenced by clients who thank and approve of them;
- Support the aims and aspirations of their clients; and
- Can become better coaches by acknowledging their own unique needs.

Drawbacks of Supporters

- May be too solicitous or possessive;
- May flatter with compliments; and
- May find it difficult to say "no."

Enterprisers

People with this coaching style motivate clients to take the initiative to produce results. Enterprisers have strong feelings about outcomes to be accomplished. Their minds are usually thinking about ways they can promote their own interests and further their own ambitions. Their practical, fast-paced thinking puts ideas into action by calculating the means necessary to produce desired results.

Characteristics of Enterprisers

- Are driven to succeed in coaching and to avoid failure;
- Set goals to be achieved in coaching and organize means to reach them;
- Focus on getting desired results with efficiency for clients;
- Become enthusiastic and excited about the task to be done;

- Influence clients by projecting a positive image and marketing themselves;

- Are ambitious in promoting their careers;

- Like to be recognized for their successes in coaching;

- Take advantage of opportunities to advance their careers;

- Are energetic and sociable with their clients; and

- Can become more effective coaches by combining short-term returns with long-range goals.

Drawbacks of Enterprisers

- May be more style than substance;

- May take advantage of clients to advance their own career goals; and

- May recommend quick-fix solutions that cut corners and produce shoddy results.

Dramatists

The style of dramatists is unique and favors doing special coaching projects. They have good intuition and are sensitive to the feelings of clients. As they process information through their hearts, they sense what is personally important to others. Their imagination enables them to come up with creative ideas.

Characteristics of Dramatists

- Like a coaching style that is a cut above the ordinary;

- Originate imaginative and creative strategies;

- See uncommon possibilities in common situations;

- Influence by listening and empathizing with clients' problems;

- Are emotionally expressive in communicating;

- Create a personal climate that is distinctive;

- Get an immediate feeling of liking or disliking a client;

- Are influenced by clients who express what is personally significant in their lives;

- Are willing to lend an ear to listen to clients' problems; and

- Can improve their coaching by stabilizing emotions and developing realistic expectations of clients.

Drawbacks of Dramatists

- May emotionally overreact and personalize minor misunderstandings with clients;

- May swing between maximum and minimum expectations of clients; and

- May recommend impractical and unrealistic solutions to problems.

Insighters

This type of coach empowers clients by giving of their own information and knowledge. They are attentive to data, grasp and reflect on ideas, and explain situations in the light of theories. They think of themselves as knowledgeable, intellectual, and insightful coaches. Their talents lie in logical and objective reasoning, uncontrolled by emotions.

Characteristics of Insighters

- Know a lot about the latest advances in coaching;

- Gather facts and reflect on ideas for sound coaching decisions;

- Construct paradigms to understand the nature of coaching;

- Analyze issues and solve problems;

- Ask significant questions;

- Focus on understanding the structure of coaching;

- Use critical thinking and logic to evaluate clients;

- Influence clients by sound reasoning from premises to conclusions;

- Are good facilitators who can readily summarize long discussions; and

- Can become more effective by developing feeling awareness.

Drawbacks of Insighters

- May not take action on ideas;

- May not be aware of their own or others' feelings; and

- May not be readily available to help clients.

Loyalists

These coaches commit themselves to their professional relationships and collaborate with clients. They like to relate to clients, especially within a group.

Clients can count on their being dependable and following through on commitments. Processing information through their heads, they deliberately weigh the pros and cons and set clear limits to their coaching.

Characteristics of Loyalists

- Respect traditions of coaching;

- Carefully fulfill their coaching responsibilities;

- Think things through to consider all aspects of the coaching relationship;

- Value a trusting relationship with clear lines of authority;

- Evaluate clients with their dedicated and reliable behaviors;

- Want to know the limits of their objectives;

- Take their duties seriously;

- Speak and listen in a friendly manner;

- Are careful about expressing their views in a group; and

- Can improve their coaching style by developing their own inner sense of authority.

Drawbacks of Loyalists

- May let self-doubts keep them from making a decision;

- May feel insecure coaching those with strong personalities; and

- May control the ideas of clients in the interest of conformity.

Strategists

These coaches promote a positive atmosphere that leads to client satisfaction. They plan for satisfactory outcomes. Outgoing and spontaneous, they usually have a variety of skills and interests. They are brainstormers who are optimistic as they create promising possibilities for the future. Very flexible, they instinctively adapt to changing times and places.

Characteristics of Strategists

- Enjoy coaching as a fulfilling experience;

- Plan the coaching activity for the satisfaction of clients;

- Explore new possibilities for coaching;

- Promote a positive, optimistic attitude;

- Develop new ideas and innovative projects for coaching;

- Use humor to contribute to an enjoyable experience;

- Easily become enthused and excited about coaching;

- Inspire clients with their upbeat behavior; and

- Can improve their coaching style by being realistic about not taking on too many projects.

Drawbacks of Strategists

- May go from one task to another without completing them;

- May dabble in many projects without being attentive to details; and

- May impulsively make commitments to clients and then vacillate.

Challengers

Challengers coach by directing and commanding. They are confident and easily assert themselves to finish a job. Seeing themselves as strong and powerful, they are ready to take risks to coach in difficult situations. Their gut instinctively processes information so they can quickly put ideas into action. Fearless and outspoken, they courageously oppose others' ideas and grapple with problems as they mobilize clients to do the job.

Characteristics of Challengers

- Take a strong lead in the coaching relationship;

- Complete tasks right away;

- Are naturally self-confident and decisive;

- Champion their clients when they are treated unjustly;

- Mobilize clients to take action and accomplish objectives;

- Emphasize the importance of power and leadership;

- Evaluate clients on their strength of will and determination to act;

- Relate by being outgoing and social;

- Challenge group thinkers to look at problems and solutions in a different way; and

- Can become more effective by thinking of power in terms of service to others, rather than dominating others.

Drawbacks of Challengers

- May come across as dictatorial and intimidating;
- May be dogmatic in giving orders; and
- May regard gentleness as a weakness.

Mediators

Mediators promote a harmonious relationship between themselves and clients. They are usually easygoing and relaxed. Their calm manner promotes harmony among diverse groups. Their patience, gentleness, and simplicity make clients feel comfortable and at ease. They instinctively smooth out disturbances and calm "troubled waters" with clients. Their holistic thinking allows them to grasp similarities and play down differences to unify diverse ideas into a harmonious whole.

Characteristics of Mediators

- Like to feel at ease with their clients;
- Are good listeners;
- Conciliate disagreements between people;
- Find the common denominator on which people can agree;
- Keep a relaxed yet steady pace in resolving conflicts;
- Are poised in critical moments that require presence of mind;
- Influence clients by accommodating their interests;
- Evaluate clients by finding the good and focusing on facts;
- Like to do routine coaching tasks; and
- Can improve their coaching effectiveness by taking control of events.

Drawbacks of Mediators

- May gloss over problems to avoid conflict;
- May find it hard to adapt to changes; and
- May procrastinate when it comes to dealing with disagreements.

Stage Two: Effective Coaching Skills

Now that you know something about your coaching style, you are in a position to advance your skills so you can be a more effective coach. The ten tips for effective coaching presented next will enable you to improve as a coach, no matter your style.

Ten Tips for Effective Coaching

Read the tips carefully and incorporate any you do not currently use.

1. Learn how clients like to be coached. Invite potential (or actual) coaches to take the Aspell Coaching Styles Indicator (2000) to identify their coaching style.

2. Develop rapport by matching your clients' behavior and the key words they use.

3. Analyze the clients' traits by considering their style of thinking, what motivates them, what they value, and what irritates them.

4. Learn whether they process information through the head, heart, or gut.

5. Determine which instincts drive the client: self-preservation, relationships, or adaptation.

6. Call clients to stretch themselves beyond their comfort zones so they can enhance their coaching experience.

7. Observe the inner natural principles of the coaching styles to appreciate the personality dynamics of the client.

8. Understand the passion (for example, anger) and virtue (for example, serenity) associated with each style.

9. Discern the spirituality of each style.

10. Facilitate transformations in thinking, feeling, and action.

Further information about Tips 7, 9, and 10 can be found in the Aspell Coaching Styles Indicator.

Tips for Dealing with the Coaching Styles

In addition to the general tips provided above, there are specific tips for coaches to deal with particular coaching styles. These tips will be useful in two ways:

- They will help you to accept clients as they are and at the same time adapt to their styles, and

- They provide ways to motivate clients to make the most of their unique styles, to challenge them to confront and overcome obstacles to their progress, and to encourage them to grow to their fullest potential.

Tips to Coach Quality Performers

- Be humorously tolerant, but be ready to challenge them to change for the better;

- Avoid arguments and power struggles at all costs, because they must be right–it's their nature; and

- Suggest they rephrase "I should" with "I want" or "I don't want."

Tips to Coach Supporters

- Recognize and acknowledge the supporters' efforts, no matter how frequently they insist, "It's nothing." Compliments may embarrass supporters, but they need to know inwardly that you notice and appreciate them;

- Facilitate their learning to be generous receivers; and

- Help them make a list of things they want for themselves and teach them how to ask for what they want.

Tips to Coach Enterprisers

- Recognize their need to be number one and to be admired. Acknowledge their gifts and the fruits of their success;

- Help them see how they react to criticism. Do they lash out, distance themselves, or dislike people who offer the criticism? An understanding of their own reactions can make it easier for them to deal with criticism; and

- Motivate them to ask questions about other people, especially about what they can do for friends or family who are closest to them.

Tips to Coach Dramatists

- Allow them their emotional freedom and enjoy the range of feelings they display;

- Don't take their emotional reactions personally. They may be emotionally stormy at one time and calm a little later; and

- Suggest that they complement their intuitive feelings with observation and judgment and by gathering as many objective details as they can.

Tips to Coach Insighters

- Accept them as they are: persons who may not mix much with others or react deeply, but who are competent and responsible with interesting inner worlds;

- Ensure that insighters have plenty of time to think things through. Appeal to logic instead of emotion. Speak to their head because they're thinkers; and

- Inform them that they can go about their own business more easily by improving their relationships with other people.

Tips to Coach Loyalists

- Reassure them that they are capable and that you appreciate their reliability;

- Take the lead in interacting with them; and

- Help them to express their opinions honestly. Invite them to tell you whatever is bothering them and to express their anger directly.

Tips to Coach Strategists

- Don't be surprised by their changing moods; remember that it doesn't take much to set them off;

- Be steady and consistent so you can keep them focused on priorities;

- Because their impulsiveness and scatteredness may take their attention in different directions, remind them often of the desired results and keep them on track. By keeping the end in mind, they are more apt to complete projects; and

- Invite them to develop detachment and restraint so they can be more in control of their impulses and desires.

Tips to Coach Challengers

- Even though you are the coach, understand and respect the power of their personalities;

- Because challengers have quick tempers, let their anger wind down before trying to solve problems; and

- Ask them to make a list of the things that bother them so they can work on managing their anger.

Tips to Coach Mediators

- Be realistic about whether you can tolerate their leisurely personalities;

- Offer to assist them with projects that need to be done; and

- Encourage them to tackle major tasks little by little, especially with people with whom they want harmony.

Conclusion

The effectiveness of a coaching relationship depends to a great extent on how well you relate to the other person. The Golden Rule states, "Do unto others as you would have them do unto you." The spirit of this principle means that others should be treated as they like to be treated. Or, more exactly, others should be coached as they like to be coached. People like others to relate to them according to who they are and to recognize their individual personalities and coaching styles.

Knowing the way others want to be treated puts you in the advantageous position of knowing what they do and do not appreciate. Other people are more apt to be cooperative and productive when you relate to them just the way they like to be related to.

Reference

Aspell, P., & Aspell, D. (2000). *Aspell coaching styles indicator.* San Antonio, TX: Lifewings.

Patrick J. Aspell, Ph.D., is a licensed professional counselor and an organizational consultant with Aspell Empowerment Enterprises, Inc. He presents workshops and seminars to public and private organizations. In addition to numerous articles, Dr. Aspell has co-authored numerous inventories and books for business and education.

Dee Dee Aspell is the founder and principal of Aspell Empowerment Enterprises, Inc. She presents workshops and seminars, specializing in leadership empowerment, team development, and conflict and emotional management. Her innovative work in the area of personality quotient (PQ) is forthcoming. She is a professional coach and the co-author of numerous inventories and books, including the Aspell Coaching Styles Indicator.

ETHICAL ISSUES SURROUNDING ONLINE RESEARCH

Heidi A. Campbell

Abstract: The online environment creates a new space for research of employee communication and work habits. However, researchers, anxious to explore people's interactions in this new environment, often fail to consider the ethical issues around participating in and publishing material from online communication forums. In this article, the author raises some key ethical issues and encourages researchers to be thoughtful about online study and research.

INTRODUCTION

Observing and researching people in the online setting brings with it a special set of ethical concerns. It has been mentioned that the nature of computer-mediated communication (CMC) allows for anonymity not only of the participants but also of researchers, who are able to "lurk" in the shadows of cyberspace. Since this field of study is still young, online researchers generally do not agree on many ethical guidelines dealing with issues of disclosure and information gathering. This article will briefly look at three key areas involving ethical decision making for those using the Internet for research or study purposes: (1) obtaining permission to conduct research, (2) level of involvement in specific online groups, and (3) issues of anonymity and privacy.

IN CYPERSPACE NOBODY KNOWS YOU ARE WATCHING

One of the first ethical dilemmas the online researcher confronts is the issue of obtaining permission from the group under study. Some researchers would argue that permission only has to be obtained for certain private contexts such as an email discussion list, while a public forum such as a bulletin board service (BBS) can be considered a public sphere. This approach is advocated by Project H Research Group, an international team of scholars who in 1993 and 1994 collaborated on a quantitative study of electronic discussion. Through much discussion, they came to the decision that it was not necessary to seek permission for recording and analyzing publicly posted messages, only those that were sent to individuals privately (Paccagnella, 1997).

This perspective raises the issue of what exactly is "public" and what is "private" in an online environment. A one-to-one email is typically considered to be a private communication between two individuals, much like a personal letter. Yet boundaries blur in publicly accessible forums such as Internet relay chat (IRC) channels or newsgroups, which are often seen as "public acts deliberately intended for public consumption" (Paccagnella, 1997). Although it is one thing to log onto one of the public forums to observe/read the interactions taking place, it is another matter to publish these interactions elsewhere.

Even if researchers feel it is essential to notify a given group of their research intentions and obtain permission, another complication may arise when trying to contact the specific group or individuals. In the case of an IRC channel, individuals often use aliases or nicknames and are able to conceal their identities behind firewalls, thus preventing the researcher from being able to find contact information. For email lists and newsgroups, it is often easier to contact individuals because the email addresses of respondents are typically listed. While this enables the researcher to contact a specific individual, it would be impossible for a researcher to contact each person on the list individually and privately without sending a post to the entire list/group. Often the group sees such public declarations by a researcher as an "unwelcome arbitrary intrusion" (Paccagnella, 1997).

One alternative for researchers is to gain consent from the list owner on behalf of the group. This approach is recommended and used by Schroeder, Heather, and Lee (1998) in their study of the social interactions within the virtual reality environment. List owners were contacted and gave consent for their groups to be studied. When material was quoted from individual participants, it was done in such a way that individuals could not be specifically identified.

To Lurk or Not to Lurk

Once permission has been obtained and access has been gained to an online group, the researcher must then decide on his or her level of online involvement. The question to be asked is: "How much participation is enough to let the members know that I am there, but not so much that it interferes with the discussion?" I posed this question to a discussion list of online researchers, the Electric Communication and Culture list, generating a lively discussion.

Researchers came out on both side of the debate. David Silver from the University of Maryland, who is conducting a four-year case study of the Blacksburg Electronic Village (a wired community in Virginia, USA), advocates participating as well as observing in the context of online ethnographic study. He comments that the "beauty" of this type of study is that it generates rich and thick description. "I don't think you should worry about going 'too deep' or 'too native'—as long as you self-reflexively chart your progress into the community" (David Silver, personal communication). Joan Biddle, a researcher with the Sociological Practice Association, supports the stance of researcher primarily as observer. As a lurker, the researcher participates "by the act of following the conversation." She feels it is important to not in any way shape or influence the conversation, "After all, if you're there to see what 'they' do, you need to let 'them' do it" (Joan Biddle, personal communication).

Within the realm of online research, there seems to be room for both approaches, depending on the community and the objectives of the researcher. As a way of offering a guideline to respond to this question, Jeffrey Weiss, a staff writer from the *Dallas Morning News*, suggests applying the doctor's "informed consent" rule. By this he means, "participate enough so that the others are aware that you are there and why you are there, but not enough to change the course of discussion" (Jeffrey Weiss, personal communication). While this guideline is helpful, it still leaves room for clarification and behavioral boundaries.

Upon reflection, I feel a position of "observer as participant" to be the best one to take in the online setting. This would involve announced presence and occasional email posts to the list to ensure members are aware of the researcher's presence. However, the researcher's primary position would be that of a lurker.

ANONYMITY FOR THE ANONYMOUS

A final area the researcher must consider is how information obtained online will be cited. This is important because how researchers treat their subjects will not only affect their personal research, but will impact on those online researchers who follow after them.

With the rise of online journals and ease in publication of materials on the World Wide Web, the probability or threat of exposure can become a critical issue for those who are subjects of an online study. This is especially relevant for online communities, "therapy," or support groups, where much of the content exchanged is highly personal or seemingly confidential. In these groups, individuals often feel freed of their inhibitions, and the Internet is used as a "confessional," enabling them to disclose issues that would be difficult for them to speak of in a face-to-face context. Therefore, the researchers' decisions concerning what information is acceptable for reproduction can have significant impact on the group and on the "safe place" created by cyberspace, again raising the issue of what is public and what is private online. This discussion was heightened recently when a man in the United States was charged with killing his daughter after a confession he made to an online support group was reported by the group's moderator to the police (After Internet confession, 1998).

The general attitude of online researchers seems to be that private communications (such as personal email) require permission from the author/originator, while public communications (messages on a bulletin board or information on a web page) are seen as fair game.

If one treats the Internet as a social space, researchers would be able to apply similar guidelines to those used in a face-to-face research setting. The common approach is to disguise the identity of research group members to the best of the researcher's ability, substituting fictional names for real names. In an online environment, this would include changing online tags or nicknames, as these created identities can be as well-known as an individual's true name. Paccagnella (1997) writes, "Changing not only real names, but also aliases or pseudonyms (where used) proves the respect of the researcher for the social reality of cyberspace."

SUMMARY

This article has presented three ethical areas to be considered by those doing online research. The Internet presents researchers with a unique and challenging new place to observe and study interpersonal interaction. It is a new space with new rules, and those who choose to engage in online study and communication must also learn to live in a space governed by new rules and ways of being.

References

After Internet confession, man charged with killing his daughter. (1998, May 1). *CNN-U.S. News Update* [On-line]. Available: www.cnn.com/US/9805/01/online.confessions.update [last accessed May 4, 2001]

Paccagnella, L. (1997, June). Getting the seat of your pants dirty: Strategies for ethnographic research on virtual communities. *Journal of Computer Mediated Communication* [On-line], *2*(1). Available: http://ascusc.org/jcmc/col3/issue1/paccagnella.html [last accessed April 30, 2001]

Schroeder, R., Heather, N., &. Lee, R.M. (1998, December). The sacred and the virtual: Religion in multi-user virtual reality. *Journal of Computer Mediated Communication* [On-line], *4*(2). Available: www.ascusc.org/jcmc/vol4/issue2/schroeder.html [last accessed April 30, 2001]

Heidi A. Campbell *is a Ph.D. candidate in computer-mediated communications and practical theology at the University of Edinburgh (Scotland), researching on-line communities and how online communication impacts interaction within a face-to-face setting. She is also an adjunct faculty member in communications at Spring Arbor College (Michigan). Ms. Campbell has worked as an experiential educator and has over ten years' experience as a freelance writer, with work appearing in publications such as* Personnel Journal *and previous* Annuals. *She has presented her research at various international conferences, including the Popular Culture Association Annual Conference, the British Sociological Association, and the Royal Geographic Society Annual Conference.*

BRAINSTORMING AND THE MYTH OF IDEA GENERATION IN GROUPS

Adrian F. Furnham

Abstract: The author reviews the business and academic literature on the benefits and drawbacks of brainstorming and concludes that it is no accident that the word "brainstorming" is derived from, and juxtaposed in the dictionary with, "brainstorm," which is defined as a "fit of insanity." He shows that the evidence from science and the evidence from practice could not be further apart and that they suggest that most business people must indeed be insane to use brainstorming groups. For the psychologist, the use of brainstorming represents an interesting problem. Why, if *all* the scientific literature shows *unequivocally* that brainstorming groups produce fewer and poorer quality ideas than a comparative group of individuals working alone, does its use continue to be popular?

Background

Madison Avenue advertising executive Alex Osborn (1957), who is credited with originating the term "brainstorm," argued that the technique increased both the quality and quantity of ideas generated by a group. Osborn developed this technique in the 1950s after concluding that typical group decision-making processes inhibit, rather than encourage, creativity. He observed that most groups discuss and evaluate an idea as soon as a group member generates it. He thought that this immediate evaluation discouraged people from developing and sharing ideas that were unusual or not yet well-thought-out, as their creativity was inhibited. He stated that the average person can think up twice as many ideas when working with a group than when working alone.

Brainstorming is thought to be best suited to finding lists of alternative solutions to problems. It is assumed that the technical details of *how to implement* these alternatives can be worked out at a later stage. Although originally developed for use in creating advertising campaigns, brainstorming is now put to such diverse uses as thinking of new products, making recommendations for new employee benefits, finding ways of raising money for a cause, and searching for new ways to lay out the work groups in a government agency.

A number of rules have been developed to ensure that a brainstorming session is properly conducted:

- Group size should be five to seven people. If there are too few people, not enough suggestions are generated. If too many people participate, the session becomes uncontrolled and uncontrollable.

- No criticism allowed. All suggestions are welcome, and it is particularly important not to use derisive laughter or disapproving non-verbal behavior.

- Freewheeling is encouraged. The more outlandish (even impractical or off-the-wall) the idea, the better. It is always easier to moderate an idea than to dream it up.

- Quantity and variety are very important. The more ideas put forth, the more likely a breakthrough idea will be suggested. The aim is to generate a long list of ideas.

The 2002 Annual: Volume 2, Consulting/© 2002 John Wiley & Sons, Inc.

- Combinations and improvements are encouraged. Building on the ideas of others, including combining ideas, is very productive. "Hitchhiking" and "piggy-backing" are essential parts of cooperation in brainstorming.

- Notes must be taken during the sessions, either manually or with an electronic recording device. One person serves as "recorder."

- The alternatives generated during the first part of the session should later be edited for duplication and categorization. At some point, the best ideas can be set aside for possible implementation.

Of course, these rules are not intended to be followed so rigidly that they stymie the process. Brainstorming is a spontaneous small-group process and is meant to be fun.

Some of the claimed advantages (Napier & Gershenfeld, 1985) of the brainstorming technique include the following:

- It reduces dependence on a single authority figure;

- It encourages the open sharing of ideas;

- It stimulates participation among group members;

- It provides individual safety in a competitive group;

- It maximizes output for a short period of time;

- It ensures a non-evaluative climate; and

- It tends to be enjoyable and stimulating.

CURRENT ORGANIZATIONAL THINKING

Most authors of books on management appear favorable to the idea of brainstorming. Consider the following two.

Davis and Newstrom (1987) say of brainstorming: "Its main advantage is deferred judgment, by which all ideas—even unusual and impractical ones—are encouraged without criticism or evaluation." They explain that the benefit of deferred judgment is that participants, free from worrying about immediate criticism, are more likely to contribute bold or unusual ideas and that, overall, the group will thus generate more ideas. They go on to list other advantages of brainstorming, including "enthusiasm, broader participation, greater task orientation, building upon ideas exchanged, and the feeling that the final product is a team solution" (p. 221).

Durham and Pierce (1989) believe that brainstorming may be more successful in generating quality ideas than other more traditional group processes. In addition, they note that participants in a brainstorming session may feel less pressure to conform and may be more accepting of others' ideas.

The authors do note some drawbacks to brainstorming, chief among them that the result of a brainstorming session is often just a list of ideas without any plans for implementation and that the presence of others may inhibit some participants from speaking. Further, these authors note that there is some evidence that "individuals 'brainstorming' alone would generate more and better quality ideas than they would in a brainstorming group" (Durham & Pierce, 1989, p. 263).

The authors conclude that individual brainstorming may be preferable in some circumstances and group brainstorming in others. Group sessions can create a sense of comradery and can improve group communication and commitment. If these elements are important, groups may be best served by a group brainstorming process.

Most textbook authors seem reluctant to discuss the damning research that explains how and why brainstorming does not deliver what it promises (Diehl & Stroebe, 1987; Robbins, 1995). Brainstorming has not fallen out of favor in the business community, perhaps because brainstorming groups overestimate their own productivity or because group facilitators are used, which tends to increase interactive group performance.

Lest business people argue that all research is unrealistic (with poor ecological validity), Paulus, Larey, and Ortega (1995) did a study on employees of a corporation that had undergone considerable training for effective teamwork. Even after the training, the brainstorming groups generated only about half as many ideas as a similar number of individuals working in nominal groups (where subjects brainstormed alone and then combined their non-redundant ideas) or working alone. They conclude, "In spite of common beliefs about the efficacy of group brainstorming, controlled research has demonstrated significant productivity losses in interactive groups. These types of findings lead some to suggest that there is little justification for group brainstorming in organizations" (Paulus, Larey, & Ortega, 1995, pp. 262–263). The authors do mention, however, that additional study of group brainstorming in conjunction with individual brainstorming should be undertaken.

EARLY RESEARCH

Evidence of the deficiencies of brainstorming has been available for some time. Taylor, Berry, and Block (1958) were the first to reject the claim that brainstorming was an efficient and effective way to generate ideas. They found that nominal groups outperformed interacting groups with the same number of participants. This finding has been consistently replicated. The most influential work was carried out in the 1970s by Bouchard and his colleagues. They manipulated, among other things, the group size and gender mix and even modified the brainstorming procedure itself in order to understand what determined the problem-solving effectiveness of groups and individuals (Bouchard, 1972).

Researchers during the 1980s and 1990s tried to answer the question as to why individuals performed better than groups (Paulus & Dzindolet, 1993). Some have attempted to specify mathematical models of group brainstorming. Brown and Paulus (1996) attempted a "simple dynamic model" based on three assumptions:

1. *Output Decay:* Over a period of time, individuals will run out of ideas;

2. *Blocking:* Working with others will serve to inhibit or prevent some ideas from being presented; and

3. *Matching:* Individuals will match the overall output rate of the group. An individual with a lot of ideas will actually present fewer ideas if the rest of the group is also presenting fewer ideas; conversely, someone with a slower rate of production will produce more ideas if the group's overall rate of production is higher.

Brainstorming experiments usually involve unstructured, open-ended, "creative" tasks. The tasks traditionally range from the "thumbs problem" (whereby the benefits and difficulties of growing an extra thumb on each hand are assessed) to the "blind world problem" (which involves thinking up the consequences of everyone suddenly going blind). The methodological diversity of these experiments makes it very hard to compare one study with another.

THREE FACTORS THAT AFFECT BRAINSTORMING EFFICACY

Reviewers of the literature have pointed out that there are traditionally three separate processes that inhibit the effectiveness of brainstorming (Diehl & Stroebe, 1987; Gallupe, Cooper, Grise, & Bastianutti, 1994): *social loafing, evaluation apprehension,* and *production blocking.*

Social Loafing

Groups have traditionally been seen to have two potentially opposing effects, social loafing and social facilitation. Social loafing is the finding that interacting group members (whose outputs are pooled) will exert less effort than will similar participants working alone. However, *individually identifiable group participants' performances* will be greater than the output from subjects working alone on tasks, depending on the task. In order to explain the latter phenomenon, investigators have argued that the mere *presence* of others leads to an increased motivation and/or competition, which, along with other things, will increase the motivation to perform. They have also argued that the possibility of other group members *evaluating* their performance also has an effect, a phenomenon that will be discussed later.

Social loafing has been found for a wide variety of tasks, including physical tasks, such as rope pulling and swimming; cognitive tasks, such as navigating mazes and identifying radar signals on a computer screen; creative tasks, such as listing thoughts and writing songs; evaluative tasks, such as rating the quality of poems, editorials, and clinical therapists; and work-related tasks, such as typing and evaluating job candidates. In the 1880s, Ringlemann examined the effects of working collectively on a rope-pulling task and noted a decrease in performance with increasing group size (Kravitz & Martin, 1986). At the time, his results were essentially ignored, regarded with skepticism, or interpreted as a mere artefact of lack of coordination among group members rather than loss of motivation. Not until 1974 were Ringlemann's findings replicated, and an additional fifteen years passed before the motivational component of this effect was understood and given the label social loafing.

Jackson and Harkins (1985) offered two explanations for social loafing: (1) hiding in the crowd or (2) the idea that people *expect* others to loaf and hence reduce their own efforts to establish an equitable division of labor. The expectation of how others behave is a crucial factor. It is what Robbins (1995) called the "fear of playing the sucker effect."

Williams, Harkins, and Latane (1981) demonstrated that being able to identify individual output was an important factor involved in evaluation. However, Harkins and Jackson (1985) tested this notion using brainstorming techniques and found that identifiability was involved in evaluation, but only when evaluation of output took place as a result of competition with co-workers.

Kerr and Bruun (1983) claimed that social loafing depended heavily on task features: whether the task was disjunctive (where only the best answers counted) or additive (where outputs were summed). They claimed that dispensability matters less with additive tasks than with disjunctive tasks (and hence the likelihood of loafing increases). The possibility of redundancy may in fact promote dispensability. Social loafing could be found responsible for only a small proportion of productivity loss, so other processes must be contributing to that loss. It may be a consequence of the nature of brainstorming, which requires little effort, as opposed to physical tasks, where loafing results in more loss of productivity (Diehl & Stroebe, 1987).

Karau and Williams (1993) reviewed studies and came up with a Collective Effort Model, which views individual effort (or loafing) as a function of three things: (1) the perceived relationship between individual performance and group performance, (2) the perceived relationship between group performance and group outcomes, and (3) the perceived relationship between group outcome and individual outcomes. The model leads to various interesting implications:

- Even if outcomes are highly valued, individual effort may lag if those efforts are not critical to obtaining outcomes.

- Communication among group members should enhance effort when it conveys positive feelings about the importance of the task, but may deter effort when it relays negative task attitudes.

- The group structure and member roles may affect collective effort in ongoing groups: "For example, leaders and high-status group members may view their inputs as more instrumental to group outcomes, and norms encouraging social responsibility and hard work within groups should have positive effects on collective effort, especially in cohesive or highly valued groups" (Karau & Williams, 1993, p.702).

Evaluation Apprehension

A second possible interpretation that has been offered to account for loss of real group productivity is evaluation apprehension, literally fear of being judged or more likely not wanting to look stupid. Many group members refrain from expressing their views in various social settings, such as the classroom or the boardroom, because they are uncertain as to how their ideas are going to be received. This notion of "the unpleasant experience of negative evaluation from other group members" has been investigated as a plausible cause of productivity loss in brainstorming groups, but the results have been somewhat contradictory. Collaros and Anderson (1969) concluded that productivity was lowest under conditions that aimed to produce the highest amount of evaluation apprehension. This finding differed from that of Maginn and Harris (1980), who found that individual productivity in the presence of observers was not significantly different from that of individual subjects working without observers.

However, the methodology of the two experiments was dissimilar in that the former induced evaluation apprehension by deceiving the subjects with respect to the number of experts who were present in the group, while the latter experiment manipulated evaluation apprehension by telling subjects that three external judges were observing them. Furthermore, the second experiment investigated only individuals working alone and sought to lower productivity (to that of real groups) with apprehension, while the first experiment dealt with real groups and sought to illustrate an increase in productivity in the "no-expert" condition. The conflicting results from these experiments indicates that a different and more powerful cause of productivity loss may exist, but the fact remains that being in a brainstorming group can, and does, inhibit certain individuals from giving their best, most innovative ideas.

Production Blocking

Production blocking occurs when group members are prohibited from airing their ideas when they think of them because of the fact that only one individual can speak at a time. Waiting can cause individuals to forget ideas or consider their idea to be less original or relevant with respect to the presently viewed idea. This contradicts the original claim that brainstorming allows individuals to express their ideas, which in turn would stimulate other members. Traditionally, brainstorming has adopted an "equal person-hour" methodology. This in actual fact allows members of real groups of size to have only one nth of the amount of speaking time of the equivalent nominal group members. Diehl and Stroebe (1987) tested whether this procedural explanation of the blocking effect was valid. They conducted two experiments in which speaking time allowance was manipulated so that real group members had the same amount of speaking time as nominal group members. Neither experiment showed a reduction in the productivity gap between real and nominal groups.

However, it has been found that a good, highly trained group facilitator can help reduce the blocking problem. In fact, one recent study showed that a brainstorming group with a highly trained facilitator did outperform groups with a less trained facilitator as well as outperform nominal groups of individuals working alone (Oxley, Dzindolet, & Paulus, 1996).

ELECTRONIC BRAINSTORMING

New computer-aided techniques to "unblock brainstorms" have recently been constructed and tested (Gallupe, Cooper, Grise, & Bastianutti, 1994). "Electronic brainstorming" aims to overcome the problems of social loafing, evaluation apprehension, and production blocking. It involves group members sitting at computer terminals and typing in their ideas, but also having full access to the others' ideas as they are produced. The technique integrates the two important and advantageous features of nominal and real group brainstorming, being able to generate ideas freely and also being able to share ideas respectfully. Seeing ideas on a screen has not been found to be distracting for participants, which was the case with traditional brainstorming (Gallupe, Cooper, Grise, & Bastianutti, 1994). Simultaneous contributions lessen the potential effect of blocking, and the anonymous nature of the technique alleviates evaluation apprehension.

In Gallupe's original, pioneering study (Gallupe, Bastianutti, & Cooper, 1991; Gallupe & Cooper, 1993) comparing electronic with non-electronic brainstorming, he found that four-person groups using electronic brainstorming outperformed four-person groups using traditional brainstorming and failed to find a difference between nominal and interacting groups using the electronic technique. In electronic brainstorming groups, performance increased with size of group. Electronic brainstorming was not found to be advantageous when only two people were involved (and thus anonymity and production blocking were at their lowest), but as group size and therefore anonymity and production blocking increased, the true potential of this new technique was exhibited. Per-person productivity and average per-person output of ideas tended to remain stable with an increase in group size (unlike non-electronic brainstorming, where a fall was noted). This was attributed to the fact that production blocking remained at a constant low level throughout different electronic brainstorming sessions. Last, satisfaction was found to be greater with electronic brainstorming groups and to increase with group size, contrary to non-electronic brainstorming.

Dennis and Valacich (1993) found that larger (twelve-member versus six-member) electronic brainstorming groups did better than smaller ones. They attributed this to the synergy obtained and the avoidance of redundant ideas in these large groups. Paulus, Larey, Putman, Leggett, and Roland (1996) noted that if computer brainstormers verbalized (spoke aloud) the ideas they were typing in, it decreased performance of all concerned, as may be predicted.

Thus, the problems with brainstorming can be overcome using computer networks. Social loafing is less likely to occur because individuals may be concerned that the ideas they key in are logged and counted. Evaluation apprehension does not occur because the source of the ideas is anonymous. Production blocking does not occur because participants can assess and attend to others' ideas when it suits them.

OTHER ISSUES

All sorts of other issues have been investigated, such as whether the personality of people in brainstorming groups has an effect of any kind (Furnham & Yazdanpanahi, 1995). Camacho and Paulus (1995) found, fairly predictably, that anxious people did less well in brainstorming groups; this may be a partial explanation for their productivity loss. Larey and Paulus (1995) found that brainstorming groups actually set fewer goals than people working alone did. The topic continues to attract researchers, partly because of the paradox noted earlier: Traditional brainstorming is held up to be a better method than nominal group brainstorming, despite evidence to the contrary.

CONCLUSION

Research in this area is particularly fascinating because so many results are counter-intuitive. What the findings seem to show is that brainstorming is most often used when it is least effective. It is odd that advertising agencies and design departments seem to rely on brainstorming techniques, when all the scientific literature suggests it is not the best strategy. It is possible that brainstorming groups function to fulfil other needs in the organization, which may or may not compensate for the resultant loss of creativity. Further fundamental processes at work in brainstorming groups appear to mitigate against good decisions being made or really creative answers being found.

When the climate is competitive and time is of the essence or when creativity is desired, individuals should be encouraged to work alone. Another option is to make ordinary brainstorming groups more productive. For instance, one could insist that individuals initially brainstorm alone in writing and then bring a certain number of ideas to the meeting. Groups could be encouraged to brainstorm different parts of "the problem" separately. Groups also produce more if they are given high targets/standards for both quality and quantity, as well as when someone keeps track of the actual numbers of ideas that they do generate. Giving the group members several breaks (from one another) has also been shown to help the process.

Certainly, as brainstorming sessions are traditionally and casually run, they are possibly the least effective way of generating ideas.

References

Bouchard, T. (1972). A comparison of two group brainstorming procedures. *Journal of Applied Psychology, 59,* 418–421.

Bouchard, T., & Hare, M. (1970). Size performance and potential in brainstorming groups. *Journal of Applied Psychology, 59,* 418–421.

Brown, V., & Paulus, P. (1996). A simple dynamic role of social factors in group brainstorming. *Small Group Research, 27,* 91–119.

Camacho, L., & Paulus, P. (1995). The role of social anxiousness in group brainstorming. *Journal of Personality and Social Psychology, 68,* 1071–1080.

Collaros, P., & Anderson, L. (1969). Effect of perceived expertise upon creativity of members of brainstorming groups. *Journal of Applied Psychology, 53,* 1159–1163.

Davis, K., & Newstrom, J. (1987). *Human behavior at work: Organizational behavior.* New York: McGraw-Hill.

Dennis, A., & Valacich, J. (1993). Computer brainstorms: More heads are better than one. *Journal of Applied Psychology, 78,* 531–537.

Diehl, M., & Stroebe, W. (1987). Productivity loss in brainstorming groups: Toward a solution of a riddle. *Journal of Personality and Social Psychology, 53,* 497–509.

Durham, R., & Pierce, J. (1989). *Management.* Glenview, IL: Scott, Foresman.

Furnham, A., & Yazdanpanahi. (1995). Personality differences and group versus individual brainstorming. *Personality and Individual Differences, 19,* 73–80.

Gallupe, R., Bastianutti, L., & Cooper, W. (1991). Unblocking brainstorms. *Journal of Applied Psychology, 76,* 137–142.

Gallupe, R., & Cooper, W. (1993). Brainstorming electronically. *Sloan Management Review, 35,* 27–36.

Gallupe, R., Cooper, W., Grise, M-L., & Bastianutti, L. (1994). Blocking electronic brainstorms. *Journal of Applied Psychology, 79,* 77–86.

Harkins, S., & Jackson, J. (1985). The role of evaluation in eliminating social loafing. *Personality and Social Psychology Bulletin, 11,* 457–465.

Jackson, J., & Harkins, S. (1985). Equity in effort: An explanation of the social loafing effect. *Journal of Personality and Social Psychology, 49,* 1199–1296.

Karau, S., & Williams, K. (1993). Social loafing: A meta-analytic review and theoretical integration. *Journal of Personality and Social Psychology, 65,* 681–706.

Kerr, N., & Bruun, S. (1983). Dispensability of members' effort and group motivation losses: Free-rider effects. *Journal of Personality and Social Psychology, 44,* 78–94.

Kravitz, D., & Martin, B. (1986). Ringlemann rediscovered: The original article. *Journal of Personality and Social Psychology, 50,* 936–941.

Larey, T., & Paulus, P. (1995). Social comparison and goal setting in brainstorming groups. *Journal of Applied Social Psychology, 25,* 1597–1596.

Maginn, B., & Harris, R. (1980). Effects of anticipated evaluation on individual brainstorming performance. *Journal of Applied Psychology, 65,* 219–225.

McGrath, J. (1984). *Groups: Interaction and performance.* Englewood Cliffs, NJ: Prentice Hall.

Napier, R., & Gershenfeld, M. (1985). *Groups: Theory and experience.* Boston, MA: Houghton Mifflin.

Osborn, A. (1957). *Applied imagination.* New York: Scribner.

Oxley, N., Dzindolet, M., & Paulus, P. (1996). The effects of facilitators on the performance of brainstorming groups. *Journal of Social Behaviour and Personality, 11,* 633–646.

Paulus, P., & Dzindolet, M. (1993). Social influence processes in group brainstorming. *Journal of Personality and Social Psychology, 64,* 575–586.

Paulus, P., Larey, T., & Ortega, A. (1995). Performance and perceptions of brainstormers in an organisational setting. *Basic and Applied Psychology, 17,* 249–265.

Paulus, P., Larey, T., Putman, V., Leggett, K., & Roland, E. (1996). Social influence processes in computer brainstorming. *Basic and Applied Social Psychology, 18,* 3–14.

Robbins, T. (1995). Social loafing on cognitive tasks: An examination of the "sucker effect." *Journal of Business and Psychology, 9,* 337–342.

Taylor, D., Berry, P., & Block, C. (1958). Does group participation when using brainstorming facilitate or inhibit creative thinking? *Administrative Science Quarterly, 3,* 23–47.

Thomberg, T. (1991). Group size and member diversity influence on creative performance. *Journal of Creative Behaviour, 25,* 324–333.

Weatherall, A., & Nunamaker, J. (1996). *Introduction to electronic meetings.* Chichester, UK: Technical Graphics.

Williams, K., Harkins, S., & Latane, B. (1981). Identifiable as an adherent to social loafing: Two cheering experiments. *Journal of Personality and Social Psychology, 40,* 303–311.

Adrian F. Furnham *is professor of psychology at the University of London. He holds three doctorates and is a self-confessed workaholic. His primary interests are in applied psychology, particularly I/O psychology. He is well-travelled and enjoys lecturing abroad. This article reflects his interest in both personality theory and applied psychology.*

SYSTEMS THINKING AND LEARNING: FROM CHAOS AND COMPLEXITY TO ELEGANT SIMPLICITY

Stephen G. Haines

Abstract: A system is defined as a set of elements or components that work together in relationships for the overall good and objective (or vision) of the whole. Thus, the focus of all systems (people, processes, departments) in an organization should be on the relationships among those elements that assist attainment of an organization-wide shared vision, values, and customer satisfaction. Systems thinking is an old, yet newly rediscovered, higher orientation to life. It is a better, more natural, and holistic view of living systems (such as individuals, teams, and organizations) that we can use as we try to survive and thrive in today's dynamic environment. It is much more than just a set of tools.

This article briefly explains the four main concepts of systems thinking and the benefits of adopting The Systems Thinking Approach℠.

OVERVIEW

Systems thinking is a heavily researched methodology and a rigorous macro-scientific, trans-disciplinary framework with its roots in the universal laws of living systems and human nature. It includes a basis in ecology, biology, psychology, and physics. An Austrian, Ludwig Von Bertalanffy, is the father of the Society for General Systems Research, which began almost fifty years ago. Systems thinking has also been a more recent focus of Dr. Russell Ackoff (1974, 1991) and Dr. Jay Forrester (1969, 1971a, 1971b), among others. In fact, the author has identified over thirty other scientific disciplines, such as electronics, architecture, complexity and chaos theory, and project management, whose leading thinkers and writers are moving in the direction of systems thinking.

Thus, systems thinking is an old, yet newly rediscovered and higher orientation to life. It is a better, more natural, and holistic view of living systems as they try to survive and thrive in today's dynamic environment. In short, it is an advanced method of critical thinking. It brings you to a higher intellect and to interdependence and deeper connectedness with others. This holistic, integrated, and more purposeful outcome-oriented approach distinguishes systems consultants from consultants whose focus is on the components or separate issues and functions of an organization.

CONCEPTS AND RESEARCH

Fifty-plus years of research on systems thinking has been translated, interpreted, and updated by the author and his colleagues at the Centre for Strategic Management. Systems thinking, as applied by the Centre, uses four interrelated concepts from the Society to clarify and simplify how one analyzes and improves individuals, teams, and whole organizations. The four concepts that follow give a broader framework, or mental map, to think, see, understand, diagnose, and act more effectively.

1. *The Seven Levels of Living Systems.* The seven levels, based on the work of James G. Miller (1995), exist here on earth and are in natural hierarchical relationships with each other (systems within systems).

2. *Standard and Predictable Organizational Dynamics.* These dynamics are based on the twelve characteristics of open/living systems from Miller's (1995) research.

3. *The Five Phases of the Systems Thinking Framework.* This model consists of a circular input-throughput-output-feedback loop within our dynamic and ever-changing environment, again based on six of the twelve characteristics of living systems above.

4. *The Rollercoaster of Change*[SM]. In addition, we use the natural and historical "cycles of change" on earth to assist management in being proactive, innovative, and more successful with their strategic and systematic change processes.

THE FACTS

The type of mechanistic, analytical thinking leading to the strategies and actions we generally use today in our social and organizational systems has led to both spectacular successes (especially in technology) and spectacular social failures (huge, intractable, and chronic problems we can't seem to solve).

Why? Our hypothesis is that:

1. The way we think contributes to the poor results we achieve;

2. Technology is being used by professionals and their organizations in new, different, and more interrelated ways; and

3. An understanding of systems thinking would dramatically improve our critical-thinking, problem-solving, and solution-seeking abilities.

In the words of John Naisbitt's (undated) well-known "High Tech-High Touch Future," as a society we are far more able to apply systems thinking to "high-tech" issues than to "high-touch" ones.

CONCEPTS EXPLAINED

Four main concepts of systems thinking must be explored further. Before we try to solve any of society's problems, we must understand these concepts and how they can simplify organizational assessment and how they improve our focus and collaboration across all aspects of any organization or team.

Concept 1: The Seven Levels of Living Systems

All systems are actually subsystems of larger systems within their environment. There is an actual hierarchy of these living systems here on earth (Miller, 1995):

1. Cell
2. Organ
3. Individual
4. Group/team/family
5. Organization
6. Society/community
7. Earth/world

Looking at these interrelated hierarchies of systems, we begin to see that they are natural and normal. We just need to focus on how to have the minimum hierarchy (not bureaucracy) working for us to achieve our goals or outcomes. Figure 1 illustrates the hierarchy of those levels most relevant for organizations.

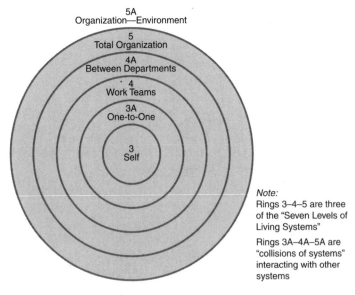

Figure 1. Hierarchy of Organizational Systems

It is the "collision of systems" within and among these system levels, especially at levels 3, 4, 5, and 6, that creates the complexity and chaos we often feel in today's world.

Concept 2: Standard Organizational Dynamics

Based on the twelve characteristics of General Systems Theory (Miller, 1995), standard organizational dynamics include the following elements (six external and six internal):

External Dynamics: The Whole System

All living systems have standard external relationships and dynamics. The whole system:

1. *Is a unique totality.* The parts do not describe the characteristics of the functioning of the entire system in its environment. We need the so-called "helicopter view" for a larger, higher-level perspective on the system in its environment.

2. *Is an open system*—in that it is continually interacting with the environment. Some systems are more open than others.

3. *Has specific boundaries.* These define the entity.

4. *Is an input-throughput-output transformation framework.*

5. *Receives feedback from its environment.* This gives it a reading on its effectiveness.

6. *Is a multiple goal seeking and outcomes/consequences oriented entity.*

Internal Dynamics

All living systems have standard internal relationships and dynamics, such as the following:

1. *Equifinality*—many ways to the same end.

2. *Entropy.* Living systems naturally run down and eventually die; closed ones die faster than open ones. This is why systems need continual reinforcement, energy, attention, and booster shots.

3. *Hierarchical relationships and elaboration.* All subsystems have natural and normal hierarchies.

4. *Interrelated components.* Parts are not separate entities; everything everywhere affects everything else inside actual systems, despite our turf and silo mentalities.

5. *Dynamic equilibrium.* Systems have a natural steady-state rhythm and try to maintain that despite all external changes and forces.

6. *Continual internal elaboration and sophistication.* These can lead to either rigidity, bureaucracy, and death or to spectacular growth.

To compare these natural laws to more typical analytical system dynamics, see Table 1.

Table 1.   Natural Laws vs. Typical Analytical Dynamics

Natural Laws	Typical Analytical Dynamics
1. Focused on the whole	1. Focused on the parts
2. Open Systems: aware of and responsive to the environment	2. Closed Systems: low environmental awareness
3. Flexible Boundaries: lead to integration and collaboration	3. Fragmented Boundaries: lead to turf battles
4. Input/Output of Data Processing: how natural systems operate	4. Sequential Data Processing: piecemeal and analytic
5. High Feedback Orientation: open to information on effectiveness/root causes	5. Low Feedback Orientation: open to financial data only
6. Willing to consider multiple goals and outcomes	6. Utilizes more rigid either/or thinking in planning goals and outcomes
7. Equifinality: flexibility and agility in meeting goals	7. Direct Cause-Effect: one best way to meet goals
8. Response to Entropy: follow-up and inputs of energy/renewal	8. Response to Entropy: rigidity and death
9. Hierarchy: flatter organization, self-organizing	9. Bureaucracy: command and control
10. Interrelated Parts: relationships/ involvement and participation	10. Separate Parts: components/ entities/silos
11. Dynamic Equilibrium: stability and balance	11. Resistance to Change: myopic view, ruts
12. Internal Elaboration: details, sophistication, and growth	12. Internal Elaboration: complexity, confusion, and death

Concept 3: The Five-Phase Systems Model

This circular way of viewing individuals, teams, and organizations as living systems is a great way to never lose your place within the context of understanding and improving organizations, teams, and individuals. These five phases, formed from characteristics 1 through 6, broaden your thinking, clarify your outcomes, improve your assessments, sharpen your designs, focus on your need for feedback, and keep you open to environmental dynamics, both on the job and as a new orientation to life overall. The five phases follow (and are illustrated in Figure 2):

Phase A. Creating Your Ideal Future (Multiple Outputs);

Phase B. Measurements of Success (Feedback Loop);

Phase C. Converting Today's Assessment to Strategies (Input to Action);

Phase D. Successful Implementation (Throughput/Actions); and

Phase E. The External Environment (or context within which the other phases operate).

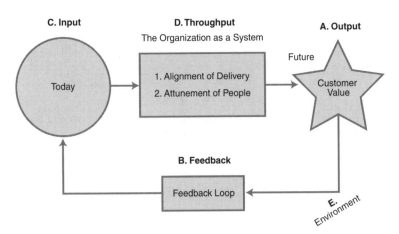

From Complexity to Simplicity

Systems: Systems are made up of a set of components that work together for the overall objective of the whole (output).

Figure 2.   The Five-Phase Systems Model

This framework is useful in analyzing and understanding any living system. It is also the key to creating a learning organization. Clearly defining your outcomes (Phase A) is the first key to learning. Feedback (Phase B) is the second key, and continually scanning the environment for new and changing events (Phase E) is the third.

Concept 4: The Rollercoaster of Change^{SM}

This model (see Figure 3) is a simple way to understand the dynamics of how to affect positive changes of all types. Cycles of stability-change-instability-new stability and change all over again are normal and natural, as Lewin showed us. Don't fight them; use them to your advantage!

Basically, you must manage and lead yourself and others through the following four stages of the rollercoaster simultaneously, although everyone goes through these stages at different rates, depths, and times.

Stage 1: Shock and Denial. As a manager, you must be prepared, give employees advance notice, and provide clear expectations regarding standards and norms of behavior during any change.

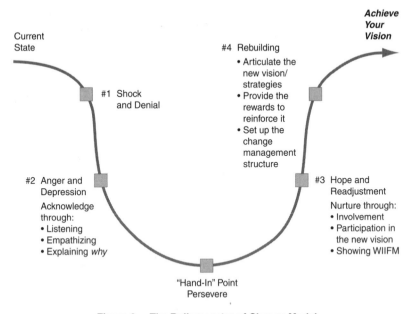

Figure 3.   The Rollercoaster of Change Model

Stage 2: Depression and Anger. As a manager, you must (a) listen, (b) empathize, and only then (c) explain why the new vision and the change are necessary (this a, b, c order is key to effectiveness).

Stage 3: Hope and Readjustment. As a manager, you must clarify each person's new role and new norms of behavior. Help others find ways to gain maximum involvement in the change and a full understanding of WIIFM (What's in It for Me?). Knowing the benefits is key for everyone to better achieve the new vision and values.

Stage 4: Rebuilding. Here you empower the fully committed individuals and teams to take on your vision and values. Then stand back, monitor, and follow up.

APPLICATIONS OF THE FOUR SYSTEMS THINKING CONCEPTS

The preceding four concepts of organization change and learning play out in the following four applications of the systems thinking approach.

Application 1: The Seven Levels of Living Systems

The seven levels of living systems are the key to comprehensive, holistic, and long-lasting learning and change competencies that encompass all the levels of an organization's functioning.

The elements of the model and their corresponding "rings" in Figure 1 are listed below, along with the elements on which systems thinking consultants should focus.

Systems Level/Ring 3—Self (Self-Mastery)

1. Improve personal competency and effectiveness.

2. Work on trustworthiness issues within oneself.

Ring 3A—One-to-One Relationships (Interpersonal Skills)

1. Improve the interpersonal and working relationships and effectiveness of each individual.

2. Work on trust issues between individuals.

Systems Level/Ring 4—Work Teams/Groups (Team Effectiveness)

1. Improve the effectiveness of the work team, as well as of each of its members.
2. Explore empowerment and role/relationship issues.

Ring 4A—Between Departments (Conflict/Horizontal Cooperation)

1. Improve the working relationships and business processes between departments to serve the customer better.
2. Work on horizontal collaboration/integration issues.

Systems Level/Ring 5—Total Organization (Fit)

1. Improve the organization's structures and processes to better achieve its results and develop its adaptive response system capacity in a changing environment.
2. Work on alignment and attunement issues in serving the customer.

Ring 5A—Organization-Environment (Strategic Plans)

1. Improve the organization's sense of direction, response to its customers, and proactive management of its environment.
2. Work on adaptation to environmental issues.

The ring model is also the key to creating a learning organization, which must receive feedback from and learn about or improve on all six of these rings—an incredible task—and install a leadership development system to prepare leaders for the 21st Century.

Application 2: Systems Dynamics and Learning

Learning about systems dynamics and understanding them is critical for maximum effectiveness. This next section is a review of the twelve laws described above and provides principles, questions, and examples of each in action (Haines, 1998).

Natural Law 1

Natural System Laws	Typical Analytical Dynamics	Systems Principles	Systems Questions
1. Focus on the whole	1. Focus on the parts	Problems cannot be solved at the level where they were created	What is our common higher-level (superordinate) goal?

Union-management fights and strikes over pay tend to amount to a win-lose game. By moving to the higher-level goal of competing and producing more profitably, both sides can make more money (increase the size of the pie).

Natural Law 2

Natural System Laws	Typical Analytical Dynamics	Systems Principles	Systems Questions
2. Open Systems: aware of and responsive to the environment	2. Closed Systems: low environmental awareness	Systems first require work and alignment from the outside in, not the inside out	What is changing in the environment that we need to consider? Is the system relatively open or closed in its environmental interactions?

In organizational terms, this means we must keep scanning the environment for changes in anything from our competition to the political scene. At a minimum, there are eight areas we need to keep an eye on. They can be remembered by the acronym SKEPTIC:

- Socio-demographics
- "K"ompetition
- Economics/Environment
- Political

- Technology

- Industry

- Customers

Natural Law 3

Natural System Laws	Typical Analytical Dynamics	Systems Principles	Systems Questions
3. Flexible Boundaries: lead to integration and collaboration	3. Fragmented Boundaries: lead to turf battles	The entity to be changed must be clearly defined	What entity (system or "collision of systems") are we dealing with? What are its boundaries? What levels of the overall entity do we want to change?

When thinking about implementing a change, consider whether you are trying to change yourself, your department, a business process, a partnership, or the entire organization.

Natural Law 4

Natural System Laws	Typical Analytical Dynamics	Systems Principles	Systems Questions
4. Input/Output of Data Processing: how natural systems operate	4. Sequential Data Processing: piecemeal and analytic	Focus on the multiple future outcomes first, then work backward to today in order to move forward to this future	Are we dealing with the ends (the what) or with the means (the how)?

What is the difference between teaching and learning? Teaching is one key way to accomplish learning: It is a set of means. Learning is the outcome;

it is the end goal of teaching. Schools often focus too much on teachers and teaching; they must keep the desired outcome in mind—the student's actual learning. Teachers and trainers of all types should ask themselves how students can learn best, not just how to teach.

Natural Law 5

Natural System Laws	Typical Analytical Dynamics	Systems Principles	Systems Questions
5. High Feedback Orientation: open to information on effectiveness/ root causes from the environment	5. Low Feedback Orientation: open to financial, direct cause-and-effect feedback only	As an input, feedback requires receptivity and for us to be flexible and adaptable	How will we know we have achieved the desired outcomes? What are our outcome performance measures?

Look at feedback as a gift. Be open and receptive to it—even encourage it. Ask for feedback from all your customers, your employees, your direct reports and peers, and anyone who can help you learn and grow as a person, as a professional, and as a leader of your organization.

Natural Law 6

Natural System Laws	Typical Analytical Dynamics	Systems Principles	Systems Questions
6. Willing to consider multiple goals and outcomes	6. Utilizes more rigid either/or thinking in planning goals and outcomes	Systems are naturally goal-seeking and will self-organize to do so	What are the desired outcomes, i.e., where do we want to be in the future?

Organizational outcomes often satisfy the needs of customers, employees, and stockholders, as well as of the community, suppliers, etc. Asking the question about desired outcomes keeps us focused on the whole rather than on isolated events.

The question "Is it X or Y?" is usually based on an incorrect assumption that there is only one answer in every case. This assumption occurs in organizations, teams, families, and interpersonal relationships and often re-sults in conflicts of need, differences of opinion, and hard feelings.

Natural Law 7

Natural System Laws	Typical Analytical Dynamics	Systems Principles	Systems Questions
7. Equifinality: flexibility and agility in meet-ing goals	7. Direct Cause-Effect: one best way to meet goals	There are many different ways to achieve the same desired outcomes; people support what they help create	What should we centralize? What should we decentralize?

Today's leadership paradigm calls for a new way of looking at organi-zations. It requires a much higher level of maturity and wisdom—a middle ground between abdicating responsibility and being all-controlling—with a focus on interdependence.

Natural Law 8

Natural System Laws	Typical Analytical Dynamics	Systems Principles	Systems Questions
8. Response to Entropy: follow-up and input of energy/renewal	8. Response to Entropy: rigidity and death	If entropy is not reversed, the system will die (and so will the change project)	What must we do to ensure buy-in over time (perseverance) and thus avoid entropy?

While human beings obviously have a finite life cycle, it doesn't have to be this way for neighborhoods, communities, and organizations. For them, the renewal process is key to long-term success.

Natural Law 9

Natural System Laws	Typical Analytical Dynamics	Systems Principles	Systems Questions
9. Hierarchy: flatter organization, self-organizing	9. Bureaucracy: command and control	All systems are linked to other systems (some larger, some smaller) in the hierarchy	How can we move from complexity to simplicity and from rigidity to flexibility in the solutions we devise?
		Multilevel systems are too complex to fully understand and manage centrally	What levels of the overall entity do we want to change?

Divisions in large companies often do not know the outcomes of the overall system. Such divisions tend to be perplexed by decisions made higher up, and higher management wonders at the decisions made on the divisional level.

Natural Law 10

Natural System Laws	Typical Analytical Dynamics	Systems Principles	Systems Questions
10. Interrelated Parts: relation-ships/involve-ment and participation	10. Separate Parts: components/ entities/silos	The whole is more important than the parts: relationships and processes are key	What is the relationship of X to Y and Z?

In organizations, the question is not: "How can I maximize my job or department's impact?" It is: "How can we all work and fit together in support of the overall objectives of the organization?" To that end, each year all major departments must share their annual plans to ensure that everyone knows what everyone else is doing and to give others a chance to critique those plans. This actually resembles a large group team-building process.

Natural Law 11

Natural System Laws	Typical Analytical Dynamics	Systems Principles	Systems Questions
11. Dynamic Equilibrium: stability and balance	11. Resistance to Change: myopic view, ruts	The steady-state equilibrium, however much we want it, can be dangerous in a changing world If you are doing things the same way you did five years ago, it's probably wrong	What new processes and structures are we using to ensure successful change?

Designing, building, and sustaining a customer-focused, high-performance learning organization for the 21st Century requires a balance in how organizations spend their time and energy among content, processes, and structure. Above all, we need to avoid content myopia (the failure to focus on process and structure).

Natural Law 12

Natural System Laws	Typical Analytical Dynamics	Systems Principles	Systems Questions
12. Internal Elaboration: details, sophistication, and growth	12. Internal Elaboration: complexity, confusion, and death	Root causes and their effects are usually not linked closely in time and space	What multiple causes lie at the root of our problem or concern, i.e., what are the root causes?

On the organizational problem-solving front, typical analytical thinking leads to the search for fast, convenient solutions—quick fixes—as if we were dealing with simple mechanical objects, not unwanted outcomes in a system within systems.

Application 3: The Five-Phase Systems Model

There are many uses of the five phases of systems thinking:

1. Coordinating a comprehensive strategic plan;
2. Creating a micro plan or a quick strategic plan;
3. Developing business unit functional plans;
4. Developing goals for an overall change plan for a major project (i.e., TQM, customer service, reengineering, etc.);
5. Creating a strategic life and career plan for a person, family, or couple;
6. Creating a plan to improve the value provided to your customers;
7. Development and implementation of a strategic HR plan to use people as a competitive edge in your organization;
8. Improving your leadership development system by enhancing leadership roles and competencies as a competitive business edge;
9. Employing an organizational systems model to assess, redesign, and implement change efforts to dramatically increase your success;
10. Enhancing team effectiveness by focusing on all aspects of departmental and cross-functional teams to dramatically enhance their outcomes; and
11. Creating a learning organization by implementing systems thinking and some of the learning/feedback concepts discussed above.

Application 4: The Rollercoaster of Change[SM]

The rollercoaster model serves as a frame of reference to guide you through every kind of change. It is particularly useful when dealing with the following situations:

1. Coaching and counseling others;
2. Working through personal change and transition;
3. Learning new knowledge, ideas, and skills;
4. Facilitating team building;
5. Guiding yourself and others through redesign and restructuring or layoffs;
6. Managing technological changes;

7. Defining and implementing new corporation strategies;

8. Learning how to hold a dialogue to truly discover new solutions; and

9. Leading organization-wide cultural changes.

The rollercoaster model can be applied almost universally in today's constantly changing environment, as any kind of major change starts the cycle. Also, keep in mind that Stages 1 and 2 are a given when change occurs. Stages 3 and 4 occur *only* with proper leadership and management (of self and others).

BENEFITS OF SYSTEMS THINKING

If you adopt systems thinking, you'll gain many benefits, including the following:

1. A framework from which to think critically and a way to make sense out of life's complexities, since all living things are systems;

2. A way to learn new things more easily, as the basic rules stay the same from system to system, team to team, and organization to organization;

3. A better way to learn and a higher order of integration of new ideas within the systems context;

4. A clearer way to see, understand, and assess what is going on in an organization or any system, that is, complex problems become easier to understand, as do the interrelationships and the multiple causes and effects;

5. A new and better (i.e., simpler) way to design solutions that last longer, create strategies, and solve problems, keeping the outcome, vision, or goal in mind at all times;

6. An unveiling of new, different, and higher points of leverage for change that might otherwise be ignored;

7. An ability of teams and people to engage in deeper analysis and to identify root problems that, when addressed, provide longer-lasting results (and fewer negative by-products);

8. Identification and resolution of those issues requiring a deeper structure and obscure relationship improvement that are not obvious by the quick-fix mentality; and

9. Development of a common language to improve communications, teamwork, learning, and results across the organization (a higher order of intellect and critical thinking).

In Summary

The comparison between systems thinking and analytical thinking in Table 2 shows the higher order of systems thinking. The four sets of concepts and applications of systems thinking must be interrelated and be used together for

Table 2.   Analytical vs. Systems Thinking

Analytic Thinking (Analysis of Today)	Systems Thinking (Synthesis for the Future)
1. We/they	1. Customers/stakeholders
2. Independent	2. Interdependent
3. Activities/tasks/means	3. Outcomes/ends
4. Problem solving	4. Solution seeking
5. Today is fine	5. Shared vision of future
6. Units/departments	6. Total organization
7. Silo mentality	7. Cross-functional teamwork
8. Closed environment	8. Openness and feedback
9. Department goals	9. Shared core strategies
10. Strategic planning project	10. Strategic management system
11. Hierarchy and controls	11. Serve the customer
12. Not my job	12. Communications and collaboration
13. Isolated change	13. Systemic change
14. Linear/begin-end	14. Circular/repeat cycles
15. Little picture/view	15. Big picture/holistic perspective
16. Short-term	16. Long-term
17. Separate issues	17. Related issues
18. Symptoms	18. Root causes
19. Isolated events	19. Patterns/trends
20. Activities/actions	20. Clear outcome expectations
Summary: Parts Are Primary	*Summary:* Whole Is Primary

the overall good of the whole system. Use these concepts and applications in combination to increase your chances of success.

Good luck on your journey!

References

Ackoff, R. (1974). *Redesigning the future: A systems approach to societal problems.* New York: John Wiley & Sons.

Ackoff, R. (1991). *Ackoff's fables: Irreverent reflections on business and bureaucracy.* New York: John Wiley & Sons.

Bertalanffy, L. (1968). *General systems theory.* New York: Brazille.

Forrester, J.W. (1969). *Urban dynamics.* Norwalk, CT: Productivity Press.

Forrester, J.W. (1971a). *Principles of systems.* Norwalk, CT: Productivity Press.

Forrester, J.W. (1971b). *World dynamics* (2nd ed.). Norwalk, CT: Productivity Press.

Haines, S.G. (1998). *The manager's pocket guide to systems thinking and learning.* Amherst, MA: HRD Press.

Miller, E.J., & Rice, A.K. (1967). *Systems of organization.* London: Tavistock Publications.

Miller, J.G. (1995). *Living systems.* Niwot, CO: University Press of Colorado.

Naisbitt, J. (undated). *Trend letter* [newsletter]. Alexandria, VA: Author.

Naisbitt, J. (1982). *Megatrends: Ten new directions transforming our lives.* New York: Warner.

Naisbitt, J. (1994). *Global paradox: The bigger the world economy, the more powerful its smallest players.* New York: William Morrow.

Naisbitt, J., & Aburdene, P. (1990). *Megatrends 2000: Ten new directions for the 1990s.* New York: William Morrow.

Vickers, G. (Ed.). (1972). *Yearbook of the Society for General Systems Research/Academy of Management Research.* Washington, DC: Society for General Systems Research.

Stephen G. Haines is a CEO, entrepreneur, and strategist. As a premier systems thinker, facilitator, and prolific author, he is recognized internationally as a leader in strategic management and in leading planning and change efforts. He is president and founder of both the Centre for Strategic Management International and its sister company, Systems Thinking Press.

BEING AN AGENT OF ORGANIZATIONAL HEALING

Beverly J. Nyberg and Roger Harrison

Abstract: The authors see a current crisis of organizational health brought on, in large part, by the trauma of rapid change. One result is a reduction in individuals' and organizations' capacities to learn and adapt. This article presents concepts of organizational health and healing and proposes how OD consultants may assist organizations to address healing and promote wholeness. Stories and examples illustrate healing interventions on the part of consultants and organization members.

INTRODUCTION

The company was obviously hurting. Stories told around water coolers and in the lunchroom were bitter and angry. Production was down. People were having trouble focusing on their work. No laughter or pleasant chatter was heard above the cubicles. Everyone was anxiously watching the clock. They scattered more quickly than usual when it struck five. The pain was palpable.

As organization development (OD) consultants, Sue and Tom had been hired to turn things around. But after the most recent round of layoffs, everyone was still reeling. Where should they start? What could they do? The organization didn't seem ready for more change, yet something had to be done to bring about healing. But how does healing happen after trauma? Is it even possible? Does time heal?

As OD consultants, we see individuals, organizations, even cultures and nations that have not healed from past injuries. They perpetuate pain and dysfunction throughout their spheres of influence, from generation to generation. What can we do as OD consultants to help hurting clients? The level of pain people experience nowadays as a result of downsizing, reorganization, mergers, and acquisitions clearly needs attention from those of us who can help. But is healing our role? And if it is, how can we as OD consultants be cognizant of the pain and find ways to facilitate healing? Is healing possible? What does it look like? What is a healthy organization, anyway?

The OD world is only beginning to explore these issues. This article expresses our thoughts on how we as OD consultants can promote healing. We hope that you will enter into this question with your whole being and will benefit with increased understanding and insight. Through continued reflection and dialogue, we trust that we will grow in our ability to facilitate healing in the organizations we serve.

THE NEED FOR ORGANIZATIONAL HEALING

We are convinced that the current crisis of organizational health is real. The accelerating demand on organizations to make monumental change (Harrison, 1995a; Kreitzer, 2000; Nadler, 1998; Smit & Schabracq, 1997) is a primary factor of the health crisis. Emerging technologies, fluctuating markets, and increasing customer demands force organizations to change, to which they often respond with repeated downsizing and reorganization. The cycle causes pain that frequently manifests in a kind of immobilization, not only for those who lose their jobs, but also for those who stay.

Globalization escalates the challenge of dealing with other cultures and communities. Cultural clashes also occur in almost all mergers and acquisitions. As people acclimate themselves to new corporate and national cultures, they have to learn new ways to act in the midst of experiencing losses of identity, relationships, and familiar and valued patterns of behavior.

People are not so much against change as against loss. But even positive change means loss of the familiar and requires readjusting one's life and identity. Traumatic changes are those that result in unacceptable losses. Traumatic losses that people in the work world currently experience include loss of security, trust in the patriarchal order, status, money, power, and influence. During such changes, people often lose feelings of adequacy, potency, and competence. They no longer find meaning and purpose. They lose identification with higher values and valued connections and relationships.

In most organizations, the traditional contract between organizations and individuals is dead or dying. Job security is lacking at all levels, as are loyalty and obedience. In search of the competitive edge, organizations are downsizing, while at the same time asking employees to work harder and smarter. Resentment and grudging compliance take the place of commitment and self-management. For many, fear of loss is a daily companion. Innovation and risk taking often give way to keeping one's head down, one's neck in, and one's nether region covered. Often, systems change so quickly that there is no time for organizations to recover from losses or to establish new identities before being catapulted into a new change.

Of course, while change doles out losses for many, it creates opportunities for some, especially for those with vision to see them. Often the difference between being traumatized by a change or excited and challenged by it is in the meaning that we assign to it. To some degree that is within the control of individuals, but it is strongly affected by the culture of the organization and by values and beliefs held in the larger society we all share.

Many other factors may diminish organizational health and wholeness. Inappropriate and dysfunctional organizational structures can result in suboptimum health (Jaques, 1976). Unhealthy environments, difficult relationships, and the highly emotional behaviors that stress arouses also add more stress and distress. Telecommuting and globalization lead to isolation. The lack of community and disengagement from friends and associates can lead to individual and organizational depression (Harvey, 1999). Organizational wounds can stem from either a lack of good things, such as not having adequate working conditions or positive support for the accomplishments of workers, or from the presence of negative elements, such as constant criticism or establishing intentionally competitive internal structures.

In summary, a significant reason that organizations experience health crises is that they lack the knowledge of how to deal with the effects of rapid change. Nor do they anticipate the impact of consequential losses on the health and well-being of their organization and its members. They lack a health-promoting approach to change, often failing to acknowledge and address the need for healing following such change. Ironically, the change that we OD consultants have traditionally pushed for has, in fact, contributed to this organizational health crisis. But whatever the source of organizational injury, woundedness weakens, disrupts, and sometimes destroys parts of the system, resulting in organizational instability and ill health.

THE COST OF NOT ADDRESSING ORGANIZATIONAL HEALTH ISSUES

What will happen if we as OD consultants fail to address organizational health issues? Does it really matter? We believe it does. We believe that neglecting organizational health and the need to heal is costly to individuals, systems, the culture, and even the nation. Such neglect results not only in ineffective organizations but toxic ones. Just as hurting people hurt others, so, too, hurting organizations hurt themselves, other organizations, and the culture at large.

The consequences of not dealing with significant health issues are the same for any organism: It will die or, at best, limp along disabled. Without organizational healing, employees live in chronic fear, anxiety, and pain. Their ability to perform, let alone learn, is seriously impaired. This is a high price to pay in a time when performing and learning are essential to organizational survival. Organizations and society suffer from the constant waste of change, lessened productivity, and the failure to learn and grow. For these reasons, we believe it is important that OD consultants and their clients learn to become facilitators of healing and promoters of wholeness in organizations. Before we actually facilitate healing, though, it is important to first have a concept of organizational health and the healing process.

Organizational Health and Healing

Understanding Health

What is a healthy organization? What do we envision when we as organization development consultants seek to optimize organizational health? What is the basis for our assessment when determining whether an organization needs healing?

Extensive study has been done on the relationship between personal health and workplace stress (Dryer, 1999; Matson, 1996; Reese, 1999). Research has recently begun on collective health and on analyzing stressors that contribute to team stress (Driskell, Salas, & Johnston, 1999; Hawk, 1998). Little has been done, however, on defining or studying health at the organizational level (Smit & Schabracq, 1997).

Organizational health is defined in a variety of ways. One concept defines organizational health as adequately functioning and fulfilling mission and goals. Another definition of a healthy organization is one that is stable enough to respond to change flexibly while maintaining its ability to function. Most stress occurs as a prolonged response to a situation that is interpreted as dangerous and demanding action. Stability for a person or an organism is freedom from the destabilizing influence of change (Ecker, 1985). A healthy organization would be one that is able to maintain its stability (functional and emotional) in the midst of change. Harvey (1999) believes that a healthy organization is one that, through community, effectively mutes the depression caused by fear of separation. Jaques (1976) holds that health depends on the organization having what he calls "requisite structure."

Our understanding is that health means wholeness. By wholeness we mean an organization whose parts operate together in such a way that the organization's tasks are performed well while contributing to one another's well-being. Although imperfect, the organization is highly self-aware. Each part has a reasonably accurate understanding of its part in the whole and how other parts function. Although parts of such a system may be in tension with one another, they are not destructive in their competition. Nor do some parts optimize their own performance at the expense of the performance of the whole. Organizational wholeness is a sustained balance and congruence among the parts of the organism. Other words that connote wholeness include integrity, consistency, fit, reciprocity, and mutual benefit.

The idea of wholeness applies both internally and externally. Internal wholeness involves the balance of power and mutual influence between parts. Top management does not disassociate from the rest of the organization. All parts of the organization communicate and are in vital relationship with one another. The organization's actions are congruent with its values and beliefs. It has sustained energy and vitality in all its parts. There is the capability to learn, adapt, and change with new experiences.

A simple model provides a framework for conceptualizing the balance and relationships among three organizational realms: structural, relational, and intentional/mission. (See Figure 1.) All three impact each other so a problem in one area will influence the other two areas. By the same token, the effects of improvement in one area may be limited by lack of health in the others. For example, it is difficult to improve communication (*relationships*) in organizations where there are great disparities in power and influence (*structure*) between people at different levels.

Externally, wholeness for an organization includes a balance between energy intake and energy output. The organization gives as much or more than it takes of the good things of this world. A healthy organization does not pollute the social and natural environment. The organization's goals are attuned to the highest good of the whole of which the organism is a part: the

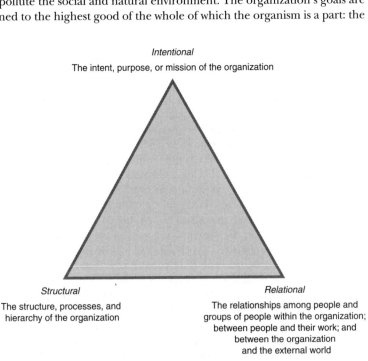

Intentional

The intent, purpose, or mission of the organization

Structural

The structure, processes, and hierarchy of the organization

Relational

The relationships among people and groups of people within the organization; between people and their work; and between the organization and the external world

Figure 1.   Three Organizational Realms

community, the larger society, the earth. The organization's purpose or mission is consistent with and furthers the good of the world it inhabits.

Differing Kinds of Wholeness

While the above concepts apply to virtually all organizations, each organization has its own unique elements of health relative to its individuality, maturity, and particular culture. We have worked with a model of four organization cultures (Harrison, 1995b) that can illuminate aspects of wholeness or its lack in any organization.[1] The four cultures are named *power, role, achievement,* and *support.* (See Figure 2.)

All organizations have some combination of these four basic organizational cultures. Each evokes different behaviors and rests on different human values. Each has a unique way of making decisions, a characteristic way of motivating people to work, a typical management style, and a set of underlying

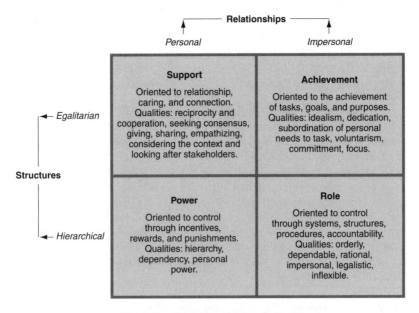

Figure 2. Four Organization Cultures

---

[1]Our discussion follows Roger Harrison's work on organization culture, especially the culture questionnaire, *Diagnosing Organization Culture,* written by R. Harrison and H. Stokes (San Francisco, CA: Jossey-Bass/Pfeiffer, 1992). Used by permission of the author.

values and beliefs about work and about human nature. The four cultures are only partially compatible with one another, and the benefits of one can only be achieved at the expense of some of the benefits of the others.

The Power Orientation.   The power-oriented organization is based on inequality of access to resources. Some "currencies" of power are money, privileges, job security, working conditions, and the ability to control others' access to these. The people in power use resources to satisfy or frustrate others' needs and thus to control others' behavior. Leadership resides in the person of the leader(s) and rests on their ability and willingness to administer rewards and punishments. People in power-oriented organizations are motivated by rewards and punishments and by the wish to be associated with a strong leader.

In more healthy power-oriented organizations, leadership is based on strength, justice, and paternalistic benevolence on the part of the leader. Leaders are firm, fair, and generous with loyal subordinates. They have a sense of obligation to their followers, and they exercise power according to their understanding of what is good for the organization and its people. This orientation toward the use of responsible power seems to be typical of some Japanese organizations. It rests on the acceptance of hierarchy and inequality as legitimate by all members of the organization. In more egalitarian societies, there is much less acceptance of hierarchy as legitimate, and there is not a strong tradition of benevolent power-oriented leadership.

At its worst, the power-oriented organization tends toward rule by fear, with abuse of power for personal advantage on the part of the leaders, their friends, and protégés. When leaders struggle for dominance, it may degenerate into a hotbed of political intrigue.

As the size and complexity of the business increases, the demands on the leadership of a power-oriented organization multiply exponentially. Large power-oriented organizations are inefficient and full of fear and confusion unless good structures and systems for getting work done supplement the power orientation. As the distance between leaders and followers increases, effective control becomes more difficult. Because followers have been conditioned to be dependent, when power-oriented organizations expand, they often run short on leadership talent.

The Role Orientation.   The role culture moderates the struggle for power through systems of structures and procedures. This gives protection to subordinates and stability to the organization. Duties and rewards of the members' roles are carefully defined, usually in writing, and are the subject of an explicit or implicit contract between the organization and the individual. People perform specific functions in order to receive defined rewards. Both the individual and the organization are expected to adhere to their part of the bargain.

The values of the role orientation are order, dependability, rationality, and consistency. A well-designed bureaucracy, in which performance is organized by structures and procedures, permits work to be reliably directed at a distance so that large, complex organizations can be created and managed. Each level in the organization has a defined area of authority, and work can continue to be done without direct supervision from the top.

At its healthiest, the role-oriented organization provides stability, justice, and efficient performance. People receive protection under the rules from the arbitrary exercise of authority, which is typical of the power orientation. They are able to spend less time "looking out for Number 1" and thus are able to devote more energy to the work.

Role organizations using stable technologies in a slowly changing environment can be very efficient because much of the routine work can be made subject to impersonal rules and a system of checks and balances. Systems, methods, and procedures maximize productivity and minimize error. Role-oriented organizations require less direct supervision compared to the "hands on" management typical of the power culture. Performance can be monitored by information systems without much face-to-face contact with people who do the work. Routine work can be standardized and broken into small pieces, which can be quickly learned by relatively unskilled workers.

The weakness of role organizations is in the very impersonality that is their strength. They operate on the assumption that people are not to be trusted much, so they don't give individual autonomy or discretion to the members at lower levels. The system is designed to control people and prevent them from committing selfish or stupid acts. It also keeps people from being innovative and from doing the right thing when the right thing is outside the rules. In the interests of rationality and order, it is made difficult to change or bend the rules. Unhealthy role organizations are rigid and resistant to change, with many barriers to communication between the parts and a tendency for each part to optimize its performance at the expense of the whole.

The Achievement Orientation. The achievement-oriented organization builds on people's tendency to want to like their work, to want to make a worthwhile contribution to society, and to enjoy their interactions with colleagues and customers. These are intrinsic rewards that are qualitative rather than quantitative and that arise from the nature of the work and/or the context in which it takes place. Traditional power- and role-oriented organizations are not designed to provide these intrinsic satisfactions.

In some work situations, these intrinsic satisfactions arise naturally. Others are deliberately designed to build them into the job and the work climate. People who have worked in such diverse situations as new business and new plant startups, nuclear test shots, intensive care units, and political and community organizing campaigns report that these work cultures can provide deep personal satisfactions and evoke personal commitment of a high order.

These "high energy" work situations are described by participants as work situations that engage the total person. People give their all, working long hours without complaint. They may willingly sacrifice their family and social lives to the demands of the work. There is a sense of urgency; people live "on the edge," putting out high energy for long periods of time. They may become addicted to stress.

There is a clearly understood mission that is articulated at the highest level of the organization. People supervise themselves, seeking out what needs to be done without direction from above. There is high morale, teamwork, and a sense of camaraderie. The group frequently feels itself to be elite or special.

The mission is emphasized and reinforced by everything upper managers do: the financial decisions they make; the questions they ask and the topics they pursue in meetings; the sorts of people they hire, fire, and promote; and the aspects of the operation they look at during field visits.

The mission is stated in unambiguous terms. There are one or two dominant values that are more important than any others in the organization. People who do not share the organization's basic values and commitments are made to feel uncomfortable and usually leave. The values embedded in the mission are larger than mere profit or growth. In pursuing the mission, organization members believe they are making a contribution to society as well as gaining something for the company.

The organization is more egalitarian than most. Employees are treated like willing contributors. Those at lower levels are empowered to make decisions that other organizations reserve for supervisors and middle managers. Positional authority does not shut off discussion or curb the expression of employees' ideas. It is easy to be heard if you have an idea or suggestion.

The unhealthy side of the achievement culture is brought on by its strengths. The high energy and involvement that the achievement orientation generates are difficult to sustain, and organization members are subject to burnout and disillusionment. Such organizations may rely on the vision to organize the work, rather than subjecting themselves to the discipline of systems and procedures. When the task is complex, and the vision takes on different forms for different parts of the organization, the organization may lose focus and unity of effort. When different groups each "do their own thing," coordination suffers and resources are wasted.

Achievement-oriented organizations are frequently under-organized; they may rely on high motivation to overcome their deficiencies in structures, systems, and planning. Although the achievement organization evokes enthusiasm and commitment, it may not have a heart. People's needs are subordinate to the organization's mission and its needs. After a time, people realize this and may begin to mistrust the organization—or they may remain committed but suffer high levels of emotional and physical stress and burnout.

The Support Orientation. The support culture may be defined as an organizational climate based on mutual trust between the individual and the organization. In such an organization, people believe that they are valued as human beings, not just as cogs in a machine or contributors to a task. A support culture fosters warmth and even love, not just driving enthusiasm. People like to come to work in the morning, not only because they like their work, but also because they care for the people with whom they work. Because they feel cared for, they are more human in their interactions with others: customers, suppliers, the public, and their fellow workers.

The support organization may be characterized in the following ways:

- People help each other beyond the formal demands of their jobs;

- Help is extended not only within one's own work group, but to other groups as well;

- People communicate a lot, not only about work, but also about personal concerns; and

- People like spending time together. They often see each other off the job, as well as on.

In hiring people, the organization gives special weight to whether the person is caring and cooperative and will fit in. People are viewed as basically good. When things go wrong, they get a second chance.

People know that the organization will go beyond the requirements of the policy or the employment contract to look after them when they need it. They feel a sense of safety. In return, they often go out of their way to take care of the organization, caring for the facilities and equipment, giving special attention to quality, conserving resources, and/or protecting the company's reputation in the community.

People celebrate together. They not only take pride in their work achievements, but they recognize such personal milestones as promotions, retirements, birthdays, and anniversaries. People value harmony and avoid confrontation, sometimes to the point of leaving important issues unresolved.

In Western societies, the support culture is the least typical of the four. It is not valued by the dominant power- or role-oriented organizations, and so it goes underground. It can be seen in relatively small groups, where people know one another personally and interact face-to-face. It tends to develop in organizations in which people work together for long enough periods of time to build personal relationships, work out their differences, and arrive at a degree of trust.

When not balanced by a thrust for success, the pure support culture is seldom found in business; it is not results-oriented enough to enable a business to be competitive. It makes its best contribution in dynamic tension with the achievement orientation. The latter releases and focuses the personal energy that is evoked for each of us by a love of doing and by a sense of high purpose and worthy mission. The support orientation taps into the personal energy present in the ties of love and trust, which bind us to people, groups, and organizations for which we care.

The emphasis on human needs by the support culture balances and moderates the single-pointed task focus of the achievement orientation. Where the one may use people up and burn them out, the other binds up their wounds, restores their energy and vitality, and heals their relationships. The achievement culture unleashes and fuses the human will of organization members in the service of the organization's task. The support culture evokes human love for the nurturing of the organization's members and the maintenance of the organization's essential fabric of relationships.

The support culture can evoke extremely strong motivation in the service of the group. We see this motivation in the sacrifices that members of groups make for one another. The willingness of people to give their lives for those of their comrades is not only known in war, but also in close-knit teams doing dangerous work such as polar exploration, police work, and fire fighting. The effects of team loyalty on productivity, quality, and absenteeism are well-publicized in recent writing on high performing organizations.

The weaknesses of the support culture are the negative side of its humanistic strengths. Organizations in which the support culture is unhealthy tend toward conflict avoidance: in the interests of harmony, difficult issues are swept under the rug. Consensus may be overvalued, hampering the organization's ability to move decisively. Sometimes, favoritism affects decisions about people, and injustice results. Backbiting, gossip, and character assassination behind one's back all tend to be rife in unhealthy support-oriented organizations. Differences in skill and ability may be ignored in the interests of "equal treatment." Tough decisions about people's performance may be postponed out of "kindness," negatively impacting the organization's effectiveness.

Unique Wholeness

From the point of view of organization culture, we consider a healthy organization to be one that exemplifies the highest form of its cultural archetype as described above. Health is not to be confused with perfection. None of the cultures we have described is ideal, and each achieves its advantages at the cost of other benefits. Health or wholeness implies congruence between the demands of the work the organization has to do and the ways it organizes to do that work. It implies clarity about its strengths and weaknesses and consistency between words and actions. From this point of view, a healthy organization is authentically and consistently congruent with its values and beliefs and aware of its strengths and limitations.

For the individuals who live and work in the organization, health or its lack often depends on the degree of "fit" between the person's character and personality and the demands the organization places on him or her. For example, dependent and authoritarian people often work well in power organizations; people who need order and stability thrive in healthy role organizations; self-starting, autonomous individuals who tolerate uncertainty well are suited to the conditions of achievement organizations; and relational focused individuals flourish in a support-oriented culture. Of course, few of us thrive on injustice or abuse of power or in chaotic situations where we have no idea how to achieve what is expected of us or how to meet our personal needs.

Understanding Healing

Organizations that are not healthy and whole need healing. Healing has the same root as wholeness, holy, holistic, hologram, and health. Organizational healing is the process of becoming whole again after a time of injury, change, or loss. Healing involves the letting go of losses following trauma and developing new connections and identities. It is moving toward integration and a bringing of the pieces together so they function as a whole, in appropriate balance, after experiencing trauma or a dysfunctional structure. Part of promoting health is giving an organization a more holistic knowledge of itself. The healing process increases self-awareness, especially of one part by another.

Healing or Cure?

A cure is a fix for a particular disease or injury. Levine (Murray, 1990) makes this distinction in speaking of individual health. Healing, on the other hand, is becoming whole. Most consultants have had clients who want a consultant to fix a specific problem. They may be looking for a cure. Fixing a specific problem often has little impact on the organization's wholeness. Finding a "fix" for a specific problem may delude some organization members into thinking that the organization is cured, and thus further healing is not pursued. Although people at the top of organizations may engage in such wishful thinking, addressing a single issue or putting a Band-Aid on a deep wound does not usually mislead people at lower levels.

The Process of Organizational Healing

How healing actually takes place is always, to some extent, a mystery. It is not a mechanical process or one to which a simple formula may be applied. People and systems are more complex than that. What will bring healing to one organization or system may not bring it to another. Healing must always come from the inside and work its way out. Yet there are certain things organizations and their consultants can do and ways they can be that we believe will be a catalyst to the healing process.

The Consultant's Role

"Physician, heal thyself." This age-old injunction applies to OD practitioners when we undertake healing roles. When we encourage organizations to become more complete and whole, we need to focus on that ourselves. We need to bring our whole selves into this healing process—not just our heads but our hearts, our spirits, our intuition, our humility, our love, our compassion. If we cannot always be models for the healthy system, we can at least try to bring all our best parts to the task of assisting in healing.

Besides doing our own inner work, OD consultants can play several other key roles in the facilitating of healing in an organization. First, the OD consultant can heighten the organization's awareness of the need and priority for healing and the costs of not addressing health issues. This in itself may stimulate the clients to begin to address their issues on their own, either directly or indirectly.

Consultants can also help their clients prepare for healing by assisting them in identifying areas of pain and obstacles to healing. We try to help our clients understand the "being" of their organization in order to appreciate what wholeness would look like for that organization. It means entering into the organization and sensing its spirit. It includes respecting the type of organizational culture one finds and helping the organization to become the best it can be of its kind. It is not something that can be discovered and then told to the organization members; rather it is mutual exploration, in which we provide tools and concepts, and our clients take active roles in the process of discovery. By entering into the organization and listening to people talk about their experiences, we may also provide time, love, and an opportunity to grieve, which are all important to the healing process. Simply being present is a healing alternative to interventions that impose more of the change from which people are already suffering.

We must be very clear that we cannot do one thing. Consultants cannot heal an organization. Because the uses of power in organizational change are so closely connected to outcomes of wholeness or suffering, we emphatically assert that consultants may not realistically aspire to heal their client organizations. Unless consultants are given discretionary decision-making authority, they cannot directly affect the establishment of the conditions that promote wholeness. Such authority is seldom given, nor should it be. The keys to healing, leading to the restoration of feelings of mastery, self-worth, potency, freedom, and control over the organization's fate, are in the hands of those who exercise power. Consultants can offer approaches to that restoration. Real healing, however, will only result from the words and deeds of those who wield the power and from the responses of those who are subject to it.

Preparation for Healing

Readiness for Healing

An initial question an organization must answer after realizing its need for healing is whether or not it is ready for healing. Almost any intervention, healing or otherwise, will require resources of time, attention, energy, and/or money from the organization. Since the chaos of change is the root of much of the trauma currently causing pain in organizations, we must ask ourselves whether our activities in the organization will be experienced as part of the solution or part of the problem. If the organization requires all its resources just to keep doing its job at the level of survival, the diversion of resources required to move toward wholeness may cause unacceptable decrements in performance, along with increased trauma and stress. In our experience, this is a question too seldom asked by consultants, for reasons that are not hard to imagine. As Schein (1988) reminds us, the less healthy organizations tend to be the more resistant to help and least open to insight. Our belief is that we should respect resistance at least until we understand its roots—the resistance may be in the service of the organization's survival.

Origins of Pain

It is tempting to approach healing the trauma of change or other wounded-ness in ways that stem from the paradigm of allopathic medicine. We know from experience and from having it hammered into our heads by exponents of systems thinking that the causes of pain and dysfunction are usually not lo-cated close to the symptoms. But it is difficult not to collude with clients and with our own hearts by directly addressing people who are hurting. Systemic approaches to healing are often a hard sell, although perhaps not so much as they used to be. It is easy to be seduced into trying to fix the people who are hurting, for example, through stress management training, instead of the much more difficult task of alleviating the sources of stress.

With that said, it is useful to have some kind of map of who or what is hurting or not working. It is useful to think about the structural, relational, and intentional/mission-related aspects of the situation. Doing so can help us and our clients to see incongruities, inconsistencies, and tensions. (See Fig-ure 1.) For example, if mission statements are proclaimed loudly, but policies and structures prevent their fulfillment, people may become depressed and hopeless.

We often use the following questions with our clients: Is there a par-ticular department or function that predominately emanates distress? Is it primarily shown in the financial performance, the service quality, the prod-uct quality, the meeting of production and delivery schedules, or the overall success in meeting customer demands?

At what organizational level does the pain reside? Does it primarily re-side at the top management level, the middle management, the first-line su-pervisors, the workforce, the entire organization, the customers/clients, or some other place?

Is the pain experienced primarily as the absence or loss of good things (loss of status, meaningful work, material compensations) or as the presence of negative or bad things (abuses of power, chaos and confusion, pressures to produce more and faster)? Are people looking for relief from something hurtful or for restoration of something lost?

What sorts of stories, fantasies, and explanations is the organization telling itself? New stories and ways of looking at the past, present, and future may need to emerge. Sometimes history needs to be reframed with forgive-ness and understanding. People may benefit from being remembered and connected in new ways with their organizational past in order to move beyond their pain.

The Culture Model in Organizational Healing

Sometimes we may use the culture model to help clients acquire concepts and language for thinking and speaking about organizational health and pain and their causes in the culture. (A culture questionnaire [Harrison & Stokes, 1992] is available to assist in the process.) The four-part culture model not only alerts us to the kinds of dysfunction we may find in a particular organization. It also provides guidance for how to work with the organization as a consultant. Each culture offers different healing options. Each poses different barriers to healing and learning. Here are some suggestions that follow from the model.

Power-Oriented Organizations.   The will, integrity, and competence of leaders are keys to healing in power-oriented organizations. Subordinates are often timid and fearful of taking initiative, and both they and the leaders may expect the latter to assume total responsibility for movement. There is security in the dependent relationships characteristic of paternalistic organizations. Where leaders are trusted and trustworthy, this leads to reduction in anxiety for subordinates.

Unfortunately, as we have seen in recent years in both public and private organizations and in government, lack of integrity and abuses of power are common. The expectations of persons with power and authority held by much of the population tend to be quite negative, and this becomes a self-fulfilling prophecy. We get the leaders we expect (deserve?) as our mistrust and suspicion become mirrored in their ways of behaving. We have in large part lost traditions of responsible and benevolent authority. Thus, leadership expectations and behaviors can often be causes of pain and dysfunction in organizations rather than sources of healing. It is important to remember, however, that these ills are aspects of recent broad social movements. Although they appear likely to be with us for the foreseeable future, they may not be universal or inevitable.

Aspects of power-oriented organizations that may be part of the problem, rather than part of the solution, include the following:

- Over-reliance on control through authority and fear;
- Isolation of those in power from facts about what is really happening and how others feel about events because bad news does not travel upward;

- Over-reliance on hard data and discounting of emotions;

- Information overload at the top of the organization and lack of information on the part of subordinates;

- Denial as a common defense on the part of leaders; and

- Few supports for the individual because people are engaged in jockeying for power and influence.

It is worth noting that it is difficult for consultants to power-oriented organizations to intervene successfully without the help and trust of powerful allies and protectors, or without a keen understanding of the realities of organizational power and politics. This goes against the grain of the strong egalitarian values many of us hold, but it is a reality nonetheless.

Role-Oriented Organizations.   The key to health in role-oriented organizations is the adequacy of systems and structures and the mutual respect for contracts and agreements (rule of law). Shoddy or unreliable systems lead to confusion, ineffectiveness, and anxiety. Given the rapid pace of change in technologies and markets, keeping structures appropriate and systems relevant and effective can be a nearly hopeless task. In such situations, role-oriented organizations that require people to operate by the rules find themselves hampered by the structures and systems that were supposed to ensure efficiency and order in the first place. Confusion and chaos are especially painful to people used to the constraints, boundaries, and security of an orderly system.

Aspects of role-oriented organizations that may contribute to dysfunction include the following:

- People's tendency not to take responsibility beyond the limits of their formal job descriptions and structural boundaries, so important tasks go undone because no one is responsible for them;

- Communication and command patterns move information and directives only up and down in the hierarchy, not across boundaries, so people who have a need to know and to cooperate with each other operate independently and in the dark;

- Lack of agreed-on procedures for rapidly changing outmoded rules, systems, and structures; and

- Fear of making mistakes on the part of people used to being told what to do, which leads to confusion and paralysis during times of rapid change.

Consultants frequently make the mistake in working with role-oriented organizations of assuming that interventions that are well-accepted by some of their clients will therefore be implemented. In role-oriented organizations, unless interventions are legitimized, they often die from neglect. They need to be made part of the systems, structures, and procedures of the organization.

Achievement-Oriented Organizations. Consultants often experience these organizations as nearly perfect clients because of the value the members give to open-mindedness and innovation. People at all levels tend to experience themselves as empowered and to have considerable freedom to innovate, experiment, and deviate from the rules. They tend to be risk takers by preference. Where the mission and purpose of the organization are known and shared by all in the organization, not solely those at the top, decisions can be debated and decided by appeals to that common vision and frame of reference. Action can be taken without reference to those who have positional power.

Competent consultants find it easier to enter and to establish their credibility in achievement-oriented organizations without the need for a powerful sponsor or a legitimate role in the system. Contributions tend to be valued on their merits rather than according to their source. Organization members may be quite competitive, but they are more likely to compete for excellence than for power and influence. When they become enthusiastic about doing something, they are willing and able to commit great amounts of time and energy in selfless dedication to the task.

Aspects of achievement-oriented organizations that may contribute to dysfunction include the following:

- A tendency toward tunnel vision, to narrowly focus on the solution of some fascinating problem while remaining oblivious to the implications of one's actions for the welfare of the larger system, so people often pursue their own personal goals without regard for the effect on the whole.

- Norms favoring personal sacrifice to the mission, which cause people to neglect their families, health, and personal lives and to burn out. The climate of the organization supports individuals in having a strong will, relying overly on reason, and having an underdeveloped heart. Pressure, lack of nurturing from others, and lack of compassion for one's own weakness and inadequacies may lead to workaholism and other addictions, including substance abuse. When people do not perform as heroes, they are easily isolated or discarded. The organization tends to use people up and spit them out.

- Norms against questioning the mission promote group think, intolerance for dissent, and a tendency to self-deception and denial of failure, dysfunction, and other bad news.

- A "whatever works" attitude may come to exist in which noble ends are believed to justify ignoble means.

- Lack of organizational memory and an arrogant "not invented here" attitude, which may lead to successful innovations at one time or place, remaining localized rather than enriching the whole. It is frequently necessary to reinvent the wheel over and over again in addressing problems.

Support-Oriented Organizations.   The powers to nurture, heal, and bring people together in cooperation are keys to the strengths of the support organization. Both love and feelings of family or community are usually characteristic of these organizations. Because love is the opposite of fear and because it overcomes alienation, members do not experience themselves as isolated or alone. Support-oriented organizations are likely to try to work with opposing forces rather than against them. Allowing and collaborating are strong work norms. There is appreciation for diversity and a wish to be inclusive. Feelings are honored as well as facts, and intuition tends to be accepted as an approach to problem solving. People are more likely than in the other organizational cultures to consider the consequences of their decisions and actions on the whole system and even beyond the system's boundaries.

Consultants often experience support-oriented organizations as warm and welcoming and as easy to engage with and establish rapport. Members are more sophisticated about process than in the other types of organizations and more accepting of consultants who focus their interventions on group and interpersonal processes. The other side of that acceptance is frequently a tendency to take a long time to decide issues, especially when there is disagreement about the right way to go.

Aspects of support-oriented organizations that may contribute to dysfunction include the following:

- The difficulty mentioned in confronting and moving through conflict and a tendency to be indecisive and slow to take needed action;

- A tendency to value kindness and tolerance over "tough love," leading to tolerance of lack of integrity;

- The well-developed heart of the organization may be combined with a weak will, leading to disastrous personnel decisions, failure to make such decisions, lack of accountability for results, and poor task performance;

- A tendency toward over-reliance on feelings to the point of disregarding facts; and

- A tendency to trust where trust has not been earned so that the support-oriented organization is vulnerable to betrayal and exploitation by unscrupulous individuals.

Other Means of Assessment

We have also had success in assisting internal teams to create their own assessment processes. In one high-tech organization, for example, a team made up of a "diagonal slice" of the organization created, with the help of the consultants, an online organizational health assessment to which everyone in the organization was invited to respond.[2] They then convened a meeting of the whole organization in the cafeteria to hear the results of their assessment and to consider in small groups what they would like to do to move toward healthier ways of doing and being.

Promoting Healing

A myriad of ideas is presented in the literature for promoting healing. Suggestions offered range from increasing communication (Harrison, 1993, 1997, 2000a; Kreitzer, 2000), reducing and managing stress (Harrison, 1984; Kreitzer, 2000; McGuigan, 1997; The Stress Doc, 1998), providing time and space for collective grieving of the losses sustained in the change (Harrison, 2000b; Kreitzer, 2000; The Stress Doc, 1998, 2000), learning to learn (Harrison, 1993, 2000a, 2000b; Kreitzer, 2000; Smit & Schabracq, 1997; The Stress Doc, 1998), and learning to forgive, to love, and to simply give time and space for healing (Harrison, 1997). Laughter, compassion, love, kindness, and understanding always contribute to healing.

Our purpose in this paper is not to survey the approaches to healing, but to advocate an approach that we feel offers a great deal of power and hope, both to consultants and, more importantly, to our clients.

Our Approach to Promoting Healing and Wholeness

We have long pondered the factors that enable individuals and organizations to go through major changes with minimal damage, disruption, and trauma. Central to the successful navigation of any change is the meanings people attribute to it. We are creatures who live on making experience meaningful.

---

[2]The project was conducted by Sandra Florstedt and Roger Harrison.

People willingly expend incredible energy and endure the most horrible suffering, even to death, when the meanings they give to their experiences are sufficiently virtuous or lofty. When meanings weaken, or shift in discouraging directions, energy flags and illness becomes more likely. Examples of this abound, both for individuals and organizations. When a group of consultants was having a conversation about organizational healing, two members shared experiences of having "panic attacks." One had been able to contain and make meaning of that experience within the framework of his religious worldview and faith and had moved through it within a couple of days. The other had no framework into which to put the experience and was in therapy for years attempting to understand and heal from what had happened.

Viktor Frankl's (1963) experiences in World War II death camps showed that those who found meaning in their experience were more likely to live. Following the war, he founded Logotherapy, a form of psychotherapy in which healing occurs through changing the meaning clients give to their experiences. In the same way, members of organizations can change the meaning they attribute to a particular change or loss.

Meaning answers the "Why?" of an experience. While finding meaning depends on an individual's or system's philosophical or theological framework, we regard four domains as central to promoting the process of helping people and systems find meaning in their experiences. Along with the domain, we have included the condition that supports healing.

1. *The Domain of Justice:* People perceive what is being done as fair and just.

2. *The Domain of Truth:* People believe they are receiving full disclosure of information relevant to the impact of changes on themselves, and they believe significant others are telling the truth.

3. *The Domain of Empowerment:* People perceive themselves as able to decide and act in ways that positively affect or ameliorate the outcomes of the change on themselves.

4. *The Domain of the Heart:* People experience significant others as caring and compassionate.

When the four conditions we have identified are met, people often endure substantial loss without suffering long-term damage. It is sadly true that the conditions are usually far from being met in changes taking place in organizations today. That is why we see so much pain and need for healing.

The four domains overlap, of course. For example, when relevant information is kept from people, they are in fact impotent to decide and act for their own interests. They come to feel that they are being treated unfairly. The use of power is key to the outcome of either wholeness or suffering when changes occur in organizations. That is most obviously true for the domains of justice, truth, and empowerment. In these domains, people are either healed or hurt, depending on how power is used in managing change.

The uses of power have more indirect consequences for the domain of the heart and are mediated through the polar opposites of fear and love. When power is used in ways that create disempowerment and fear, then hearts become closed, and the healing expression of softer, more expansive feelings of love and compassion becomes difficult and infrequent.

We disavow the notion that power is necessarily corrupting or that those who hold it are less sensitive, aware, compassionate, and open to learning than are those who are subject to their exercise of authority. It is true that the possession of a longer, broader vision of possibilities can blind executives to the short-term effects of the implementation of strategy. They may also collude in their own blindness out of a wish to avoid the experience of others' pain, anger, and disappointment. It is also true that the planning and implementation of change is frequently carried out by a small group of people who sequester themselves in order to focus on their task, communicating primarily with one another and thereby insulating themselves from the chaos and pain occasioned by their activities. With the rapport that well-established coaching relationships can provide, these blind spots can often be illuminated, and the eyes, ears, and hearts of those in power may open.[3]

Fostering Healing

Of the four domains, the domains of truth and of the heart are the most accessible to consultants. We ourselves place most of our emphases in our work with these two domains. Our intervention in the domains of justice and empowerment must take place indirectly through education and other kinds of influence on those with organizational power. Of course, it is true that what happens in the justice and empowerment domains constrains the impact of any interventions in the domains of truth and of the heart. That said, we hold firmly the vision that consultants can become effective agents for healing, both through coaching those who hold power and by working in the domains of truth and of the heart.

Our first commitment in fostering wholeness in organizations is to assist our clients in building a climate in which it is safe to speak one's mind

---

[3]For a good introduction to the practice of executive coaching, see James Flaherty's *Coaching: Evoking Excellence in Others* (Woburn, MA: Butterworth-Heinemann, 1998).

and heart, including both positive and negative feelings. Of course, all of us have experienced the formidable barriers against telling the truth that exist at the best of times in most organizations.[4] As consultants, our commitment to clients is first and foremost to tell the truth and to ask the same of them. When people act in ways that suppress truth telling, we try to uncover the underlying fear and confront it with compassion and honesty.

The establishment of dialogue among participants in organizational change is a major healing resource that consultants can provide. Dialogue can profoundly affect the meanings that people attribute to changes going on around them. Creating the conditions for effective dialogue directly and positively affects the domains of truth and the heart, thus fostering healing.

We use the term dialogue broadly to include any conversation within a safe social container that enables participants to speak their minds and hearts regarding what is going on and what it means. We especially recommend the circle processes developed by Christina Baldwin (1998, 1999) of PeerSpirit. In PeerSpirit circling, there are four basic agreements to establish and maintain mutual respect:

1. What is said in the circle belongs to that circle.

2. We listen to each other with discernment, not judgment.

3. Each person asks for the support he or she needs and offers the support he or she can.

4. When the group is uncertain how to proceed or in need of a resting point in the group's process, we will stop action, observe a pause, and self-reflect.

These agreements form the basic structure of PeerSpirit circling, together with three principles:

1. Leadership and facilitation rotate among the members.

2. Everyone shares responsibility for the task and for the maintenance of a safe, supportive container for the work.

3. We rely on our highest goals and our common purpose, and we return to those in times of uncertainty and conflict.

These make the circle a safe place where people, no matter what their initial views, can search for shared understanding while deliberately refraining from both polarization and polite surface agreement. PeerSpirit circling pro-

---

[4]See, for example, the writings of Jerry B. Harvey, notably *The Abilene Paradox and Other Meditations on Management* (San Francisco, CA: Jossey-Bass, 1998) and *How Come Every Time I Get Stabbed in the Back My Fingerprints Are on the Knife?* (San Francisco, CA: Jossey-Bass, 1999).

vides powerful help for finding shared meanings in experiences of change and loss. Such experiences can enable people to move from being stuck in their feelings about the past to being fully present in the moment and ready to commit to realistic action.

Many consultants have had the experience of trying to facilitate a group-planning effort in which it seemed the participants just couldn't come to grips with the task, and the work kept getting sidetracked and going nowhere. This is often a signal that the group members are enveloped in negative feelings and meanings about their experience. We have had good results by postponing the task and dropping into a deeper conversation in circle. Feelings of anger, grief, and loss that may be under the surface can then be shared, honored, and released, at least for the time being. After such sharing, the task often moves ahead quickly.

An understanding of PeerSpirit circle practices of creating safe spaces for speaking and listening, combined with a strong commitment to truth telling, empowers any consultant or organization member to be an agent for wholeness. Such conversations can truly foster improvement and opening in the domains of truth and the heart, given a reasonable amount of freedom to meet with others, and given enough time for the processes to work. These conditions are, unfortunately, often scarce in organizations today, and vigilance and determination are called for to seize the day (or moment) for healing.

Neither our clients nor we can do anything simpler or more effective to promote organizational healing than to provide a safe climate for truth and compassion. At the same time, there is probably nothing harder for clients or for us. Clients are often anxious about inviting people to share their feelings and perceptions about changes that are clearly creating losses for organization members. They fear that people will generate negative thoughts and feelings about one another and then become stuck in those feelings. Our experience is that most people do not enjoy wallowing in despair and, having plumbed the depths, they spontaneously seek positive ways of dealing with the situation. People are more likely to become stuck in negativity when free expression of their darker feelings is suppressed or punished.

What Does It Take?

So what does it take for a consultant or organization member to be an agent of healing in the workplace? First, although experience is always useful, this work is not about techniques and methods of consultation and management. The fundamental requisites are courage, compassion, and the ability to listen without judging or taking precipitate action. It requires courage to stand, often alone, and speak truth and to persevere when others counsel prudence or deny awareness of what we are speaking about. It requires courage to place wholeness first and expediency second—never more so than when an organization is in crisis or plunging headlong into a quest for some vision of organizational excellence.

It requires compassion to be present to pain, anger, resentment, and self-pity in us and in others, while maintaining rapport with people who are doing or saying bad things to others and to us. Without compassion and a genuine interest in listening to others, truth telling becomes a challenge for others to defend themselves, rather than an invitation to sit together in council. We have learned that it is possible to speak almost anything without breaking rapport and trust, so long as we are able to speak without a strong charge of anger, resentment, or judgment. The way we learned this truth was through suffering the consequences of our own inadequate compassion on numerous occasions.

STORIES OF HEALING

Our interest and personal commitment is first to establish safe conditions for speaking and listening. However, it is true that both consultants and organization members have employed other means of implementing change in ways that have been good for an organization's performance and healing, both for the organization's members and for the organizational system as a whole. One of the authors polled a cross-section of OD consultants in the United States and the United Kingdom for examples of managing change that contribute to wholeness and healing. As we reviewed these, we observed that the majority of them gave examples of the four domains outlined above. We are heartened by what our correspondents sent us. We offer a paraphrased selection of their stories in the hope that they will encourage our readers and their clients to try their own approaches to healing and to fostering the conditions of justice, truth, empowerment, and heart that support healing.

Justice and Empowerment

One story that illustrates a company's desire to promote justice and empowerment in the process of change comes from David Francis in the UK. Smokestack Ltd. is a manufacturer of precision metal components.[5] In 1990, they

---

[5]This and the following examples were received via email as personal communications to Roger Harrison. They are in some cases paraphrased for clarity and brevity.

were operating at a loss. The changes were carried out during the recession of the early 1990s, with Smokestack Ltd. taking increased market share during that period. By 1997, they were profitable. It was all done through a tough approach to problems, a tender approach to people, and a willingness to risk.

The change was led by a steering group that interfaced closely with the union. The top team committed itself to develop a "partnership" with the workforce over a period of four to five years. Although the original change was initiated and driven by the top team, a major aim of the program was to push responsibility for future change activities down to second-tier management. Specific detail work was undertaken by working parties involving about fifty people in all. A weekly bulletin was used to keep people up-to-date on the development of the thinking. The whole process took about a year to work through and gain agreement.

A "change agreement" was negotiated with the union, featuring a job security guarantee, commitment to fair pay rates, a new pay structure, phased manpower reduction through wastage, and early retirement provisions. Teamwork was introduced, along with definitions of training requirements and a progression through acquisition of validated skills. Training is encouraged even if it does not relate to the current job—the idea being to sponsor development, not stifle it. However, the main emphasis has been on job-led training where there is an immediate use so that the lessons are not lost. Job swaps, mutually agreed between the people concerned, have been introduced to allow people opportunities to develop. People are encouraged to do jobs differently so long as the job gets done. There are no job descriptions as such. A "responsibility initiative" encourages individuals to take initiatives and "step out of the box."

One outcome of the process was a Partnership Statement, which the top team did not originally envision. It sets out the two sides of the bargain: what the company can offer and what is expected of staff in return. Another outcome of the agreement was Partnership Awareness Days, which are run jointly by the management team and personnel, along with union involvement, for groups of twelve people at a time. Everyone on site is to have participated by the end of the year. The use of cross-sections in the groups has been particularly useful, and the small size allows good two-way discussion of issues. The message of partnership is being successfully communicated to people, and they are very receptive.

The motto is, "Don't bitch—talk." It is accepted that people have minds of their own, and they will do more when they want to than they will because they are told to. The emphasis is "to try to allow people to do their own thing within a framework of controls."

Truthfulness and Disclosure

The need for truthfulness and full disclosure is illustrated by its lack in the following story told by one of our respondents:

> In the early 1980s, we did all of our change planning with a major oil company behind closed doors and in secrecy. We did not want to unduly worry those who might be affected by the change. When we had all of the plans in place, we announced the complete package. Although this caused pain, we rationalized that it was better to have a short sharp shock than a drawn-out period of uncertainty. My attitude and behavior changed when one manager who experienced our process confronted me. "What would you like your father's doctor to do?" he asked. "For six months he knows your father is dying, but he doesn't tell you until the day before he dies, as he does not want to worry you unduly. Would you have preferred the longer period of uncertainty so you could have planned for your loss and enjoyed the remainder of the time together?" Since then, I have always seen the benefit of early and open, honest communication about the possibility of change rather than the announcement of a fait accompli, and I counsel this approach whenever I can.

Less Task Orientation

A manager in an international youth-oriented organization spoke of the healing effects of departing from task-driven ways and seeking deeper honesty and truthfulness:

> I've just returned from a two-day retreat of our two top management teams. The key to the healing that happened was our determination, in this case, to *not* have a prescribed agenda. For the two CEOs, this was a rather big risk. We had a general direction and a few key questions—beyond that, we were guided by a shared commitment to pursue "big questions," but not to leave the meeting with anything like a "to do" list. This led to an openness and honesty that is too rare in our meetings. Our habitual "task drivenness" leads to a mindless quantity-over-quality orientation that precludes creativity and, ironically, appreciation of our significant successes. With less premeditation, there was more presence, more honesty, and more willingness to remember basic principles and also—of all things—to share a few dreams. By being ourselves during this time, we moved a few steps from being managers toward being leaders.

Other colleagues shared these examples of managers' behaviors that fostered a healing environment through speaking the truth and demonstrating leadership in honest self-disclosure:

- A division manager publicly acknowledged at a retreat that the management group had failed to follow through on previous commitments to improve workplace conditions and that he would find it perfectly understandable if employees were skeptical about any new commitments.

- A team leader was willing to show strong emotions (cry) in a team meeting, acknowledging deeply felt anguish over her inability to better manage conflicts between work and family commitments.

- A senior manager in a training program for junior managers acknowledged the dilemma that, while it will in the long run be to the advantage of the junior members to invest in teamwork, they will predictably under-invest because of pressures and contradictions from the company's reward structure.

- In a situation in which a company was being sold, senior people shared their own fears and sadness instead of staying in their "strong and in-charge" role.

- A senior manager took the risk of giving some very painful personal feedback to her boss about his destructive behavior and the impact that it was having on others. It resulted in drawing them closer and in his opening up his floodgates to share his own distress.

Empowerment

An example of fostering empowerment came to us from the recent closing of all C&A clothing stores in the UK (Cox, 2000). At C&A, from the date of the closure, the managing director of the UK operation, Neil McCausland, tells of losing all of his authority over the five thousand staff overnight. Why should they listen to someone who has just told them they were all going to lose their jobs?

One key opportunity that McCausland seized was to offer greater empowerment to his staff. Knowing that they were going to close gave him the occasion to take risks that might not be tolerated in normal trading environments. So McCausland offered staff a choice: be demotivated and angry or try out new strategies to achieve success in the final months. He pointed out that the chances of taking these attitudes into job interviews was very high, so the better option for them personally was to adopt the positive strategy.

Focusing on the immediate concern, he promised help in finding new jobs. Then he told the store managers to tear up the rule book. No longer would they have to follow corporate guidelines; they could run their stores individually, just focusing on making a profit. A monthly bonus for managers and staff based on that store's success replaced previous Europe-wide performance payments.

The result for C&A in the UK was a 50 percent increase in sales, with the added irony that trucks had to be brought in from the group's European operations (which were being kept open) to help with distribution!

Special Techniques

Another correspondent pointed to ways in which using Appreciative Inquiry,[6] Future Search,[7] and Open Space[8] provide safe containers for exchanging thoughts and feelings and empower people as an organization prepares for change:

> I have been using Appreciative Inquiry with groups undergoing or contemplating change. I find that the focus on appreciation and reflections on success makes a considerable difference in attitudes to the change. People become more positive and committed and feel in control of where they are going. The visions or propositions are reality based and are more empowering than "blue sky" projections. Appreciative Inquiry is based on storytelling, and it is a safe place to share feelings. I also find that, because the picture painted by the process is positive for the organization, it is easy for managers to share their power and authority when Appreciative Inquiry is used.
>
> I have also participated in Future Search conferences and find that they provide similar encouragement for those in power to find it easy to give freedom for decisions to the group as the leaders gain confidence in the process. Open Space is another technology that I have found particularly empowering for helping to deal with the tensions and fears of change.

---

[6]A recent treatment of Appreciative Inquiry can be found in *Appreciative Inquiry: Rethinking Human Organization Toward a Positive Theory of Change*, edited by D.L. Cooperrider, D. Whitney, & P. Sorenson (Champaign, IL: Stipes, 1999).

[7]For a complete guide to the philosophy and practice of Future Search, see Marvin R. Weisbord and Sandra Janoff's *Future Search: An Action Guide to Finding Common Ground in Organizations and Communities* (San Francisco, CA: Berrett-Koehler, 1999).

[8]Practical help with Open Space can be found in Harrison Owen's *Open Space Technology: A User's Guide* (San Francisco, CA: Berrett-Koehler, 1997).

A colleague in a multinational accounting and consulting firm shared this touching example of an organization facilitating healing by living from the heart: The firm was in the process of a significant change to its approach to consulting. The managers from around the world who were "responsible" to embed the new way of working back in their local offices had gathered in the United States. When they shared the successes and difficulties they were having in implementing the new approach, the last person to speak stood up in front of forty of her peers to tell her story. She was shaking as she spoke about her "lack of success" and the reasons behind it. Her peers listened intently.

The facilitator turned to the group and asked, "What does she need from you right now? She does not need your strategic minds; she needs your caring and love." The woman who was sharing her story broke into uncontrollable tears. The facilitator sat down on the floor with her, in the middle of the circle of her peers, and asked if she would be okay sharing with the group where her tears came from. She agreed. With the help of the consultant, and the caring of the group, she talked about working in a place where there was no space to do the kind of work she so wanted to create—wanting to change the unhealthy patterns and dynamics that were at play, yet feeling helpless and alone. Healing, I believe, came not only to the woman who shared her story, but also to many of her colleagues as they experienced the depth of pain one can endure in the midst of change.

Healing Through Change

Another consultant shared some thoughts on encouraging healing during the change process:

> Consultants talk of three basic stages: the first is to dismantle, unfreeze, discredit, and separate from the old ways of working. The second is to cross the "abyss of uncertainty" as quickly as possible and get through the "neutral zone" so we can climb the learning curve. The third is to make the change operational and arrive at the promised land of outrageous goals, higher profits, and market dominance. Most practitioners of change management focus on creating the new vision (and discrediting the old) and on measuring the results of the change.
>
> The aspect of change management I am most interested in is the second: the neutral zone.[9] In contrast to trying to get through

---

[9]This is a term coined, so far as we know, by William P. Bridges and discussed in his excellent little guide to finding meaning in change: *Transitions: Making Sense of Life's Changes.* (Boulder, CO: Perseus Publishing, 1980).

this as quickly as possible, this may be the stage of change that holds the most promise for creativity and innovation, depth and stability of change, and the making of real meaning in people's work. It may also be a source of real damage if it is not sufficiently lived through.

The Jungians call this second stage liminality (Stein, 1986). It is the break in continuity between the old way and the new, the experience of what was once solid becoming insubstantial. It is separation; it is the place where the soul can enter consciousness, where grief, mourning, and acknowledgment of loss can be allowed conscious experience, therefore integration. Liminality is the womb through which innovation is born, where half-baked ideas are allowed to exist and develop into full-fledged innovations, where people's minds float through a sea of possibility.

I now believe that if the psyche or soul of the people being asked to change is not invited to change as well, psychological damage will be done. If the liminal stage of change is paved over by outrageous goals, fear of job loss, and especially the lack of time, real change will not hold. It will not integrate into the depths of the soul. Meaning is the real glue that binds change together, and the source of meaning is the soul.

Finally, some interesting insights into the healing power of starting over afresh come from two more respondents:

I am learning a process for healing the wounds caused by mergers and takeovers from a person skilled in helping the re-marriage of divorced or separated partners. In helping to create a new family group, this counselor advises couples not to move into either of the existing homes, but to set up a new one. That way they have to negotiate roles and agree to color schemes and layouts together. No one has to compromise or is forced to live with the other's existing layout and design. So with merging organizations, it is better to set up a new organization somewhere else than to try to consolidate two sets of staff into one existing structure. Whenever possible, new offices are ideal, but even symbolic new homes are effective: new organization structures and job titles/roles that are new to both original organizations, etc.

An example of helping healing by letting go of the past in a symbolic way comes from a client in Denmark. They reorganized radically in the mid-1990s to an organization with no structure, no paper, and no job descriptions. On D-Day, everyone renegotiated roles and found himself or herself a space to work. To symbolize the new start, an auction of the old office furniture was held, and new furniture was provided for the new working space.

Conclusion

These examples of being agents of healing in organizations illustrate some ways in which an open heart, a desire for truth and justice, an empowering of people, an inquiring mind, and the willingness to take personal and organizational risks can bring healing to those in difficult and demanding organizational and personal circumstances. These stories offer hope in the face of the magnitude of pain and wounding that takes place daily in organizations and the difficulties that consultants encounter in making a difference for wholeness and health expressed in the earlier part of this paper.

In spite of all the adverse and dire realities, we believe, to paraphrase a cynical bumper sticker, that "Healing Happens." It happens when courageous and conscious managers and consultants have the temerity to tell the truth, to listen deeply and non-defensively to others, and to open their hearts and express the love and compassion that dwell therein. It happens when some of us OD consultants risk responding to the call to move beyond our traditional roles of being catalysts for change to beginning to learn to facilitate healing as well. It happens when those who carry grave and weighty responsibilities decide to empower others, at the risk of seeing them fail to take up the slack. It happens when those who control scarce organizational resources direct them into nurturing and supporting the people as well as into fixing the organization. It happens when we can trust that what is good for one will be good for the whole.

Healing occurs when we allow the latent love and respect we have for our fellow humans to overcome our cynicism and self-protection and move into action—action that may at times only manifest as listening deeply and being present to others. Each of us may choose to open to this longing of our hearts at any time or place. Some times and places, of course, are more challenging than others.

References

Baldwin, C. (1998). *Calling the circle: The first and future culture.* New York: Bantam.

Baldwin, C., & Linnea, A. (1999). *PeerSpirit council management.* Langley, WA: PeerSpirit.

Bridges, W.P. (1980). *Transitions: Making sense of life's changes.* Boulder, CO: Perseus.

Cooperrider, D.L., Whitney, D., & Sorensen, P. (Eds.). (1999). *Appreciative inquiry: Rethinking human organization toward a positive theory of change.* Champaign, IL: Stipes.

Cox, G. (2000, December). *Cuttings: Learning from crisis: Closing down can be inspiring.* Available: www.newdirections.uk.com/cuttings37.htm [last accessed 4/27/01]

Driskell, J.E., Salas, E., & Johnston, J. (1999). Does stress lead to a loss of team perspective? *Group Dynamics: Theory, Research, and Practice, 3,* 291–302.

Dryer, J. (1999). Hard work never killed anyone? *Works Management, 52*(9), 52–55.

Ecker, R. (1985). *The stress myth: Why the pressures of life don't have to get you down.* Downers Grove, IL: InterVarsity Press.

Flaherty, J. (1998). *Coaching: Evoking excellence in others.* Woburn, MA: Butterworth-Heinemann.

Frankl, V.E. (1963). *Man's search for meaning: An introduction to logotherapy.* Boston, MA: Beacon.

Harrison, R. (1984). *Guidelines for fear reduction in conflict situations.* Unpublished manuscript.

Harrison, R. (1993). *Quotes on healing and learning.* Unpublished manuscript.

Harrison, R. (1995a). *Consultant's journey: A dance of work and spirit.* San Francisco, CA: Jossey-Bass.

Harrison, R. (1995b). *The collected papers of Roger Harrison.* San Francisco, CA: Jossey-Bass.

Harrison, R. (1997). *Becoming an agent of healing in the transformation of business.* Unpublished manuscript.

Harrison, R. (2000a). *Organizational healing.* Unpublished manuscript.

Harrison, R. (2000b). *Towards the learning organization.* Unpublished manuscript.

Harrison, R., & Stokes, H. (1992). *Diagnosing organization culture.* San Francisco, CA: Jossey-Bass/Pfeiffer.

Harvey, J.B. (1988). *The Abilene paradox and other meditations on management.* San Francisco, CA: Jossey-Bass.

Harvey, J.B. (1999). *How come every time I get stabbed in the back my fingerprints are on the knife? And other meditations on management.* San Francisco, CA: Jossey-Bass.

Hawk, K. (1998). Maintaining a winning team. *Catalog Age, 15,* 163–164.

Jaques, E. (1976). *A general theory of bureaucracy.* Burlington, VT: Ashgate.

Kreitzer, D. (2000, May 13). *What I learned about change I learned in practice, not from the literature.* Available: www.bsu.edu/teachers/department/edld/conf/ [last accessed 4/27/01]

Matson, E. (1996). Special work-stress section. *Fast Company, 6,* 142–147.

McGuigan, F.J. (1997). Edmund Jacobson award and memorial lecture. *International Journal of Stress Management, 4*(4), 291–295.

Murray, W. (1990, July). True healing: An experience of the heart—An interview with Steven Levine. *Science of Mind Magazine,* 18–29.

Nadler, D.A. (1998). *Champions of change: How CEOs and their companies are mastering the skills of radical change.* San Francisco, CA: Jossey-Bass.

Owen, H. (1997). *Open space technology: A user's guide.* San Francisco, CA: Berrett-Koehler.

Reese, S. (1999). Healthy minds have great ideas. *Business and Health, 17*(12), 16–17.

Schein, E. (1988). *Process consultation, Vol. 1: Its role in organization development.* Reading, MA: Addison-Wesley.

Smit, I., & Schabracq, M. (1997). Stress, performance, and organizational culture. *International Journal of Stress Management, 4,* 275–295.

Stein, M. (1986). *In midlife: A Jungian perspective.* Dallas, TX: Spring Publications.

The Stress Doc. (2000, May). *Five keys for managing change and reducing burnout.* Available: www.stressdoc.com/five_keys.htm [last accessed 4/27/01]

The Stress Doc Letter. (1998, February). *The stress doc letter.* Available: www.stressdoc.com/news2982.htm [last accessed 4/27/01]

Weisbord, M.R., & Janoff S. (1999). *Future search: An action guide to finding common ground in organizations and communities.* San Francisco, CA: Berrett-Koehler.

Beverly J. Nyberg *is currently a doctoral student in the Graduate School of Education and Human Development at the George Washington University in Washington, D.C. Her focus is on organizational culture, health, and healing. She has thirty years of experience working with not-for-profit service agencies, much of which has been in an international setting. She has also facilitated reconciliation dialogue.*

Roger Harrison *is a pioneer practitioner in the field of organization development. He has participated in and contributed to nearly every phase of its growth—from survey research and team building to large systems change and organization transformation. He is a noted author of training programs, books, and articles, including* Collected Papers of Roger Harrison *(Jossey-Bass, 1995) and* Consultant's Journey: A Dance of Work and Spirit *(Jossey-Bass, 1995). Retired from his consulting practice, Dr. Harrison is active in community organizing from his home on Whidbey Island, Washington.*

THE ROLE OF THE EXECUTIVE COACH

Barbara Pate Glacel

Abstract: Executive coaching allows high-potential managers and executives the opportunity to learn faster, perform better, and obtain more job satisfaction. Coaches act as counselors, confidants, teachers, advisors, sounding boards, reality checks, or extra eyes and ears. The foundation for executive coaching is built on trust and confidentiality. When performed correctly, coaching provides a return on investment with better decisions, better planning, better interpersonal skills, improved leadership, and higher productivity.

EXECUTIVE COACHING

In 21st Century organizations, the use of an executive coach is becoming more commonplace. The increased use of executive coaches reflects the current times, which are characterized by constant change and by executives and informal leaders facing situations they have not encountered before, where there is no set pathway to success. Moreover, the profile of those in management positions in organizations is more often that of a technical wizard than of someone with management and leadership training. A coach offers an organizational and strategic perspective to the application of technical know-how.

WHY COACHING IS NEEDED

Organizations invest in coaches for their executives and high-potential performers for one simple reason—an immediate return on investment. A coach offers a test bed to analyze potential actions, both before and during implementation. In the chaotic business world of continuous change, situations without precedent are often confronted. The organization's goal in handling these situations is to minimize the chance of making mistakes and to maximize the opportunity to learn from mistakes. As an objective outsider, the coach often sees both advantages and pitfalls not foreseen by inside executives.

An executive coach shortens the learning curve for new employees and high-potential employees in new positions. A coach works specifically with an individual to introduce new information, organizational know-how, or advanced technical expertise to bring a new employee or new manager quickly up to speed, decreasing the time required before an employee can make an effective contribution.

An executive coach helps to broaden the executive's view. By looking systemically across the organization or at the organization in relation to the marketplace, the coach offers a different perspective to the insider. This brings more data to decision making, allowing for more informed decisions.

A coach works individually with clients on specific behavioral goals and skill building. This focused approach makes the most of the executive's time by addressing individual needs, rather than using a broad approach to general leadership development. By setting specific time-bound goals, the coach works continually to assess an individual's progress and to evaluate achievement of goals.

The coach provides a sounding board to executives who find it lonely at the top. Often, sensitive business and personnel decisions cannot be discussed within the organization, so a coach becomes a confidential advisor to executives to prevent decisions being made in isolation.

Finally, a coach helps the transition from specialist to generalist. Organizations typically promote outstanding performers in areas of their particular specialty. The skills that made these specialists top performers are not the same skills they need to be successful as managers of people and organizational decision makers. A coach offers a broader perspective to the specialist, teaching in real time as new organizational challenges are confronted.

WHO CAN USE AN EXECUTIVE COACH?

The use of an executive coach is a sign of strength, not a sign of weakness. Knowing what one does not know and seeking assistance is more realistic and leads to greater success than pretending that one knows all—an impossibility in today's business environment.

High-potential employees who are on the "fast track" are ideal candidates for executive coaching. A high-potential employee who is given too much responsibility too soon may well derail and never achieve his or her potential. A coach can provide added insight, allow reflection about the lessons of experience, and even slow down the too-fast promotions that leave a void in one's leadership foundation.

High-tech experts are often promoted because of their technical brilliance. However, at higher levels in organizations, a different kind of know-how is the key to success. At these levels, leadership skills, the ability to build teams, and strategic vision are the most important. A coach can be used to help high-tech experts make the transition from the narrow view of technology to the broader view of organizational success.

For those with little practical experience in a career field, an executive coach can provide a personalized acclimatization. For instance, an academic moving into industry or a government employee moving into the private sector might have the perfect set of skills for a position, but not the practical experience to deal with the environment. The coach adds insight and a reality check as to whether particular actions fit within a new culture or career field.

Executive coaching is also often effective for high performers who have poor interpersonal skills. In environments in which work is accomplished in teams, in which influence skills are important, and in which one is dependent on others to accomplish a task, interpersonal skills may make or break an executive. The coach can teach such skills as communication, listening, conflict resolution, negotiation, and influence techniques.

Executive coaching may sometimes be paired with executive search. When a senior person is hired through a search firm, there is little time for the new employee to get up to speed. One is expected to "hit the deck running." By pairing a new executive with an executive coach for the first few months of the job, the new employee becomes immediately productive at the task, while the coach is able to scope out the landscape of the organizational politics and advise the executive along the way.

What Executive Coaching Includes

Executive coaches must be good listeners, have good experience in business or a particular skill in which they coach, and the ability to reflect on experience to learn from it. Often, however, a coach is chosen because the "chemistry" between the coach and the client just seems right. A very skilled coach may not be successful with some clients because there is a personality "disconnect." So both skills and chemistry are important in choosing an executive coach. After that, there are two basic tenets to successful executive coaching: trust and confidentiality. The client must be assured that conversations with the coach remain absolutely confidential. As that behavior is proven, then trust grows.

If, after the coach and client have had an opportunity to meet and get to know one another a bit, they both decide that they want to pursue the coaching relationship, then the coach needs more in-depth information about the client, and the client may need more information about what it will be like to be coached. A good introduction to a coaching intervention is a behavioral interview between the coach and the executive. Information learned during the interview will allow the coach to get to know the client, to understand holistically who the person is, both at home and at work, and to hear how the client defines himself or herself. Suggested questions and discussion starters for the interview include the following:

- Describe your personal background.
- How do you describe yourself?
- How would others describe you?
- Describe your strengths.

- Describe your weaknesses.

- What has been your greatest success?

- What has been your biggest failure?

- Describe a typical interpersonal transaction with someone at work.

- What makes you angry or frustrated?

- What are your personal goals?

- Describe the balance in your life.

- Describe your family relationships.

- Describe your key business relationships.

- What feedback have you received in previous jobs and on performance reviews?

Another method for getting to know the client is through the administration of a personality inventory such as the Myers Briggs Type Indicator® or another typological questionnaire. An understanding of the client's preferences for behavior provides a basis for recommending individualized activities, skill development, or training. Another helpful survey for a coaching client who has been in the job for a period of time is a 360-degree assessment survey. Feedback on the survey from boss, subordinates, and peers provides specific areas for focus.

A coach will be most effective with knowledge of the business situation and the key players. This information can be gathered through interviews with those individuals, through briefings on the organizational mission, or by reading annual reports and organizational documents. A thorough indoctrination might include 360-degree interviews with the client's boss, subordinates, and peers. Such interviews would provide the coach with an understanding of the business, the business relationships, and the client's strengths and weaknesses and could offer a snapshot of organizational health.

The coach may employ a shadowing technique to see the client in action. Two or three days of accompanying the client to meetings, watching interpersonal interactions, analyzing communications, and looking for behavioral patterns provides information for valuable feedback to the client. The coach may offer specific advice on meeting management, time management, interpersonal communication, presentations, and a variety of real-time management needs.

Having established a firm foundation of trust with a thorough knowledge of the client's work behaviors and business environment, the coach may then begin the regular practice of coaching. For best results, coaching should last for a minimum of six months; it can last longer at the client's request. The coach and the client should meet on a regular basis, preferably weekly. Coaching sessions may be done in person or by telephone. Topics may be real-time situations for which the client wants a sounding board or particular advice. Over time, skill development may be undertaken. The coach and client set specific goals and set a time line for implementing new behaviors, learning new skills, or assessing ongoing needs.

Over time, the coach may be a counselor, a confidant, a teacher, a sounding board, a reality check, an advisor, or an extra pair of eyes and ears.

POSSIBLE PITFALLS OF EXECUTIVE COACHING

An executive coach must remember at all times that the goal is to make the executive more successful. The coach must not become more visible than the client. The client may learn from the coach and may take advice from the coach, but the client is always the one to act. The coach must stay in the background.

The coach must always maintain complete confidentiality. Although the coach may know or even work with others in the organization, it is never acceptable to talk about a client to anyone else. By drawing firm boundaries around the coach-client relationship, a coach can continue to be effective, even with multiple clients in the same organization. Breaking confidentiality is a breach of trust.

The coach is not a therapist. In filling the roles of counselor or confidant, the coach may sometimes flirt with the practice of therapy. However, effective coaches recognize the line between business advisor and psychological analyst. Coaches may work on such personal issues as balance, satisfaction, or motivation, but coaching is not therapy.

It is important for the coach to remain objective and impartial. The coach can present alternatives and analyze the advantages and disadvantages of particular actions. The decision maker, however, must be the client; he or she must decide what action to take based on reasons that make personal sense.

RETURN ON INVESTMENT

Executive coaching produces measurable business results by way of increased productivity, higher job satisfaction, and better decision making. Executives who utilize coaches do less "shooting from the hip" when making business decisions. They tend to have more well-thought-out plans because they have discussed them with an impartial and objective outsider.

New executives learn their jobs and their organizations faster by working with coaches to assess the lay of the land. They become productive faster because they are more comfortable in the new setting.

High-potential managers become more confident as they learn the skills required to perform at higher level jobs. Job satisfaction increases as managers and executives improve their skills, their relationships, and their decisions and see positive results of their actions.

Barbara Pate Glacel, Ph.D., is principal of Glacel Development Group of Virginia. She is author of a business best-seller on teams. She works with individuals, teams, and organizations in the Fortune 500 and not-for-profit arenas. She has over thirty years' experience in coaching and teaching leaders at all levels of organizations. Dr. Glacel is a well-known author and public speaker and has consulted in Europe, Asia, and South Africa.

TWENTY-ONE WAYS TO DELIGHT YOUR CUSTOMERS

Peter R. Garber

Abstract: Truly delighting customers must be the ultimate goal of anyone who works in business today, especially consultants. A delighted customer is better
advertisement than any amount of money could buy.
A delighted customer keeps doing business with you
and tells others to do the same. But delighted customers don't just happen. The twenty-one ways to
delight customers presented in this article help ensure that consultants are doing the right things. As
the article shows, delighting customers doesn't have
to be overly complicated or complex. Often the simplest things are ultimately most important to customers. These twenty-one ways are presented to help
consultants achieve the level of customer service and
satisfaction that will not only delight customers but
keep them calling for consulting services for many
years to come.

1. Exceed Your Customers' Requirements

It isn't often that we are pleasantly surprised by getting more value from a purchase than we expected. Unfortunately, too often it is just the opposite. We find that we are disappointed with what we get for our money and most likely take our business elsewhere. But what happens on those rare occasions when someone does exceed your expectations? You probably continue to do business with that supplier and tell others about your delightful experience!

Exceeding customers' requirements can help ensure their continued business more than any other single factor. Give customers more advice and services than contracted for and you'll see great returns on this investment. However, to achieve this goal, you must fully understand customers' expectations and requirements. Find out exactly what service each customer expects of you. Ensure that you know what materials are desired and the amount of time you are expected to spend on a particular project. If a customer wants ten copies of something, bring a few extra just in case someone else shows up and needs one. You might even throw in some extra consulting time just to make sure you are exceeding a customer's expectations.

Often customers' expectations are not met because of a lack of understanding of what their requirements might be, rather than from a supplier's lack of ability to achieve the objectives. Do you fully understand your customers' expectations? First, develop a clear understanding of their expectations and then develop plans to not only meet but to exceed them. Give customers a pleasant surprise and deliver more to them than they expect. Both of you will be delighted with the results.

2. Be a Good Listener

Most people would say that learning to be a good listener is the greatest challenge they face in communicating with others. Being a good listener is not always something that comes naturally to people. Listening is a learned skill that requires both time and patience to acquire. One must really want to listen to what the other person has to say. As Stephen Covey (1990) explains in his book, *The 7 Habits of Highly Effective People*, we must seek first to understand, then to be understood. It is only then that we really understand what others are trying to tell us.

As a consultant, it is even more important that you be a good listener. Through communicating with your customers you can learn what they really want and how to keep their business. All you really have to do is listen. It is important that your customers feel you understand their needs. If not, they may seek out another consultant who does. To be a better listener, try this exercise. Restate exactly what you believe the agreement is between you and your customer. Ask the customer if what you've just said accurately reflects the agreement as he or she understands it. If not, discuss any issues that the customer raises and then restate the agreement until the customer is satisfied. This way, you can both be sure that you have a completely accurate understanding of your agreement. Make sure there are no misunderstandings about time, place, duration, materials, and so on.

Your customers need to know that you care enough to listen to what they have to say. Although it may not always seem like it, the best way to communicate your commitment to the customer is by listening, rather than by talking. This way the customer will know that you are interested in his or her needs. Remember that God gave you two ears and only one mouth. Perhaps He was trying to give you a message about the importance of listening.

3. Take Care of the Little Things

Often the little extra things truly delight the customer. To benefit from this idea, you must first determine what these seemingly little but important things might be and then ensure that you provide them. It might be nothing more than remembering a certain detail concerning a product specification or some other aspect of their business. It might be remembering someone's name or something that someone told you. It might be some small detail that could easily have been forgotten. Keep a notebook to record details and stay on top of them.

Your taking care of little things also gives the customer more confidence in you. It shows the customer that you are paying attention to his or her needs and are interested in doing the best job that you possibly can. Just think about how it makes you feel when a supplier misses a detail or forgets something, even if it is relatively small or insignificant. You might start wondering what other more important things this supplier has forgotten! Your customers feel the same way. Make sure that you are paying attention to all of their needs and requirements, especially the little things. Customers remember personalized treatment most when making future decisions about where to take their business.

4. BE INNOVATIVE

Being innovative means that you think "outside the box," that is, you go beyond the usual constraints or limitations that might exist. Innovators are never satisfied with the status quo. They look for different ways to do things. Innovation is what allows us to grow and develop continually.

Your customers want you to be innovative when it is appropriate to do so. You must recognize those circumstances. Perhaps you need to provide a different type of training than in the past. Or you might recommend an entirely different set of goals relating to a problem or project. Take your consulting to a different place or at different times with different goals in mind. You might just surprise everyone with the results. One consultant took a team of managers to the top of a mountain with breathtaking vistas to develop the company's long-term vision. Inspired by this setting, they set more aggressive goals than ever before and reached every one of them. Innovation is what can help you stand out in the crowd. *Innovation can put you a step ahead of the rest. It allows you to provide tomorrow's solutions to your customers' problems today.*

Dare to imagine what is possible. Think of ways in which you could provide your customers with an innovative approach to serving their needs. Who knows? You might just come up with a new idea that completely changes the way everyone does business in the future!

5. PAY ATTENTION TO DETAILS

An old television commercial company proudly proclaimed, "We sweat the details!" This ad was effective because it told the company's customers that the company was committed to taking care of all the many details necessary to provide a quality product and service. From the customers' perspective, these are details that they assume will be taken care of. Make sure that you meet customer deadlines, complete reports when due, and perform any set-up activities or research that you can. The more details you can take care of for a customer, the more he or she can focus on other more strategic matters. Become an expert on the details that your customer has to deal with, and that customer will never want to be without your services.

The bottom line is that customers don't want to worry about details contracted to a consultant. They feel, rightfully so, that this is what they are paying for. The ultimate goal should be that your customers are not even aware of the details.

But of course, details don't take care of themselves. Paying attention to details does require a certain amount of hard work on your part, but it can yield excellent results, including customers who feel assured that there won't be any unpleasant surprises. As a result of their confidence in your ability to take care of details of the consulting contract, they can focus on details concerned with delighting their own customers.

6. KNOW YOUR CUSTOMER'S BUSINESS

It is not enough to simply have an understanding of your customer's business. You also must understand how that business interrelates with their customers' businesses. Thus, knowing your business also means knowing your customer's customers' businesses. *This is one circumstance where "Mind your own business" does not apply.* Be mindful of your customer's business just the same as you would your own. Learn about the most important elements and keep current.

Learning as much as you can about your customers' businesses helps you earn their trust and confidence. It also shows that you care and are motivated to serve their needs. Frequently ask your customers about their businesses. Add to their own understanding of the variables in their businesses whenever possible through your other contacts and sources. Read the customers' literature and company reports, look them up on the Internet, visit their home pages, be knowledgeable about their products, services, locations, and operations. Learn the terminology that people in the company use and be prepared to "talk the talk." This will make you an even more valuable resource. You may be able to bring to light ideas not apparent to your customers. This is perhaps the most important service you can provide for your customers—providing an outsider's point of view. This would be analogous to preventing your customers from not being able to see the "forest for the trees." Help your customers see forests of opportunities. This will surely be a source of delight for them.

7. Be Accessible

Don't play hide-and-seek or hard to get; be as accessible as possible. Today this doesn't mean that you have to sit by the telephone waiting for a customer to call. *Particularly with all the communications technology available today, there really isn't any reason for you to be out of touch with your customers, no matter where you are.* Tools such as pagers, voice-mail systems, electronic mail, cellular phones, and fax machines can help keep you available.

Let your customers know how to reach you via these tools. If you are not immediately available when a customer tries to reach you, get back to the customer as soon as possible. If there will be any significant delay before you can respond to the customer, let him or her know this as well. Send the customer an email or leave a voice-mail message that you are not available at the moment but will contact him or her as soon as you are able. It is also a good idea to let customers know when they can expect to hear from you; be sure to make contact by the time promised. When you are able to reach the customer, as a courtesy you may want to explain what you were previously committed to doing that prevented your immediate response, particularly if you were being of service to someone else. This way your customers will know that they can expect this same commitment when you are being of service to them.

8. Find Ways to Save Customers' Money

Nothing delights customers like saving money. *The more ways you are able to save your customers money, the more delighted they will be with you and your consulting services.* The best way to do this is to think of your customers' money as if it were your own.

If you know of a more economical or efficient way of providing your service, then by all means suggest it. If you know of discounts, rebates, government financial aid, special loans, shortcuts, contacts, brokerages, licenses, and so on that could save your customers money, be sure to tell them. Explain how and why these methods will save them money. Of course, also assure your customers that saving money does not mean that they have to sacrifice quality. If there is any change in your services as a result of these savings, then communicate this to the customers, who can decide whether the savings are of value to them or not. This last point is very important. Don't ever surprise your customers with any change in services without first advising them about the change, even if it saves them money. If they are not informed ahead of time, they may be less than delighted. They may have reasons that you are not aware of for keeping things the same. Thus, discuss the issue from the very beginning!

9. Don't Waste Customers' Time

As they say, time is money. Time is one of the scarcest resources available in business today. For the same reasons you shouldn't waste a customer's money, you shouldn't waste his or her time. It seems that there is so much to do in order to operate a successful business and so little time to do it. This is particularly true in streamlined and downsized organizations that many of your customers may operate today.

Because your customers are so busy, it is more important than ever that you not waste their time. *Treat your customers' time as being as valuable as your own.* Only ask your customers to invest their time with you if it is important and beneficial for them to do so. Once you have your customers' time, use it wisely and to their advantage. Get straight to the point. Don't make customers spend more time than is absolutely necessary. Do your homework and don't ask questions you could research on your own. Let the customer know just how resourceful you can really be. For example, one consultant found out important information about his customer's own capabilities that the customer wasn't even aware of, which in turn resulted in an important project being completed more easily and quickly.

10. Synergize with the Customer

When you have synergy, the whole is greater than the sum of its parts. In other words, synergy means $1 + 1 > 2$. When you and your customer create synergy, both of you are better as a result. *Synergy can allow both you and your customer to achieve goals not possible if you were working independently.* It is like what happens when you nail two boards together. The combined strength of the boards will hold more weight than the combined weight of what each board could support alone. Similarly, synergy between you and your customer can help make both of your businesses stronger.

Synergy creates the strongest customer and supplier partnerships. It is the ultimate win/win relationship you can have with your customers. Look for opportunities to create synergy. Sometimes this may require you to be creative or imaginative. Or you may offer your customer additional resources, such as clerical support or technical expertise, to help you both achieve your goals. Synergy doesn't always come easy, but the results are well worth the effort.

11. BE PROACTIVE

To be proactive means that you are always looking ahead and anticipating problems before they occur. A good consultant stays one step ahead of the game, stays on top of things, and prevents problems before they occur. *It is still true that an ounce of prevention is worth a pound of cure.* Sometimes being proactive involves anticipating your customers' needs before they even realize what they are! Your customers will appreciate your being proactive and even learn to depend on that. They will look to you to let them know what they need to do to avoid problems.

Sometimes being proactive may be difficult. There are seemingly more urgent things to attend to that will push your proactive efforts to the back burner. But being proactive may be the best thing you can do for your customers. For example, you might suggest that the customer offer a particular training program to employees months before it is absolutely needed. This way, when the need for the training does arrive, the customer won't be in a state of panic trying to put everyone through the program. Your customers may never fully understand just how many problems you helped them avoid as a result of your foresight, but nevertheless they will be delighted.

12. APPRECIATE YOUR CUSTOMERS' PERSPECTIVES

Sometimes, we only appreciate our own perspective on things. We look only at how we are personally affected. This is a natural tendency. However, when interacting with customers, you need an appreciation for their perspectives as well as your own. Put yourself in your customers' shoes to see how you would feel in their situations. Don't just view your business interactions from a consultant's point of view, but look at them from the customers' as well. *Ask yourself this question: "If I were in this customer's situation, would I listen to this advice?"*

Think about the factors that would affect a particular decision. Which of them influence a customer's decision to use a consultant? Which would influence a customer not to use your services? How many of these influencers are within your control and what can you do to change them? How can having a better understanding of your customer's perspective help to provide him or her with better services or products?

13. Value Your Relationships with Your Customers

If you expect any repeat consulting business, value your relationships with your customers. Invest time building these relationships and getting to know them better. Customers also like to know something about the consultants to whom they give their business. The more your customers feel you know about them, the more they will feel that you understand their needs and can meet these needs.

Show your customers that you appreciate working with them. This may involve a simple thank-you gesture or some other appropriate recognition that demonstrates your appreciation. Perhaps you could give a customer some kind of incentive to do future business with you. Whatever the case, the most important thing is to let customers know how important they are to you and how much you value your working relationships.

14. Reduce Hassles for Your Customers

One of the most important things you can do for your customers is to make it easy for them to do business with you. The last thing a customer wants is more hassles. Reducing hassles might involve eliminating excessive paperwork, steps, processes, approvals, or other red tape. Search for ways to simplify things for your customers. The more hassles you can eliminate, the happier they will be.

"Don't worry about that; I'll take care of it" are some of the most delightful words *that your customers can hear.* Say this to them as often as possible. Of course, just saying it isn't enough; you also must make good on your promises. Ultimately, your ability to provide the most hassle-free consulting services possible determines whether you will get return business.

15. Be Honest (It's Still the Best Policy)

Although we read and hear about crime, scandals, and fraud nearly every day, honesty is still the best policy, not only in business but in our personal lives. Treating customers honestly should be a priority. *Customers want and deserve to be treated honestly. They must be assured that they are receiving their money's worth and are receiving exactly what they were promised.* Nothing displeases customers more than to feel they are being "ripped off" or cheated in some way. Under these circumstances, not only will they take their business elsewhere but they will tell others to do the same. Honesty goes beyond delivering what a customer paid for; it also involves being honest in your communications and relationships. For instance, if you make a mistake or inadvertently give a customer incorrect information, let him or her know about it as quickly as possible. Customers will generally forgive an honest mistake, but not an outright deception. Always be completely honest with your customers. Do exactly what you say you will do, and don't commit to that which you cannot do. A consultant's livelihood is based on reputation. Getting a reputation for being anything less than honest is disastrous.

16. Link with Your Customers Electronically

Just as there are any number of ways to be accessible to customers via the high-tech communications equipment available today, so too are there countless ways to be linked electronically with your customers. These new tools provide ultra-convenient methods to transfer information. Both you and your customers can have the benefit of immediate access to "real time" data. This can provide tremendous advantages over the old days, in which data was compiled into reports that were frequently outdated before they were received.

The Internet has forever changed the way we access information. Whole new worlds of information are now instantly available to us. Many companies are also creating their own intranets, secure sites on which they provide information about their organizations to their employees. Assuming your customers will grant you access to their intranets, this is an excellent source of information that can allow you to serve your customers' needs better.

There are also many other electronic communication tools that allow you to link with customers, including voice-mailbox telephone systems, electronic organizers, and local area computer networks. *Your customers want you to keep current with these new technologies in order to stay in touch with them.*

17. Add Value for Customers

You need to add value for your customers, rather than becoming just an additional expense. There is a big difference between the two. Expenses are simply costs that customers pay without any expectation of return for their money. *When money is spent on something that adds value for a customer, something positive is gained as a result.* Your customers should view doing business with you as adding value. If they do, they will continue to do business with you.

Find ways to add value for your customers. Think of ways that customers can obtain a greater return on their investment. Suggest ways that customers can maximize the services you provide. Help customers measure the effectiveness of your services and/or any training you provide. Show customers ways that the benefits of your services could be communicated to the top management of their organizations. One consultant developed an Excel® spreadsheet showing all the various calculations and computations that could go into measuring the effectiveness of his consulting services, such as time saved and increased efficiencies. The customer continued to use the spreadsheet every time he utilized the services of any outside sources.

How can you help your customers turn expenses into investments? Sometimes this might involve spending even more money. Although this might sound contradictory, it isn't so far-fetched. Are there circumstances in which this might be the case for your customers? How can you help them realize this added value? Sometimes the best service you can provide is helping customers realize that value isn't always what's cheapest or what has the most immediate returns. Ultimately, they will appreciate your helping them realize the difference.

18. Honor Your Commitments, Big or Small

Make good on your promises to your customers, big or small. *The little things we say we will do are often most important to other people.* The problem is that these also are the types of things that are easily overlooked or forgotten in the midst of the myriad of other commitments. So if you said you would make a call or check on something, then do it. Remember, those who are expecting you to follow through won't so easily forget, especially your customers.

Think about some of the commitments that you may have made to your customers. Do you only pay attention to the big commitments and overlook the smaller ones? Might your customers not notify you about these oversights because they're small or relatively insignificant? Or might they be upset that they didn't get something promised to them or that they expected? Your not remembering or fulfilling a small commitment could cause a customer to question your ability to honor a more significant commitment. Remember, big or small, a commitment is still a commitment.

19. ALWAYS FOLLOW THROUGH

It is important to follow through when providing any consulting services. *Without follow-through, you only have completed half the job.* Sometimes follow-through might occur immediately. For example, you might provide your customers with additional information about using your service or request that they complete a questionnaire for quality assurance purposes. At other times follow-through may need to occur after some period of time. Follow-through also involves closing "loops." This means that you make sure that there isn't anything left undone, particularly something that could cause future problems for a customer. Give your customer a follow-up call to ensure everything is going the way he or she expects. Check on the results of your work and update the customer frequently on the status of your project.

Your customers will also appreciate the fact that you continue to show interest in them, even after the consultative services are completed. This type of service keeps customers coming back and brings new ones in the future. Follow-through is one of those things that can really delight your customers.

20. KNOW WHEN "NO" MEANS "NO"

There is an old saying in business that you should never accept a customer's first "no." When a customer says "no," it is sometimes said, what he or she really means is, "I don't yet have enough information to make a buying decision, and you need to provide me with more facts about your consulting service."

Although there may be some benefit and even truth to this advice, it may not always serve you well. Learn the difference between when a customer needs more information and when a customer really means that he or she isn't interested in buying. This can be a very difficult distinction to make. Sometimes failing to try to help a customer understand the benefits of your consulting service could cost you a sale. On the other hand, becoming a nuisance or even an irritant to a prospective customer would obviously also negatively affect future chances of doing business with this customer. To understand the difference, listen very carefully to what "no" really means and react accordingly. If you are told "no," ask whether you can help in some other way not directly related to your consulting services. This will let a customer know that you are interested in helping him or her under any circumstance. *If a potential customer really isn't interested in your consulting services today, don't ruin your chances of doing business together in the future. If you can't make a sale, then make a friend.*

21. Be a Contingency Thinker

Being a contingency thinker means always having a back-up plan. This way you are fully prepared for anything that can happen. This is not to say that you should expect problems to occur—actually quite the contrary. As part of your contingency thinking, look for ways to prevent problems from occurring in the first place. *The best contingency plan is the one that you never need to use.*

Sometimes it may be beneficial to let your customers know about your contingency plans. For instance, tell them exactly what they should do if the original plan doesn't work out. Be ready to step in with another plan developed for just such a situation. For example, one consultant helped launch the introduction of a new product for a large customer. At the press meeting announcing the product, the computer they were going to use for the presentation wouldn't work. The consultant had pre-loaded the presentation on another computer just in case and saved the company a great deal of embarrassment and possible harm to the rollout of the new product.

This kind of forethought will ensure that customers feel confident that you are able to provide them with uninterrupted service. Your customers will learn that they can depend on your delivering the quality they have become accustomed to receiving from you. Contingencies are like a safety net for your customers. Just like a high-wire circus act, you work hard every day to make sure you don't lose your balance. But if you ever do, it is nice to know there is something to catch your fall. Your customers will feel better too!

CONCLUSION

Twenty-one ways to delight your customers were presented to help you build stronger working relationships with customers. Ultimately, your customers' delight will be based on their relationships with you. These relationships must be built on trust, and you must earn this trust each and every day you do business together. The twenty-one ways represent many of the most important qualities that your customers expect of you as a consultant. *Use these twenty-one ways on a regular or, even better, on a daily basis to help keep your customers delighted with you.*

Good luck and keep on delighting your customers!

Reference

Covey, S. (1990). *The 7 habits of highly effective people.* New York: Fireside.

Peter R. Garber is manager of Affirmative Action for PPG Industries, Inc., in Pittsburgh, Pennsylvania. He is the author of five management books, including his most recent work, Turbulent Change: Every Working Person's Survival Guide, *and is a regular contributor of activities and learning instruments to the* Annuals.

INFLUENCE:
KEY TO THE DOOR OF LEADERSHIP

Marlene Caroselli

Abstract: Yesterday's command-and-control management style no longer works. Today's empowered
employee responds less to demands and more to
direction. Being empowered, that employee is ready,
willing, and more than able to assume a leadership
role. Consequently—whether you serve in a managerial capacity and/or in a leadership capacity—you
need to influence others in order to effect the outcomes you envision.

In this article, you'll learn the importance of
defining terms; making choices; influencing 24/7;
speaking the languages of influence; leading by influence, not authority; getting results by improving
relationships; and developing influential and ethical awareness.

DEFINING TERMS

It's easy to influence. It's much harder to influence with integrity. Part of the difficulty lies in the many possible definitions of key words, such as "integrity." Is it, as the dictionary denotes, a question of honesty? Is it a matter of sincerity or of uprightness, as the dictionary also suggests? Would you perhaps equate integrity with sound moral principles? If so, what exactly are those principles?

Some people regard integrity as the decision to live according to the Golden Rule: "Do unto others as you would have them do unto you." Is this your belief as well? And what if you were seeking to measure your degree of integrity as well as define it? Would you assess your actions as ethical ones if they brought improvement to existing situations? If not, what gauge would you use? The questions leading to a definition of integrity are multiple and mingled; they overlap with many other factors.

In the simplest sense, "integrity" means living according to specified values. But, of course, simplicity is usually deceptively complex. Living by specified values involves complex ramifications and interpretations. The definition of integrity that we endorse has ever-widening circles. The more integrity you demonstrate, the more widespread the benefits to others.

In other words, when you act with integrity, you are widening the sphere of influence; you are using power tools to achieve powerful benefits for those who "buy" your concepts or your commodities. If your actions are taken for your own advantage exclusively, you are following a narrow moral code, one that places your needs above all others. You no doubt operate within the letter of the law, but perhaps not within the spirit of the unwritten laws that govern our behavior as human beings. If your actions are self-serving, you are not concerned with serving others. Consequently, your ethical influence is limited.

On the other hand, when your actions benefit other people, you are operating from a higher-level moral code; you are living by and influencing others with generally accepted principles of correctness, rather than by your own interpretation of specific rules.

Unlike morality, which implies a codified sense of ethics—an acknowledged system to which many people subscribe—integrity is an individual consideration. Consequently, achieving clarity on integrity is much harder than achieving clarity on influence. But once you have made the choices that lead to clarity, you can consciously take ethical actions—actions that reflect the principles by which you wish to live. Having grasped what integrity is, you'll proceed to use it in your efforts to influence others in honorable ways.

Remember though, the second sentence in this article: "It's much harder to influence with integrity." Don't think that, once you have managed to define "integrity," the definition will last a lifetime. Integrity, in truth, is a slow-moving target. Think about it. Over the years, haven't you shifted some of your views, in keeping the maxim that "a foolish consistency is the hobgoblin of little minds"? Some of those views probably involved the definition of what it means to act with integrity.

MAKING CHOICES

The events or encounters that occur even after you have finally defined integrity to your satisfaction keep the target in a state of slow flux. These events and encounters may be significant enough to force you to rethink your definition. You may have determined your personal set of principles, but when those principles are put to the test, you may find they are not steadfast after all. Or you may find that your principles do not apply to other people. Or that certain factors cause a given principle to recede in importance. You may even modify your definition to include certain behaviors that have gained greater significance in your life. Having been betrayed by a friend or an employer, for example, you may now decide that keeping one's word is a critical aspect of integrity.

Psychologists have a name for these below-the-surface rumblings in our mental terrain: "cognitive dissonance." In other words, you may have determined for yourself what actions fall within the acceptable realm as far as integrity is concerned. To be sure, it is important to make these determinations. Otherwise, you may find yourself in a state of emotional disequilibrium. But then you receive information that upsets what you've come to believe is true. You are thrown off balance, so to speak, by the information that runs contrary to the belief system you've established. Your ethical "wholeness" now has a crack in it.

To illustrate, let's assume you have placed various individuals in either the acceptable or the non-acceptable area on the integrity spectrum on the basis of their actions. Then you learn that someone you regard as a person of high moral character has done something you consider unethical. You actually have several options available to you in order to change your mental "dissonance" to "consonance."

You can refuse to believe the story you are hearing, thus maintaining the image you have of this person. Or you can relax your standards, perhaps even redefining what integrity means to you, in order to keep this person's behavior within the realm of acceptability. Finally, you could decide to shift your opinion of this individual from the high end of your integrity scale to the lower end. But resolution of some kind is necessary. Otherwise, you will continue to experience psychological discomfort. Such discomfort makes it difficult to lead or to be led.

Let's look at another example. If you were asked what core values you abide by, would you be able to express them without hesitation? Many people would find this question a challenging one, to be sure. Having lived through recent eras such as the Me Generation, the Greed-Is-Good era, and a Scandal-in-Government era, you may find yourself wondering more than ever before how steady your moral compass really is. When you read that approval ratings for dishonest politicians continue to soar or that stock prices continue to climb despite charges of unethical practices against corporate leaders, you may even wonder if the integrity component of the leadership personality is as important as you've always thought it was.

Current events force us to grapple with questions just like these. We choose our leaders in part because we believe them to be men and women who act with integrity, which in the eyes of many is an integral aspect of leadership. When we learn they are alleged to have done things we regard as unethical, perhaps even immoral, we have to make some tough choices. Do we still support such individuals? Do we revamp our opinions of them? Do we widen the borders surrounding appropriate behaviors? Do we remove certain actions from our previous definition, regarding them as unimportant after all? Do we decide that the person can still be an effective/successful leader despite transgressions because the economy is strong and/or because the nation is at peace?

Our basic moral foundation was formed early in our childhood. But experience and events cause it to undergo periodic revisions. Think of the childhood and young-adult experiences that shaped your ethical view of the world. Would you want your children growing up with the moral outlook that you depended on to guide your actions? In what ways has your belief system changed to accommodate today's world? Once you entered the world of work, did you find a fit between your beliefs and the culture in which you worked? Depending on your answers to these and other questions, you make choices—important choices—about the way you choose to live and work. The choices bring you closer and closer to the target that represents your ethical core.

The choices, as we've mentioned, cannot be made collectively. Yes, you may be swayed by the results of polls, you may engage in discussions of these issues, you may learn how others are leaning. But in the end, you must decide for yourself what constitutes integrity. The decisions are seldom simple and almost never quick. But they must be made. Otherwise, you will find yourself foundering in a sea of decisions each time a new scenario presents itself. (You probably know some metaphoric boats that have capsized or sunk because there were cracks in the hull. In reference to the integrity of boats and individuals alike, the literal definition of "wholeness" or "soundness" is a good one to use.)

First, though, decide whether you think lying is wrong. Then consider the following situation and decide whether the woman involved influenced with integrity, even though she lied as she did so.

A perfectly healthy woman is dining in a restaurant with signs on the wall that clearly state "No smoking permitted." She sees a rather surly looking man blatantly light up a cigarette. There is no waiter or waitress nearby and so the woman approaches the man. She does not wish to start an argument, she does not wish to be rude, but she does want to influence him to put out the cigarette. Fearing that a simple request—"Could you please not smoke?"—will yield an antagonistic response—"Make me!"—she decides to tell a white lie: "I suffer from bronchial emphysema and the cigarette smoke causes me to gasp for air. Would you mind not smoking in here?"

It works. The man immediately crushes the cigarette and even apologizes to the woman. Would you have taken a similar influencing course given these circumstances? Was the woman dishonest and thus lacking integrity as she influenced the man? Or was she successful in her influence objective: making him stop without causing an unpleasant exchange?

Think long and hard about the positive elements associated with influence—integrity, leadership, trust, appropriateness, style, impact, vision, visibility, and values. They represent the ammunition to steady your aim as you focus on that ever-moving target known as your ethical core.

As we've noted, choosing an operational definition of "integrity" is a personal matter. By contrast, when we work collaboratively and collectively, it's fairly easy to establish standards to govern us. As team members, for example, we have ground rules that promote ethical treatment of one another. As organizations, we have mission, vision, and values statements that guide our operations. As members of one religious group or another, we have holy books and golden rules that encourage ethical practices. As members of a reading society, we are able to purchase books that encourage us to adopt specific behaviors. While we can, as a society, as a nation, as a member of one group or another, establish agreed-on principles that overarch our collective behaviors, it is much more challenging to know and articulate our own core values.

In addition to the questions regarding integrity, consider these regarding influence: What does it take for you to be influenced? How do you feel when someone has influenced you unethically? What led you to believe it was unfair or unethical? Do we have a right to influence those who hold onto their viewpoints as firmly as we hold on to our own? What role does "manipulation" play in ethical influencing?

Think of what life would be like if integrity did not govern the actions of those with whom you come in contact, especially those attempting to influence you. Speculate for a few moments about the results of a world in which ethical questions had not been answered, had not, perhaps, even been asked. Consider the products you buy, the services you receive, the work that you do, the community in which you live—if there were no moral premise governing decisions, the world would be in a sorry state indeed. The best business practitioners operate from a high sense of morality and a strong adherence to social values.

Exploring the links between influence and integrity requires effort. Is the effort/investment worth the return? We believe it is. Expending the time and energy to explore these issues results in the formation of those sound moral principles that serve as a base of operations. Without this foundation, we lack the higher purpose that makes us feel good about what we do—as individuals, as corporate citizens, as citizens of even larger communities. As you study the questions and answers associated with influence and integrity, you'll be adding to your store of knowledge. And the greater the array of choices on the shelves of that store, the more carefully and correctly you can select the ones allowing you to influence with integrity.

INFLUENCING 24/7

Each day, we hear of situations that are easy to identify as unethical, immoral, or illegal. Such situations require little thought or effort from us in terms of separating right from wrong. Actions involving murder or theft or abuse or drug activity, for most of us, fall clearly in the "wrong" end of the ethical spectrum. But when we influence others, there are multiple shades of gray associated with our actions.

Because you are influencing all day long, you may not be paying attention to the ways in which you exert influence over others. But in truth, you cannot *not* influence. Everything about you influences others, whether or not you are aware of the impact you are having. The way you dress, the way you organize your workspace, the way you speak, the way you decorate your home, the way you drive and the car you drive—all of these and more send out messages that influence others, be it negatively, minimally, optimally, or ideally. That influence may be intended or inadvertent, effective or ineffective, correct or incorrect, positive or negative, driven by ethics or by self-aggrandizement. But you are indeed sending out non-verbal messages all of the time. Consequently, you influence the way others think and act, based on their perceptions of both your message and your motivations.

The most effective influencers use a honed, not a haphazard, approach to interpersonal interactions. They weigh the possible outcomes of the words they've chosen to speak and the actions they've decided to undertake. You may be starting to equate such deliberation with manipulation. Realize there *are* some parallels. Those who "sell" with standards know that "object language" can easily influence the impression others have of you and may even be a factor in their decision to hire you or to do business with you. Do decisions to put your best foot forward mean you are behaving improperly? Absolutely not. They simply mean you are doing all you can to influence the outcomes you believe are directly advantageous to you and indirectly advantageous to others.

If you've ever watched a courtroom drama or served on a jury yourself, you know that lawyers make special efforts to relate to the jury. They may speak in a certain way, cite particular references, dress in a deliberate fashion, carry a certain kind of briefcase. Would you regard their efforts as dishonest manipulation or deliberate influence? You must judge for yourself, of course. But if such actions were immoral, then salespeople, leaders, ministers, managers, teachers, attorneys, and a host of others—including those who spruce up their home before selling it—would be guilty of unethical influence.

SPEAKING THE LANGUAGES OF INFLUENCE

Effective influencers are multi-lingual: They use the language of objects and a variety of other languages to lead others to think or act in a certain way. As long as the purpose behind their use of those languages is an ethical purpose, designed to benefit someone or something beyond the influencer, then the influencers are acting with integrity. To effectively employ body language and paralanguage and silence and neurolinguistics and proxemics (the use of space) is to understand that different folks need different strokes. Your ability to use a wide range of tools is a tribute to your understanding of human dynamics.

LEADING BY INFLUENCE, NOT BY AUTHORITY

Influencing with integrity, not surprisingly, means exerting positive leadership, effecting positive change. If you wish to lead others, you can no longer depend exclusively on the power of your position. Your authority, such as it is, carries less weight today than it did in times past. Because the "quality movement" emphasizes empowered behavior and because flattened organizations spell leadership opportunities for everyone, you are probably eager to learn how to lead by influence—no matter what degree of authority you have in the organization or in the other structures in which you participate. Leading means effecting positive change. What change would you like to see take place in your workplace? And what is the likelihood that you can be influential and instrumental in achieving that change? Once you are certain you can make a difference, make your proposal to both the individuals who will be impacted by the change and to those you'd like to participate in it.

Realize that the initial reaction to your leadership proposal might be a healthy skepticism. Most people are slow to change. They have adopted an "if-it-ain't-broke-don't-fix-it" attitude. Thus, to be effective, you must withstand and overcome the reluctance that is the usual response to a leader's initial suggestion. You and your ideas must be strong enough to withstand a range of negative reactions—from apathy at one end to complete refusal at the other. Influencing with integrity may mean overcoming objections, or igniting passions, or changing minds. It may be convincing through information, or persuading through personality, or swaying through strategic alliances.

GETTING RESULTS THROUGH RELATIONSHIPS

No matter what means or combination of means you use, the purpose behind your influence efforts must be an ethical one—to effect positive change for both yourself and others.

If your efforts are less than admirable, others will sooner or later learn of the unethical stance you have taken. Not only do you stand to harm your reputation, but you may harm your career as well. Every action you take has consequences—positive or negative—sooner or later. Sometimes you will not learn of the ripple effect you have created until long after you have spoken or acted. Whenever you set out to influence, you will be tossing words onto smooth surfaces of paper, computer screens, or minds. There is no telling how far your influence may extend, no foreseeing how wide the audience may become. If only for this reason, integrity should guide all your influence actions. And the more tools you have at your disposal, the more effective your influence can be. Those who are limited to the metaphoric hammer view every influence situation as a nail. The more effective influencers, though, have acquired several different integrity tools and several different influence techniques.

You know from personal experience that positive outcomes are usually the result of positive working relationships. You may be able to maintain your professional relationships by operating in an integrity vacuum for a while. Sooner or later, though, some of the people who cannot be fooled all of the time will see through the threadbare mantle of non-principled behavior worn by those with few scruples in order to cloak ulterior motives. And when that happens, the consequences are usually dire. If you are interested in results, you need good relationships. And to sustain those relationships, you need to influence with integrity, to take a standards-driven approach.

DEVELOPING INFLUENTIAL AND ETHICAL AWARENESS

As you build mutually beneficial relationships, develop awareness as well. Undertake a program of continuous questioning: Do you know when you are acting with integrity? What leads you to your conviction that your actions are proper? On what basis do others view your actions? How can you expand your influence without lessening the ethical component of it? Ideally, in exploring these issues, you will simultaneously be developing:

- Your own definition of "integrity,"

- Your own philosophy for integrating integrity into your influence endeavors, and

- Your own practical approach for operating from an ethical stance whenever you seek to influence others.

Because the "nanosecond nineties" have yielded to a culture of chaos, in the opinion of many, the need for frequent updates and calibrations is critical—whether we're looking inside ourselves or outside the organization. With corporate, societal, and communications structures being revamped daily, if not completely replaced, it's easy to feel rudderless and then to feel that leadership is a waste of time.

Remember, though, that certain things remain constant in this change-driven era. Change requires influential people to manage it. And the importance of treating one another and the environment itself with respect is a constant as well. So is the need for values and for vision, which has been defined as "the art of seeing the invisible." As you work to make the ideal vision real, as you strive to bring value to undertakings, you will be gaining visibility yourself.

Know that every action in which you engage has consequences, many of which are unanticipated, some of which cannot be anticipated. Your words and actions may have far-reaching consequences. And so ethical behavior assumes special significance, given the intensive and extensive ramifications behavior has in this wired world. It behooves each of us to seek many-layered benefits for our actions, to ensure that an ethical outcome is designed for every step of the journeys we propose others take with us.

Finally, recognize the merit in the assertion that results depend on relationships. You may be able to maintain those relationships for a while without exercising integrity. You may be able to operate with less than full disclosure; you may be able to sell a shoddy product or disguise a true intent. Sooner or later, though, people will discover your less-than-ethical ways. And when that happens, the consequences may easily doom the unscrupulous influencer.

Lead by ethical influence. Stand resolute in these millennia-straddling days, when the very concept of employment has changed. If you become a "portfolio" employee—someone who contracts with various companies for the skills and competencies amassed in a professional portfolio—your reputation will be more important than ever. If the prediction of a portfolio'd workforce is correct, then developing your ability to influence with a fine sense of ethics will surely lend weight and breadth to your portfolio. And to paraphrase a popular bumper sticker, "The person with the fattest portfolio wins."

Marlene Caroselli, Ed.D., conducts corporate training on a variety of subjects. She also presents motivational keynote addresses and writes—forty-five books to date. View them at her website, http://hometown.aol.com/mccpd, or at Amazon.com.

SPIRITUALITY AND BUSINESS: WHERE'S THE BEEF?

Gary Schouborg

Abstract: Taking a "spiritual" approach to business is an increasingly popular concept that can easily waste corporate resources unless properly understood. It is filled with high-minded ideas, but where's the beef? That is, how is it really useful? Transcendence, connection, and presence (TCP) is a model for the productive use of spirituality in the workplace. The TCP model shows that spirituality is not something separate from, but a natural part of business that enhances both performance and job satisfaction. TCP uses psychological language, rather than traditionally spiritual terms. Thus it connects to the various spiritual traditions that employees may follow so they can apply the teachings directly to business. TCP displays the relationship between spirituality and business through a performance matrix, a material focus (traditional business factors) and a spiritual focus (openness and flexibility with regard to business factors). The article shows how spirituality contributes to business performance and job satisfaction and how to enhance both.

Introduction

Traditionally, businesses have focused on relatively straightforward things such as customer satisfaction, productivity, market share, and profits. Spiritual approaches to business are more vague, but are often thought to express high-minded, non-material values such as the following:

- Meaningfulness;
- Job satisfaction;
- Work that makes sense;
- A felt connection between a company and its employees;
- Integration of head and heart;
- A common goal or vision;
- Avoidance of burnout;
- Ethics;
- Contributions to the common, social good;
- Respect for the environment;
- Open and honest communication;
- Humane treatment of employees;
- Work with dignity;
- A living wage;
- Humane productivity;
- Creativity;
- Flexibility;
- Team spirit;
- Employee empowerment; and
- Mutually supportive communication.

To the extent that these have inspired widely employed practices, business has already become progressively, although covertly, spiritual. Recent talk about spirituality both supports the trend and makes the connection between these concepts and traditional spirituality overt (Covey, 1989; Elkins, 1998; Hawley, 1993; Needleman, 1991).

Explicit reference to spirituality allows you to do several things: (1) identify what the above concepts have in common; (2) understand the nature of the organization that employs them; (3) assess the effects of a trend, for good or for ill, on business performance and job satisfaction; and, (4) understand the relationship of that trend to traditional spiritual teachings and practices and thereby apply them to business effectively.

However, talk about spirituality also creates at least two problems. First, the vagueness of the term makes it difficult to measure how a spiritual approach contributes to business productivity. Second, its high-mindedness can seduce some individuals into promoting spirituality divorced from its contribution to legitimate business goals or, in the worst case, in opposition to them.

You can adequately address these problems only by making the concept of spirituality clear, operational (tied to business goals and functions), and therefore useful.

SPIRITUALITY DEFINED

Three key aspects of spirituality are *transcendence, connection,* and *presence.* Although these qualities sound abstract, they can be explained in down-to-earth terms that make them practical for business. In fact, the TCP model (transcendence, connection, presence) can guide your thinking and performance.

Briefly, a spiritual approach to business is being as open and responsive as possible to *all* the factors that contribute to business performance. A spiritual approach is *transcendent* in that it urges you to grow beyond the status quo—beyond your current business thinking, strategies, and practices. A spiritual approach is *connected* in that it leaves you involved—looking for and motivated to deal with the many interrelated factors that contribute to achieving your business goals. Together, your transcendent openness and connection make you *present* and fully engaged in your work.

The framework offered here builds on traditional notions of spirituality, allowing you to apply the depth and scope of traditional spiritual energy to your business in two ways. First, if you are religious, it alerts you to how spirituality is *part* of business. It helps you see a depth to the business enterprise that may have been previously hidden to you if you thought of it as "only" business, an activity distinct from and perhaps even opposed to spiritual activity. Second, even if you have no interest in religion or think that it has no place in the business world, by clearly focusing on openness and flexibility, the framework presented here offers a dimension of business that is essential to your success. It provides a criterion for assessing the effectiveness of policies and training efforts that claim to be spiritual: Do they result in more effective performance by encouraging employees to consider and respond to important business factors?

CLARIFICATION BY CONTRAST

To understand any concept, it is often helpful to contrast it with something else. To emphasize that spirituality is an essential part of productive business, let's contrast our TCP model with three mistaken notions of spirituality. These three notions err in seeing business and spirituality as two separate entities, like food and drink (or worse, like oil and water). Having separated spiritual and business needs, those who believe these myths then disagree as to whether spirituality or business has priority.

Myth 1: Spiritual Needs Take Priority over Business Needs

According to this myth, when business and spiritual needs conflict, it is assumed that you should address spiritual needs first.

Take the example of XYZ Corporation, which can continue to operate (business need) only by employing workers for $1 a day (less than a living wage, which is often assumed to be a spiritual need). According to Myth 1, XYZ should disband itself rather than continue to exploit its workers. That is, the spiritual need for not exploiting workers is more important than the business need for making a profit.

Myth 2: Business Needs Take Priority over Spiritual Needs

This view says that you should address business needs first, because it's hard enough just to meet a payroll and survive against accelerating competition, but it's asking too much of management to consider spiritual needs too. Holders of this belief say that, if employees have spiritual needs, they should satisfy them off the job, just as they do other personal needs.

According to Myth 2, it's enough that XYZ management keeps the enterprise going, without asking it to address its workers' spiritual needs (assuming that a living wage counts as a spiritual value). In the final analysis, it's better for the workers to have a job, rather than none at all.

Myth 3: Spirituality Is in a Business's Enlightened Self-Interest

This view is that spirituality and business are separate, but it is in a business's enlightened self-interest to attend to both. Accordingly, a spiritual approach does not take away from, but enhances, productivity. This myth comes the closest of the three to the TCP model. But, unlike TCP, Myth 3 still treats spirituality and business as separate.

Those who espouse Myth 3 refuse to accept the assumption that XYZ Corporation cannot continue operating while paying employees a living wage. They argue that improving wages is a win-win strategy that will boost employee health and morale, and thus improve productivity. The value of Myth 3 is that it brings our attention to win-win solutions that we might otherwise overlook, helping us identify situations where we really can increase productivity if we address spiritual needs. The problem, however, is that there is no guarantee that spirituality and business will *always* be congruent. For example, in some cases increasing wages *will* put you out of business. The profit margin of the business simply does not allow employees to make a living wage or to work under humane conditions. In situations like that, where spirituality and business conflict, believers in Myth 3 point to no way of deciding which takes priority.

Shall XYZ management continue current wages in order to maintain operations (and jobs)? Or shall it improve wages and go out of business (and destroy jobs)? Is it better for the employees to enjoy more humane conditions for a short time and then lose their jobs? Or are they better off suffering less humane conditions indefinitely but keeping their jobs? On the one hand, how can a spiritually sensitive person sleep nights on profits earned by something close to slave labor? On the other hand, how are the employees helped by a morally righteous owner who simply disbands business and leaves them unemployed? After all, the employees themselves seem to be voting that even "inhumane" conditions are better than unemployment simply because they come to work every day.

Supporters of either side of this issue will argue endlessly without achieving consensus, since the root cause of the conflict is the question of the separation of spirituality from business. Once that Humpty Dumpty has fallen, no one will put him back together again.

THE TCP MODEL

The TCP model reconciles the three myths, providing a more integrated view. Using this model, spiritual approaches to business are seen as a part of business itself. Business is seen as a function of two factors, spiritual and material, just as a statue is a function of shape and material or a computer is a function of software and hardware. *Spirituality is not separate from business, but one of its components,* just as the shape of a statue is part of the statue itself or software is an integral part of a functioning computer.

The *material dimension* of business includes factors such as products, assets, cash flow, market share, and profits. The *spiritual dimension* involves one's relationship to those factors—one's openness and responsiveness to them and whether one uses them appropriately to achieve business goals. You can no more separate business and spirituality than you can separate a statue and its shape or a functioning computer and its software, for you can't separate business factors from your relationship to them.

TCP offers no easy answers for what XYZ Corporation should do. But it does offer a framework that increases the chances of an optimal solution and enables us to deal with the emotional effects of irreconcilable conflict when it occurs.

WHAT TCP MEANS IN PRACTICE

TCP is pragmatic in the best sense of the word. Following it, you (as a business person) work out your spirituality by being as open and responsive as possible to your material circumstances (traditional business factors such as products, assets, cash flow, market share, and profits). The matrix in Figure 1 illustrates your options: you can operate along a continuum from high to low in two dimensions, spiritual and material, resulting in four kinds of performance. (Although the matrix visually suggests four separate compartments, they really differ only in degree.) Notice that spirituality is no longer separate from business; rather, *optimal business performance results from the synergy between spiritual and material business factors.*

Business performance is a function of a material focus (traditional business factors) and a spiritual focus (openness and flexibility—how you intellectually and emotionally relate to business factors). Low material and low spiritual focus generate poor performance. High material focus and low spiritual focus create good performance that is unsustainable. High spiritual focus

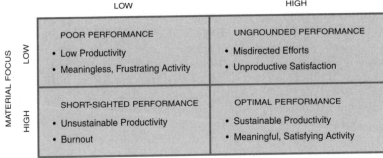

Figure 1. Matrix of Material Focus and Spiritual Focus

and low material focus result in misdirected performance. High material and high spiritual focus produce optimal performance.

Poor Performance

To the extent that you inadequately respond to traditional business factors (low material) and do that without being open to feedback and ready to revise your operations (low spiritual), you generate *poor performance*. Productivity is low and employees experience their work as meaningless and frustrating. Many companies have been initially successful, even while inadequately responding to traditional business factors, because they rode the wave of their industry growth. But if they did not eventually acknowledge and correct their mistakes, they failed to maintain their success.

Short-Sighted Performance

If you adequately respond to traditional business factors (high material) but are not open to feedback and ready to improve your operations (low spiritual), your performance is *short-sighted*. It will produce burnout and work against you in the long run. Certainly, there are high material, low spiritual systems that are extremely successful, but no one seriously expects to maintain that success unless he or she adapts to changing circumstances. The history of American enterprise is filled with companies that flourished and then declined because they did not acknowledge and adapt to changing circumstances.

Ungrounded Performance

If you inadequately respond to traditional business factors (low material) but emphasize openness and responsiveness (high spiritual), your performance is *ungrounded*. It is *ideological* if your focus is on abstract principle. It is *sentimental* if your focus is on feeling good without adequately considering consequences. In either case, your efforts are misdirected and what satisfaction you derive from your "ideals" is illusory and unproductive. Even the strongest advocates of a spiritual approach to business do not seriously suggest that the finest ideals are sufficient if traditional business factors are inadequately addressed. The TCP model points out that the authenticity of your spirituality in business should be assessed in terms of effective performance rather than of good intentions.

Optimal Performance

If you adequately respond to traditional business factors (high material) and also remain flexible and open to improvement (high spiritual), performance is *optimal.* You are performing adequately now and are alert both to improving and to adapting to changing circumstances.

Because these four categories are not watertight compartments, consider the center as a gray area of development or decline. For example, if you inadequately respond to traditional business factors (low material) but are *genuinely* flexible and open to learning (high spiritual), you can improve your material dimension and move toward optimal performance.

PRACTICAL GUIDELINES

The performance matrix in Figure 1 shows the interplay between the material and spiritual dimensions of business in general. More concretely, here are seven guidelines for applying TCP to your particular situation.

1. Express Your Spiritual Approach Completely in Business Terms. Remember, the TCP model says that spirituality is not something separate from business. It is your relationship to traditional business factors such as customer satisfaction, productivity, market share, and profits. Therefore, talk of spirituality that is separate from business falls under one of the three myths previously mentioned, with all their resulting problems.

2. Identify All the Stakeholders of Your Business. The stakeholder system includes not only shareholders but management, employees, suppliers, and customers. It even includes social and physical environments insofar as they affect the business. No enterprise is an island. You must identify all the stakeholders in order to understand the system of which your business is a part. All stakeholders have some interest in your business because they are affected by it. They will not passively accept your decisions forever. They will affect your business in turn, for good or ill.

3. Assess Recommended Spiritual Policies and Training by How Much They Help All Stakeholders Consider and Adequately Respond to All Important Business Factors. This guideline tests the mettle of any talk about spirituality. To satisfy *transcendence,* you must open stakeholders to interests other than their own. To satisfy *connection,* you must help stakeholders see themselves as a part of an interrelated system. Shareholders supply the capital, management the direction, employees the products and services, suppliers the more basic products and services, and customers the revenues. The social environment provides shareholders, managers, employees, suppliers, and customers themselves. And it supplies the infrastructure that enables all of them to interact productively. The physical environment functions like the social environment, one level removed.

Together, transcendence and connection make stakeholders *present* to one another as interrelated parts of a system that they all share. Presence means that stakeholders are increasingly aware of their interdependence, so that no contributor to the system is overlooked and system performance thereby harmed. Guideline 3 avoids both extreme individualism that neglects the whole and totalitarianism that neglects the contribution of any individual.

4. Make Stakeholders, Not Profits, Your Priority. Profits are important. They are a direct goal of the shareholders. They are an indirect goal of employees, whose direct goal of wages depends on profits. They are also an indirect goal of suppliers, whose profits depend on yours. They are an indirect goal even of customers, whose immediate goal of receiving a valued product or service is unlikely to be met by an unprofitable business. Even social and physical environments are indirectly interested in business profits, since a profitable company creates wealth for society and is more likely than an unprofitable one to respect the physical environment. Management has the most complicated relationship to profits, as it is directly responsible for creating them but can do so only if it adequately addresses the goals of all the stakeholders. Profitability cannot be maintained unless the system is honored, which means that the needs of every element must be addressed.

Therefore, profits are just one part of stakeholder requirements. To understand the role of profits in the whole system, you must first identify all the stakeholders and their objectives. Then you can understand the different ways in which profits help achieve those various objectives.

5. Negotiate from Self-Respect. Although you should respect the system and all its stakeholders, you do not have to sacrifice yourself on the altar of respect for others. Indeed, the best long-term guarantee that you will respect others is for you to respect yourself. The reason is that self-respect (from the Latin, meaning "look back on one's self") is the awareness of what you are as an individual, which includes your participation in countless interconnected systems. Your awareness of that interconnection compels you to take others into account, to respect them, because you and they are connected.

Negotiating from self-respect is therefore a deeply spiritual approach because it opens you up to yourself, the system of which you are a part, the other stakeholders of the system, and all the interrelationships involved. In other words, self-respect itself generates a sense of interconnection, which is a core feature of spiritual experience. Furthermore, it helps you make a spiritual approach to business genuinely operational, because it ties all talk about spirituality to the system and its stakeholders.

Recall XYZ Corporation's dilemma of being unable both to give workers a living wage and to maintain profitability. Guideline 5 says that you cannot deny the humanity of the workers without hardening yourself to your own humanity. The reason is that your own self-respect requires you to acknowledge that you are a part of a system composed of fellow human beings. You cannot deny their humanity without diminishing your awareness of the kind of system of which you are a part, that is, without reducing your own self-respect. Negotiating from self-respect demands that you be honest and forthright. It does not mean, however, that you indulge your employees, since customers, suppliers, management, and shareholders, as well as the social and physical environment in which you operate, have their different interests. That fact, of course, leaves you with no easy answers. However, *the role of spirituality is not to provide easy answers, but to give you the spirit and courage to be open and responsive, so you can make optimal decisions in a complex world.* As you will see in the section on "Spirituality and Suffering," stakeholders in a system seldom if ever get everything they want. A key function of spirituality is to help you cope with those limits.

6. Require that All Stakeholders Meet Their Commitments. You are part of a system composed of human beings, who, if they are rational, will not continue to do business with others who fail to keep their commitments. The reason is fundamentally more pragmatic than moralistic: They cannot achieve their objectives if they depend on unreliable associates. Honoring commitments is the glue that keeps systems together. Being open and responsive to the system(s) of which you are a part requires that you honor your commitments and insist that others honor theirs. At the same time, your commitments are not ends in themselves, but have value insofar as they contribute to the system. They are not rigid; you should renegotiate them as changing demands are put on the system.

This analysis explains why honoring commitments is a key part of every spiritual tradition. The interconnection of all to all is at the core of spirituality, and human beings cannot nurture their mutual interconnection if they fail to meet their commitments. You make your participation in your business system spiritual by serving the system with integrity, by giving 100 percent of what you have contracted to give.

Here again we see that spirituality is a natural part of the system, not something "higher" and added to it. If any of the participants in the system—shareholders and managers who sacrifice the system for quick profits, employees and suppliers who do not perform or who demand recompense that destroys sustainable profitability, customers who demand products and services at unprofitable prices, environmental demands that ignore economic laws of how human goods are created—ignore other parts of the whole system, each group risks killing the goose that lays the golden egg.

7. Broaden Your Perspective and Foster a Climate for Others to Do So as Well. Guidelines 1 through 6 are hard-headed counsels to make a spiritual approach operational. Guideline 7 is the soft-hearted advice to open up—the most challenging guideline of all. All spiritual teaching boils down to this: Personal, spiritual development is continuously opening yourself up to broader perspectives and a wider emotional world—in other words, becoming increasingly aware of, and concerned about, the systems of which you are a part. This is just good business.

Your current situation is not set in concrete. It is in your interest that you improve your workers' conditions as opportunities permit in order to make them more productive. It is in their interest that they grow in understanding of the realities of their situation in order to accept with dignity what they cannot change and to make good use of opportunities for improvement as they present themselves.

This guideline provides a two-edged corrective. If you are an exploiter of labor and you want an easy answer that ignores the plight of the less powerful, Guideline 7 urges that you open your mind and heart to explore whether you are acknowledging the workers' rightful place in the whole system. And if you are a champion of the downtrodden and you want an easy answer that ignores business realities, the guideline urges that you open your mind and heart to explore whether you are acknowledging the rightful place of other stakeholders as well as of employees.

SPIRITUALITY AND SUFFERING

Even in a flourishing economy, you can seldom achieve all stakeholders' goals, and never for long. Circumstances change. Or the desires themselves change as current satisfaction wanes. Suffering or disappointment is therefore inevitable. A key function of spirituality is to help people cope emotionally; to heal the hurt and disappointment that failed dreams bring; to summon the courage to make necessary changes and risk the unknown. TCP speaks not only to intellectual and policy requirements, but to emotional needs as well.

In the happy circumstance where individual interests also promote the system, everyone wins and the business can satisfy customers and generate profits. A business that can offer good wages, benefits, and a stimulating and enjoyable work environment can attract and retain productive workers. A business that is profitable can attract good suppliers as well as eager investors. A business that has efficient processes and is continuously improving them can be responsive to the marketplace, increase profits, stimulate productivity further, and attract more customers, better employees and suppliers, and more capital. Such a business is a boon to the community and is in the best possible position to honor the demands of the physical environment in which it operates.

However, even in that best of all possible worlds, circumstances are constantly changing, demanding that you be flexible, that you not be wedded to your present way of thinking and doing things. Changing circumstances demand that you risk change, that you risk moving into an uncertain future. To do that requires moral courage, letting go of the familiar and venturing into the unknown. Such moral courage is at the heart of every spiritual tradition.

FROM TRADITIONAL SPIRITUALITY TO TCP

Traditional spirituality has three defining characteristics: transcendence, connection, and presence. Whatever form a particular spiritual tradition may take, it serves all three.

The 2002 Annual: Volume 2, Consulting/© 2002 John Wiley & Sons, Inc.

Ethical systems that arise from spiritual traditions commonly teach brotherhood. Examples include Christian charity and Buddhist compassion (Pargament, 1997). Their teaching urge us to move beyond narrow self-interest (transcendence), often giving the reason that we are "children of the same God" (connection). The spiritual traditions that produce those ethical systems usually promise that those who honor transcendence and connection in their behavior will be present to one another in satisfying ways. TCP teaches the same thing, but uses psychological language rather than traditional spiritual terms such as "God," "soul," and "prayer." This allows TCP to connect to various spiritual traditions and to apply the teachings directly to business.

Prayer in many forms reminds you that you are not self-sufficient (connection). This is often an anxiety-provoking realization that prayer helps many people admit and accept. Prayer also reminds you that you are dependent on powers greater than your own (transcendence) and helps you reach deep within yourself for resources that you may not have known were available to you. Whether you attribute those resources to God or to your unconscious or to something else, prayer helps make them available to you by helping you acknowledge that your ordinary way of doing things is inadequate to the present situation. Whether you call it prayer or meditation or just plain quiet time, prayer is how you occasionally dwell quietly within yourself (presence) to understand and apply to your life both your limitations and your inner resources. Again, TCP does no more than state this in simple, psychological terms.

Even mysticism, which might seem to be the most unworldly, most unbusinesslike of experiences, dovetails with the TCP model. Not every form of mysticism is a withdrawing from the everyday world; it can be the intense and concrete realization of transcendence, connection, and presence in daily life. Such "everyday" mystics are taken beyond their ordinary way of thinking and behaving (transcendence). They usually realize the interconnection of things (connection). And through these twin realizations, they feel themselves vitally present to the world around them (presence). Their language often sounds exotic, as if they are transported to a world completely unrelated to the ordinary one in which business exists. But careful reading reveals that their core mystical realization is that nothing is profane, that the divine is found in how we relate to what we are doing in our ordinary, daily lives (Trasi, 1999). Again, TCP merely translates the insight of those mystics into ordinary terms that can be directly applied to business.

The error called materialism is not in loving profits, but in relating to them narrowly, obsessively, so as to rob ourselves of both satisfaction and flexibility. Rather than moving beyond this world to a higher one, the transcendence of the TCP model is moving beyond one system to another of which we are a part or subsystem. This movement opens us up to ever more comprehensive systems, including all of humanity—and ultimately to all of reality as a system that encompasses all others. As our perspective broadens, it moves along a continuum from specific and easily identifiable systems to less identifiable but more inclusive ones. Our sense of system moves correspondingly from tangible to intangible, ultimately to mystery—a generalized sense of an all-inclusive but undefinable system variously called God, Allah, Great Spirit, Brahman, or other names. Even when we are addressing a specific business system, a similar but inward movement opens us to mystery, since relating spiritually to anything opens us to energies within ourselves that are increasingly intangible and less readily identified and explained: Tao, Self, Non-Dual Consciousness, No Mind, God's presence within (Bowker, 1997; Trasi, 1999).

Accompanying increased transcendence is a growing sense of connection—to all the elements of our business system (customers, employees, suppliers, management, shareholders, and their social and physical environment). Since none of these elements is an isolated atom, each connects us to yet further systems. As with transcendence, our sense of connection becomes increasingly comprehensive and intangible until it moves into mystery.

This spiritual focus sensitizes us to connections, but does not tell us their nature. Our material focus tells us that *connection is not necessarily warm and fuzzy*. Although business realities demand that we cooperate with others, those same realities also reveal that the others have interests that often conflict with our own. Even when we share common interests, others often have opinions that conflict with ours as to how to achieve them. Connection is neither a simple matter of giving ourselves over to the will of others (group think) nor of blaming them for being so unselfish as to not yield to us. It is finding the most mutually productive way of cooperating, negotiating fairly when our interests conflict, and emotionally accepting the situation with dignity when we cannot achieve everything we want. TCP spirituality is not found in the impossible dream of eliminating conflict, but in working through conflict productively, with mutual respect, and with emotional equanimity.

As all members of the system *transcend* their narrow self-interest and work out their *connection* productively, they become *present* to one another in a more gratifying way. They win the respect, perhaps even the affection, of one another because they are increasingly alert to one another's needs. They are authentically in the world, because they are connected to it and open to adapting to it as it changes.

LOOKING TO THE FUTURE

This account of spirituality opens up at least two issues that are beyond the scope of this article. The first is the question of whether economic progress can replace win-lose with win-win competition. It is worth exploring to what extent operating spiritually enhances the odds of win-win situations. It would seem that openness and proactive creativity are inclined to find ways for conflicting parties to team together rather than focus on defeating one another. To know how far this can go requires both further research and further entrepreneurial creativity. Secondly, this account opens up a fertile area for assessment. Empirical evidence must be found to confirm that certain policies and training are more effective than others in leading stakeholders to consider and effectively respond to all-important contributors to business performance.

References

Bowker, J. (Ed.). (1997). *The Oxford dictionary of world religions.* Oxford, England: Oxford University Press.

Covey, S. (1989). *The 7 habits of highly effective people: Restoring the character ethic.* New York: Simon & Schuster.

Elkins, D.N. (1998). *Beyond religion: A personal program for building a spiritual life outside the walls of traditional religion.* Wheaton, IL: Quest.

Hawley, J. (1993). *Reawakening the spirit in work.* New York: Simon & Schuster.

Needleman, J. (1991). *Money and the meaning of life.* New York: Doubleday Currency.

Pargament, K.I. (1997). *The psychology of religion and coping: Theory, research, practice.* New York: Guilford.

Trasi, N. (1999). *The science of enlightenment: Enlightenment, liberation, and God—A scientific explanation.* New Delhi, India: D.K. Printworld.

Gary Schouborg, Ph.D., is a partner of Performance Consulting, a Walnut Creek, California, firm that improves developmental processes for both individuals and organizations. He has been a Jesuit priest and has taught philosophy, psychology, and mathematics. He has also been a telecommunications consultant with sales management responsibilities and has published academic research in philosophy and religious studies, practical business manuals in performance improvement, and poetry.

CONTRIBUTORS

Kristin J. Arnold, MBA, CPCM
Quality Process Consultants, Inc.
48 West Queens Way
Hampton, VA 23669
  (757) 728–0191 or (800) 589–4733
  fax: (757) 728–0192
  email: karnold@qpcteam.com

Dee Dee Aspell
Aspell Empowerment Enterprises, Inc.
P.O. Box 460688
San Antonio, TX 78246–0688
  (210) 930–4664
  fax: (210) 828–0965
  email: info@aspell.com
  URL: www.aspell.com

Patrick J. Aspell, Ph.D.
Aspell Empowerment Enterprises, Inc.
P.O. Box 460688
San Antonio, TX 78246–0688
  (210) 930–4664
  fax: (210) 828–0965
  email: info@aspell.com
  URL: www.aspell.com

Lynn A. Baker, Sr.
10004 Hefner Village Boulevard
Oklahoma City, OK 73162
  (405) 722–7394
  fax: (405) 720–7393
  email: Blynn@OU.edu

Ralph R. Bates, M.A., M.HRD
3816 Dade Drive
Alendale, VA 22003
  (703) 354–0669

Amy M. Birtel, M.S.
Department of Psychology
Virginia Commonwealth University
VCU Box 842018
Richmond, VA 23284
  (804) 225–3866
  email: psy2ambirt@titan.vcu.edu

Robert Alan Black, Ph.D.
Cre8ng People, Places & Possibilities
P.O. Box 5805
Athens, GA 30604–5805
  (706) 353–3387
  email: alan@cre8ng.com
  URL: www.cre8ng.com

Heidi A. Campbell
University of Edinburgh
New College—Mound Place
Edinburgh EH1 2LX
Scotland
  011 44 131 650 8945
  email: Heidi.Campbell@ed.ac.uk

Marlene Caroselli, Ed.D.
Center for Professional Development
324 Latona Road, Suite 1600
Rochester, NY 14626
  (716) 227–6512
  fax: (509) 696–5405
  email: mccpd@aol.com
  URL: hometown.aol.com/mccpd

Phyliss Cooke, Ph.D.
1935 Harton Road
San Diego, CA 92123–3819
  (858) 569–5144
  fax: (858) 569–7318
  email: phyliss6@earthlink.net

Adrian F. Furnham
Department of Psychology
University College London
26 Bedford Way
London WC1 0AP
England
011 44 171 504 5395
fax: 011 44 171 436 4276
email: ucjtsaf@ucl.ac.uk

Peter R. Garber
Manager, Teamwork Development
PPG Industries, Inc.
One PPG Place
Pittsburgh, PA 15272
(412) 434–3417
fax: (412) 434–3490
email: garber@ppg.com

Barbara Pate Glacel, Ph.D.
12103 Richland Lane
Oak Hill, VA 20171
(703) 262–9120
fax: (703) 264–5314
email: bpglacel@aol.com
URL: www.glacel.com

Stephen G. Haines
Centre for Strategic Management
1420 Monitor Road
San Diego, CA 92110–1545
(619) 275–6528
fax: (619) 275–0324
email: csmintl@san.rr.com
URL: www.csmintl.com

Edward L. Harrison, Ph.D.
Mitchell College of Business
Department of Management
University of South Alabama
Mobile, AL 36688
(334) 460–6715
fax: (334) 460–7241

Roger Harrison
3646 East Redtail Lane
Clinton, WA 98236
phone/fax: (360) 579–1805
email: rogerh@whidbey.com

Nancy Jackson, Ph.D.
592 South Victor Way
Aurora, CO 80012
(303) 340–8518
email: Nansolo@aol.com

M.K. Key, Ph.D.
Key Associates, LLC
144 Second North, Suite 150
Nashville, TN 37215
(615) 255–0011
fax: (615) 665–1622
email: keyassocs@mindspring.com

Valerie C. Nellen, Ph.D.
Leadership & Team Development
Conexant, Inc.
4311 Jamboree Road
Newport Beach, CA 92660
(949) 483–4600
email: valerie.nellen@conexant.com

Niki Nichols
P.O. Box 40
Buchanan Dam, TX 78609
(512) 793–2014
email: niki.nichols@tpwd.state.tx.us

Bevery J. Nyberg
950 25th Street NW #116N
Washington, DC 20037–2157
(202) 965–2553
email: bjn@gwu.edu

Karen Ostrov, Ph.D.
KONECT
402 Gammon Road, #290
Madison, WI 53719
   (608) 233–6225
   fax: (608) 236–4909
   email: ksostrov@facstaff.wisc.edu

Paul H. Pietri
College of Business
University of South Alabama
Mobile, AL 36688
   (334) 460–6130
   fax: (334) 460–7241
   email: ppietri@usamail.usouthal.edu

Kevin J. Pokorny
Pokorny Consulting
3209 Ingersoll Avenue, Suite 103
Des Moines, IA 50312–3920
   (515) 277–5228
   fax: (515) 277–3554
   email: info@pokornyconsulting.com
   URL: www.pokornyconsulting.com

Yvette Delemos Robinson
12902 Federal Systems Park Drive
Fairfax, VA 22033–4412
   (703) 633–4123
   email: yvette.d.robinson@
   us.pwcglobal.com

Gary Schouborg
1947 Everidge Court
Walnut Creek, CA 94596–2952
   (925) 932–1982
   fax: (925) 932–1982
   email: garyscho@att.net

Bob Shaver
Fluno Center for Executive Education
University of Wisconsin
601 University Avenue
Madison, WI 53705
   (608) 441–7334
   fax:(608) 441–7325
   email: bshaver@bus.wisc.edu

Lori Silverman
Partners for Progress
1218 Carpenter Street
Madison, WI 53704
   (800) 253–6398
   fax: (608) 241.8092
   email: pfprogress@aol.com

Steve Sphar
2870 Third Avenue
Sacramento, CA 95818
   (916) 731–4851
   fax: (916) 739–8057
   email: sphar@pacbell.net

Ed Werland
2649 Barton Hills Drive
Austin, TX 78704
   (512) 443–1491
   email: ed.werland@tpwd.state.tx.us

Susan B. Wilkes, Ph.D.
Virginia Commonwealth University
VCU Box 842018
Richmond, VA 23284
   (804) 828–1191
   email: swilkes@vcu.edu

Sherene Zolno
25900 Pillsbury Road SW
Vashon, WA 98070
   (206) 463–6374
   fax: (206) 463–6328
   email: coachpb@worldnet.att.net

CONTENTS OF THE COMPANION VOLUME, THE 2002 ANNUAL: VOLUME 1, TRAINING

Preface   v

General Introduction to *The 2002 Annual: Volume 1, Training*   1

EXPERIENTIAL LEARNING ACTIVITIES

Introduction to the Experiential Learning Activities Section   3

Experiential Learning Activities Categories   6

* 696. The Imposter Syndrome: Getting in Touch with Success
Adrian F. Furnham   11

697. Cultural Triangle: Determining the Effect of Values on
Customer/Client Perceptions *Homer Warren,
Anne M. McMahon, C. Louise Sellaro, and Carol Mikanowicz*   19

698. Speed Up! Increasing Communication Skills *Marlene Caroselli*   29

699. Memories: Influencing Others *Saundra Stroope*   51

700. Electric Company: Deciding by Consensus *John E. Fernandes*   55

701. Power Poker: What's in It for Me?
Linda Raudenbush and Steve Sugar   69

702. Sweet Tooth: Bonding Strangers into a Team *Robert Alan Black*   85

703. Puzzles: Practicing Team Process *Kristin J. Arnold*   91

704. Interrogatories: Identifying Issues and Needs *Cher Holton*   95

705. Crochet Hook: Learning How We Learn *Lynne Andia*   99

706. Certificates: Appreciating Oneself *Lois B. Hart*   111

707. Selection Interview: Practicing Both Roles *John E. Oliver*   115

708. Second to None: Electronically Mediated Personal
Leadership Planning *Robert C. Preziosi*   127

709. The Alphabet Game: Developing Confidence and
Spontaneity Through Improv *Izzy Gesell*   137

---

*See Experiential Learning Activities Categories, p. 6, for an explanation of the numbering system.
**Topic is "cutting edge."

Inventories, Questionnaires, and Surveys

Introduction to the Inventories, Questionnaires, and Surveys Section   143

The Archetype Inventory for Organizations
    Patrick J. Aspell and Dee Dee Aspell   145

Organizational Values and Voice Audit *Diane M. Gayeski*   161

Why Don't They Do What I Want? Understanding Employee
    Motivation *Janet Winchester-Silbaugh*   171

Empowerment Inventory *K.S. Gupta*   185

Presentation and Discussion Resources

Introduction to the Presentation and Discussion Resources Section   197

Hurling Kindness Rather Than Stones *Marlene Caroselli*   199

Developing Interpersonal Intelligence in the Workplace
    Mel Silberman   207

Voluntary Industry Skill Standards: Valuable Tools for
    Workforce Professionals *Eleazar O. Velazquez*   215

Email Basics: Practical Tips to Improve Communication**
    Kristin J. Arnold   227

The Effective Protégé *H.B. Karp*   241

Implementing E-Learning *Brooke Broadbent*   251

The Rhyme and Reason of Improvement and Innovation
    Mark W. Smith, with comment by George Land   259

Planting the Seeds and Cultivating the New Workforce
    Harriet Cohen, David B. Johnson, and Debbie Newman   267

Action Learning at Finco: A Learning History *Andy Beaulieu*   279

Teaching How to Learn Through Online Discussion *Zane L. Berge*   307

Contributors   315

Contents of the Companion Volume, *The 2002 Annual:
    Volume 2, Consulting*   319